OVER THE MOUNTAIN MEN

THEIR

EARLY COURT RECORDS

IN

SOUTHWEST VIRGINIA

Compiled by

ANNE LOWRY WORRELL

CLEARFIELD

Reprinted for Clearfield Company by
Genealogical Publishing Company
Baltimore, Maryland
2004, 2010

Originally published: Hillsville, Virginia, 1934
Reprinted by Genealogical Publishing Co., Inc.
Baltimore, Maryland
1962, 1975, 1976, 1979, 1983, 1991, 1996
Library of Congress Catalogue Card Number 63-495
ISBN 978-0-8063-0671-1

Made in the United States of America

INDEX TO COUNTY RECORDS

Marriage Records

In 1784 the general assembly made it lawful for an ordained minister of any christian society to celebrate a marriage in Virginia, provided the minister receive a license to do this. Even Quakers and Mononites could solomonize their own marriages, with, or without, a ceremony, provided it was done publicly.

The form used in the following marriage records is very plain: first, the groom; next the bride; and lastly, either the surety, or minister followed by the date. The abbreviations used are the simplest: min. for minister; dau. for daughter; sur. for surety, etc. I have only named the surety as the parent when I was assure of this fact by it being stated in the bond, or by written consent accompying the bond. When record is from ministers' return, I have used initial of minister, adding a list of these ministers at end of each group.

BEDFORD COUNTY.

The following list is from ministers returns, and have not been included in any list published heretofore.

Adams, Millijah, and Elizabeth Holeson. By J. M.—Oct. 31, 1785.

Alexander, Andrew, and Elizabeth Black. By J. M.—Nov. 8, 1792.

Allen, Thomas, and Mary Craghead. By J. A. —Dec. 23, 1790.

Ashwell, John, and Elenor Stump. By N. S.— June 30, 1785.

Blades, George, and Nancy Epperson. By J. A.—Jan. 30, 1791.

Bryan, John, and Catherine Evans. By J. A. —Sept. 2, 1788.

Claytor, Samuel, and Martha Mitchell. By A. H.—Oct. 25, 1788.

Crump, Thomas, and Permelia Thorp. By E. C.— ...., 1787.

Dawson, Jeremiah, and Agnes Dollard. By J. H.—Mar. 28, 1787.

Dawson, John, and Elener Williams. By J. H. —Nov. 25, 1790.

Dooley, John, and Mary Forsee. By J. H.— Mar. 16, 1786.

Drake, Clayton, and Sary Meador. By J. A.— July 25, 1791.

English, Charles, and Jane Robertson. By J. A.—Oct. 16, 1792.

Evans, Anthony, and Mary Bowyers. By J. M. —Oct. 20, 1792.

Ewing, John, and Mary Ewing. By Jos. M.— Nov. 21, 1790.

Goggins, Robert, and Sally Irvine. By J. M. —Feb. 4, 1794.

Gord, Thomas, and July Toler. By J. A.— —Jan. 31, 1793.

Greer, Asa, and Rebeckah Neighbors. By J. A.—July 25, 1791.

Hale, William, and Sarah Quarles. By Jos. M. —May 4, 1791.

Huddleston, Henry, and Martha Pate. By N. S.—Jan. 11, 1791.

Huddleston, William, and Rachel Newgeon. By Jos. M.—Dec. 25, 1790.

Irvine, William, and Patsey Burton. By A. H. —Dec. 8, 1788.

James, Joseph, and Elizabeth Ballard. By J. A.—Dec. 19, 1793.

Johnson, Thomas, and Mary Robertson. By J. A.—Jan. 27, 1791.

Jones, Henry, and Betsy Weaver. By N. S.— Jan. 26, 1786.

Jones, Lewis, and Elizabeth Bowcock. By J. H.—Sept. 6, 1792.

Jones, William, and Nancy Kimbron. By J. H.—June 19, 1790.

Kemp, William, and Susannah Hale, By J. A.—Dec. 30, 1791.

Maxey, Hale, and Dicie Craghead. By J. A. —Nov. 3, 1789.

Maxey, John, and Sary Green (or Greer) By J. A.—Aug. 7, 1794.

McMurray, John, and Elizabeth McClellon. By J. M.—Oct. 6, 1785.

Moodey, John, and Mary Lilley. By N. S.— Feb. 3, 1785.

Morris, Hudson, and Elizabeth Smith. By J. A.—Feb. 19, 1791.

Moseley, Edwin, and Sarah Galright. By N. S.—July 21, 1785.

Nickolls, Nehemiah, and Elizabeth Blades. By J. A.—Mar. 17, 1791.

Oliver, John, and Catherine Grigg. By Jos. M.—Apr. 5, 1787.

Parker, Henry, and Elizabeth Dorrothy. By J. A.—July 14, 1791.

Payne, Frayl, and Elizabeth Pollard. By J. A. —Oct. 19, 1790.

Pryor, Samuel, and Mary Wimbush. By Jos. M.—Apr. 5, 1787.

Radford, John, and Gastry Truman. By J. A.—Oct. 23, 1794.

Rifler, John, and Caty Radford. By J. A.— Nov. 7, 1793.

Roberson, John, and Elaner Russell. By J. M.—Oct. 9, 1792.

Robertson, John, and Cena Hix. By J. M.— Jan. 12, 1792.

Robertson, John, and Sukey Theman. By N. S.—Oct. 10, 1785.

Shear, James, and Mary Martin. By A. H.— July 22, 1789.

Shewsberry, Benjamin, and Nancy Richardson. By N. S.—Jan. 24, 1785.

Warren, John, and Elizabeth Fuqua. By Jos. M.—Apr. 5, 1787.

West, Thomas, and Betsy Hogan. By J. A.— Sept. 2, 1790.

Westland, George, and Sarah James. By N. S.—Nov. 20, 1785.

Wheat, Zacheriah, and Edith Chastain. By J. H.—Jan. 20, 1791.

White, Obediah, and Rhodea Arther. By N. S.—Apr. 24, 1785.

Wright, Thomas, and Betsy Pullen. By N. S. —Mar. 31, 1785.

Bedford Ministers.

John Ayres: A. Clay; Andrew Hatcher; Jeremiah Hunter; James Mitchell; Joseph Mitchell, and Nathaniel Shewsberry.

Franklin County Marriage Records

1786 Through 1806

—A—

Abshire, Abraham, and Susannah Vinson (own cons.) —Jan. 14, 1801.

Abshire. Edward, and Dinah Short; dau. Winny Short. Sur. John Abshire. Mar. by R. H.—Nov. 23, 1790.

Abshire, James, and Elizabeth Overholts,—Mar. 6, 1804.

Abshire, John, and Elizabeth Bermion (?); Wm. Pottet, sur.—Sept. 11, 1796.

Abshire, Peter, and Nelly Doran; dau. Mary Doran: Sur. Peter Doran—Aug. 19, 1787.

Adams, Elisha. and Elizabeth Newton; H. Nele. sur.—June 14, 1798.

Adkins, John. and Elizabeth Adkins. dau. David Adkins—Apr. 24, 1788.

Adkins, (See Atkins.)

Adney. Daniel, and Anna Coger. Mar. by Jacob Miller—Feb., 1798.

Adney. John, and Barbary Lesene, dau. Elizabeth Lesene..Jan. 11. 1797.

Adney, Thomas, and Polly Rose, dau. Gabriel Rose—Feb. 19, 1803.

Agee, Ephrean, and Elizabeth Dunn, dau. Thomas Dunn—Apr. 6, 1801.

Akers, Daniel. and Rebeckah Webster, dau. Luke and Sarah Webster,—Dec. 2, 1800.

Akers, James, and Lucy Webster, dau. Luke and Sarah Webster—Jan. 24, 1792.

Akers, John. and Sarah Brown. Mar. ret. by R. H.—Aug. 8, 1793.

Akers, Nathaniel, and Elizabeth Akers. John Akers, sur.—Oct. 7, 1806.

Akers, Samuel, and Sarah Highly: James Highly, sur.—Aug. 2, 1802.

Aleck. Daniel, and Elizabeth Bowsman: Lawrence Bowsman, sur.—Aug. 17, 1797. (In the mar. ret. by R. H. it is David Alick, not Daniel)

Aleck. David, and Hannah Shueman, dau. Mary Shueman—Mar. 25. 1796.

Aleck-see Altic.

Allaway, Abner. and Polly Kent. Peter Bernard. sur—Nov. 10, 1805.

Allen, Stephen. and Sally Radford; dau. James Radford—Sept. 12. 1792.

Allen, Thomas. and Mary Craighead, dau. John Craighead—Dec. 5. 1790.

Alley, David, and Charity Bybe. Nicholas Alley, sur.—Dec. 4, 1786. (Written Bybe Charity, in Mar. ret.)

Alley, John, and Mildred Laurence. Nicholas Alee, sur.—Jan. 1, 1786.

Alley, William, and Sukey Biby: Sherod Biby, sur.—Nov. 10, 1802.

Allman, Sabastian, and Sally Webb. Sam'l Webb. sur.—Aug. 25, 1797.

Altic, Abraham, and Elizabeth Reed. John Altic, sur.--Apr. 2, 1806.

Altic, Jacob, and Elizabeth Sink: Abraham Sink, sur.—Dec. 22, 1803.

Altic, Solomon, and Elizabeth Michael: John Michael, sur.—Mar. 11. 1806.

Amoss, ..., and Henny Boswell,—Nov. 5, 1805.

Anderson, George, and Millia Jones. Mar. ret. by Robt. Jones—1787.

Angell, James, and Patty Simmons: Joseph Simmons, sur.—Oct. 20, 1810.

Angle, Jacob, and Caty Snider: John Snider, sur.—Sept. 27, 1803.

Angle, John, and Fanny Rudy: Daniel Rudy, sur.—Apr. 3, 1798.

Archer, Chapman, and Suffy Beckelhymer; dau. John Becklehymer. July 16, 1802.

Armstrong, Thomas, and Mary Allin: Wm. Drake, sur.—Dec. 28, 1786.

Armstrong. Thomas, and Jane Daughton. Sam'l Duvall, sur.—June 21, 1797.

Armstrong, William, and Alianah Hill, dau. Thomas Hill—Dec. 26, 1792.

Arrington, Samuel, and Elizabeth Greer, (owns cons)—Dec. 20, 1800.

Arrington, Thomas, and Milly Coleman, James Coleman, sur.—Sept. 27, 1791.

Ascue, Phillip, and Ruth Vanover: George Vanover, sur.—Jan. 3, 1804.

Atkins, Henry, and Susanna Bradshaw. Mar. ret. by R. Hall.—May 29, 1790.

Atkins, Jacob, and Phebe Bradshaw, dau. Susannah Bradshaw.—Mar. 28, 1791.

Atkins, Littlebury, and Nancy Atkins, dau. Mary Atkins.—May 29, 1790.

Atkinson, Charles, and Rebeckah Haslip: Henry Haslip. sur.—Oct. 7, 1799.

—B—

Bailey, James, and Elizabeth Wright, dau. Elizabeth Wright—Dec. 11, 1798.

Bains, Tuishitha, and Nancy Highly, dau. Wm. Highly—Dec. 18, 1797.

Baker, Edward, and Susannah Mullins: Wm. Mullins, sur.—Apr. 24, 1793.

Baker, Peter, and Anne Lezemy, dau. Elizabeth Lezemy—Apr. 1, 1805.

Ball, John, and Amiah Shockley, dau. David Shockley—Dec. 22, 1800.

Ball, Joseph, and Elizabeth Perdue. Meslick Oerdue, sur.—Sept. 15, 1804.

Ballard, Charles. and Mary Craghead. Nathan Swanson, sur.—Aug. 6, 1787.

Ballard. James, and Rachel Howzer: Jasper Howzer. sur.—June 26, 1787.

Bandy, Cary, and Frances Woods, dau. Peter Woods—Nov. 14, 1791.

Banks, John. and Agnes Marcum; Thos. Marcum, sur.—Dec. 19, 1789.

Banks, Samuel, and Elizabeth Markham: Thomas and Phebe Love, sur.—Apr. 3, 1787.

Banks, William, and Elizabeth Harris. Mar. ret. by R. H.—Jan. 10, 1793.

Barnerd, Benjamin, and Sarah Betz: Conrad Betz, sur.—Sept. 1, 1806.

Barnes, James, and Permelia Lain: Alexander Lain, sur.—Aug. 6, 1798.

Barnhart, Daniel, and Elizabeth Nave, dau. Jacob Nave—Feb. 24, 1788.

Barret, George, and Nancy McCormack: Macakah McCormack, sur.—Nov. 3, 1800.

Barret, William, and Mary Craig; Thos. Craig, sur.—Oct. 29, 1801.

Bartle, George, and Elizabeth Highly: Wm. Highly, sur.—Nov. 8, 1796.

Bartle, John, and Dicey Kirby; Francis Kirby, sur.—Sept. 4, 1786.

Barton, Joshua, and Jane Hale; sur, Thomas Hale—Jan. 11, 1800.

Basham, John, and Franky Meadors· Jesse Meadors, sur.—Jan. 13, 1804.

Basham, Uriah, and Rhoda Simmons, dau. Chas. Simmons.—May 27 1804.

Basham, William, and Anna Meador, dau. Jesse Meador,—Dec. 4, 1797.

Bates, Daniel, and Lydia Bradshaw; mar. ret. by R. H.—Aug. 22, 1793.

Bates, William, and Elizabeth Harris, dau. John Harris.—Jan. 7, 1793.

Beck, Edward, and Nancy Oldakers; Jacob Oldakers, sur.—Sept. 2. 1799.

Beck, John, and Frankey Oldakers: sur. Jacob Oldakers.—May 4, 1801.

Beck, Moses, and Ann Richards; Isaac Lemons, sur.—Aug. 29, 1791.

Becklesimer, Adam, and Betsey Prater. Thomas Prater, sur.—July 25, 1800.

Becklesimer, John, and Cahrity Harger, dau. John Harger.—Sept. 7, 1803.

Beek, Joseph, and Isabella Bohannon; Jeremiah Bohannon, sur.—Feb. 3, 1791.

Beheler, George, and Mary Doss. Mar. ret. by R. H.—Jan. 8, 1794.

Belcher, Isham, and Patsey Hodges. Isham Hodges, sur.—Jan. 3, 1791.

Bell, George, and Rachel Goudy, (own cons.) —Dec. 7, 1800.

Bell, James, and Frankey Meddows, dau. James Meddows.—Jan. 31, 1798.

Bell, William, and Lucy Law: Henry Law, sur.—May 6. 1805.

Best, John, and Lydia Meador; mar. ret. by John Saunders.—May 24, 1801.

Bibee, John, and Elizabeth Kelley; Min. ret. by R. H.—May 12, 1791.

Billups, Edward, and Susannah Webster, dau. Sam'l Webster.—Dec. 18, 1788.

Billups, Richard, and Margaret Webster, dau. Luke and Margaret Webster.—Dec. 3, 1799.

Billups, Thomas, and Sally Webster. Mar. ret. by R. H.—Nov. 28, 1793.

Binnion, John, and Milly Dehaven. Abraham Dehaven, sur.—Jan. 23, 1804.

Bird, Abner, and Jane Jameson, dau. Thomas Jameson—Mar. 4, 1791.

Bird, James, and Fanny Mason: Robt. Mason, sur.—Sept. 3, 1787.

Bird, John, Sr., and Mary Davis. ("of age"); dau. Williamson Davis—Nov. 22, 1798.

Bird, Thomas, and Susannah Broady: John Broady. sur.—Apr. 29, 1806.

Bishop, Joseph, and Elizabeth Bishop. Isaac Bishop, sur.—Dec. 21, 1805.

Blankenship, Barnett, and Bathsheba Meador, dau. Jesse Meador: Hezekiah Blankenship, sur.—Oct. 15, 1792.

Blankenship, Hezekiah, and Rhoda Meador, dau. Joel Meador. Feb. 28, 1791.

Blankenship, John, and Rhoda Blankenship; Isham Blankenshin, sur.—Aug. 29, 1798.

Blankenship, Presley, and Frankey Ross, dau. Mourning Ross. Elisha Blankenship. sur.— Dec. 24, 1791.

Blankenship, Shadrick, and Edey Perdue (own cons.)—June .. 1792.

Blankenship, Smith, and Jemima Charlton. Alex. Ferguson, sur.—Dec. 2, 1794.

Blaydes, George, and Nancy Epperson: Benj. Booth, sur.—June 6, 1791.

Bocock, John, and Lucy Hughes, dau. Nancy Hughes "by her first husband". Wm. Bocock, sur—Dec. 29, 1800.

Bolling, Joseph, and Rebecca Maddox. Min. ret.—Mar. .. 1795.

Bolling, Joseph, and Rebecca Davis. Sam'l Davis, sur.—Feb. 1, 1796.

Bondurant, Joel, and Sally Wheat: sur. Guy Smith—July 11, 1800. Enclosed with mar. bond was following note: "Kind Sir; I have known this Sally Wheat for many years, and her family people, and her family connection, has all left this part of the world for some years past, and do believe her parents to be goan to the world of spirits. Sir, I do believe this Sally Wheat to be between 28 and 30 years of age.
Richard Mitchell." This bond badly worn—Apr. 15, 1803.

Bond, Benja-, and Thea- Ross.

Bond, Robert, and Sally Ann Starkery; Sam'l Ozburn. sur.—Oct. 18. 1796.

Boon. Abraham, and Susannah Kelly. Wm. Kelly, sur.—Dec. 31, 1806.

Booth, Benjamin, and Elizabeth Devers: John Devers. sur.—Dec. 16, 1795.

Booth, James, and Frances Ferguson, dau. Wm. Ferguson—Apr. 6, 1805.

Bowles, David, and Elizabeth Clower. John Clower. sur.—May 20, 1803.

Bowles. William, and Sally Preston. John Preston. sur.—Jan. 23, 1797.

Bowles, William, and Nancy Bolling. John Bowles, sur.—Dec. 27, 1800.

Bowman, Peter, and Mary Saunders: John Saunders, sur.—Sept. 3, 1804.

Bowsman, Adam, and Susannah Crowl; Devault Crowl, sur.—Jan. 30, 1805.

Bowsman, George, and Elizabeth Pool. Mar ret. by J. M.—1794-95.

Boyd, Henry, and ....Wood. John Wood. sur.—June 28, 1800.

Boyd, William, (son Wm. Sr.) and Sary Newberry, dau. William Newberry—Mar. 23, 1805.

Bradshaw, Allen, and Mourning Richardson dau. Lucy Richardson.—Jan. 26, 1793.

Bradshaw, Charles, and Hannah Boles. John Boles sur.—(Bates, in mar. ret.)—Mai. 15, 1790.

Brammer, Noah, and Caty Jones, dau. Jehu Jones—Mar. 5, 1803.

Branson, Hezekiah, and Agnes Preaddy, dau. Nancy Preaddy—Sept. 3. 1789.

Bridcett, George. and Catherine Eads. John Adkins, sur.—June 22. 1797.

Bristow, Benjamin. and Sarah Miles, dau. Sam'l Miles—Dec. 7, 1796.

Bristow, William, and Martha Beek, dau. Martha Beek—Oct. 3, 1796.

Britton, Richard, and Susannah Turnbull. George Turnbull, sur.—Feb. 9, 1804.

Brock, Joshua, and Fanny Estes. dau. Elijah and Marraret Estes—Dec. 28, 1800.

Brock, Jubal, and Doshia Stuart. David Stuart, sur.—Dec. 9, 1796.

Brock, Moses, and Susannah Dyer. Elijah Brock, sur.—May 5. 1795.

Brogin, Robert, and Grace Allen. Jos. Underwood, sur.—Feb. 18. 1794.

Brooks, Jeremiah, and Catherine Mclewain. Mar. ret. by J. M.—Aug. 18, 1794.

—7—

Brooks, William, and Mary Sellars. Wm. Scott, sur.—Nov. 14, 1798.

Brower, John, and Rebecca Harter. Christian Harter, sur.—Sept. 5, 1803.

Brower, John, and Elizabeth Rinehart. Jacob Rinehart, sur.—Sept. 2, 1805.

Brown, Abram. and Betsy Horten (or Horter), Geo. Horte-. sur.—Nov. 3, 1800.

Brown, Henry, Jr., and Hannah Dillman. Jacob Dillman. sur.—Aug. 4, 1800.

Brown, Jacob, and Anny Rudy. Daniel Rudy, sur.—July 17, 1798.

Brown, John, and Sarah Rives. Unsigned min. ret. July 8. 1793.

Brown. Maraduke. and Mary Wever, dau. Jacob Wever: Rodman Felso Brown, sur.—Dec. 16. 1802.

Brown, Ruffin, and .... Jamison. Mar. ret. by R S.—Nov. 8, 1794.

Brown, Samuel, and Martha Holt Thompson, dau. Thos. Thompson. Apr. 19, 1804.

Brown. Skelton, and Mary Napier, dau. Ashford, and Mary Napier.—Dec. 22. 1796.

Brown. Thomas, and Sarah Smith. Nar. ret. by R. H.—Jan. 2, 1794.

Brummit. .... and Mary Estes; min. return—Apr. 10, 1790.

Bryant, James, and Sally Brumut. James Brumut. sur.—July 7, 1788.

Buchanan, Jeremiah, and Sarah Jones, dau. Thomas Jones.—Dec. 25, 1786.

Burdel. William. and Rachel Osburn, dau. John Osburn—Dec. 6, 1794.

Bunnion, Isaac, and Elizabeth Poteet. dau. William Poteet—Apr. 13, 1789.

Burton, William, and Hannah Lykins. Mar. ret. by J. M.—1797-98.

Burwell. John, and Elizabeth M. Wood. Josiah Wood. sur.—June 2. 1806.

Byars, David, and Roable Wimmer. Jacob Wimmer. sur —Sept. 16. 1796.

Bybee, Allin. and Sarah Linkens, dau. Sarah Linkens. Allin, son of John and Betty Bybee.—Mar. 13, 1786.

Bybee. John, and Elisabeth Colley, dau. Wm. Colley. Sherod Bybee, sur.—May 6, 1791.

Bybee. Neil McCan and Mary Evans. dau. John and Betsy Evans.—Sept. 15, 1792.

Byrd, John, and Mary Stewart. James Byrd, sur.—Oct. 7, 1792.

—C—

Camp, John, and Milly Edmondson, dau. Richard Edmondson,—Oct. 2, 1786.

Camp, William, and Susannah Hail, dau. Stephen Hail,—Dec. 4, 1790.

Campbell, John, and Elizabeth Nowlin, ("of age")—- ...., 1799.

Campbell, Thomas, and Charity Price—Feb. 16, 1804.

Campbell, William, and Mary Hale, dau. William Hale,—Feb. 25, 1789.

Canady, William, and Mary Douty, dau. Elizabeth Parker,—May 23, 1798.

Canter, Turman. (See Carter, Turman.)

Canterberry, Samuel, and Lucy Webb, dau. Loncey Webb,— ...., 1796.

Capper, Samuel, and Darbara Prillaman: Jacob Prillaman, sur.—Feb. 11, 1806.

Capper (Caper), Thomas, and Elizabeth Craven. David Overholt, sur.—Nov. 23, 1799.

Carley, Chatham, and Delilah Basham. Bartlett Basham, sur.—Dec. 27, 1804.

Carrico, Vincent, and Frances Estes, dau. Widow Frances Estes.—July 5, 1791.

Carter, John, and Fanny McCutchen, dau. James McCutchen—Nov. 19, 1795.

Carter, Phillip, and Sarah Prunty, dau. James Prunty—Jan. 9, 1804.

Carter, Traves, and Mary Sneed, (Nancy and not Mary, in consent) dau. Nancy and John Sneed.—Nov. 24, 1804.

Carter, Turman, and Cintha Harris, dau. John Harris—Mar. 19, 1792.

Carter, Walker, and Frances Steagall. Geo. Rives, sur.—Jan. 31, 1803.

Carter, William, and Mary Huff, dau. Mary Huff—Oct. 13, 1802.

Carver, Willian, and Elizabeth Prunty. James Prunty, sur.—Mar. 5, 1794.

Cassetty, Thomas, and Sarah Thomas, dau. William and Deborah Thomas,—Feb. 25, 1796.

Caufman, Benjamin, and Hannah Nofsinger. John Nofsinger, sur.—Oct. 16, 1798.

Caylor, Jacob, and Elizabeth Holderman, dau. Christian, and Elizabeth Holderman.—Sept. 3, 1800.

Cemp, Robert, and Sally Mattox, dau. Nathan Mattox. Jordon Cemp—Dec. 6, 1802.

Chambers, John, and Agnes Moore, dau. Agnes Moore— ...., 1799.

Chambers, Samuel, and Nancy Nabours—Dec. 25, 1805.

Chandler, Benjamin, and Jane Fallis—Jan. 23. 1793.

Cahdler, Daniel, and Margaret Roan. John Stone, sur.—Jan. 2, 1797.

Chandler, Shadrack, and Ann Brummit, dau. James and Agnes Brummit.—Oct. 8, 1789.

Chandler, Thomas, and Cahrity Elliot. Dan'l Browm, sur.—Mar. 13, 1787.

Chandler, William, and Jane Douglas, dau. Thomas Douglas.—May 24, 1788.

Chapman, Nathan, and Betsy Colenan. James Coleman, sur.—Feb. 12, 1791.

Chartain, George, and Rebeckah Staton. Mar. ret.—Aug. 18, 1791.

Chartain, Renny, and Massey Robins, dau. Jacob and Mary Robins.—Sept. 19, 1795.

Chartain, Robert, and Maylin Moore, dau. Jane Moore— ...., 1799.

Chartain, Valentine, and Mary Robins. Mar. ret.—Sept. 19, 1791.

Charter, Jonathan, and Margaret Brockman —Aug. 9. 1800.

Charter, William, and Jean Read, dau. Sam'l Read. Thos. Charter.—Sept. 28, 1787.

Chasteen, Barnet, and Sarah Hixon. Daniel Hixon sur.—Dec. 19, 1795.

Chavers. Benjamin, and Anna Beverly. Silvester Beverley, sur.—Aug. 24, 1801.

Chitwood. Joel, and Sally Short, dau. Winaford Short—Jan. 6, 1800.

Chitwood, Squire, and Mary Wray: Benjamin Wray, sur.—Jan. 5, 1801.

Choat, Austen, and Theadocia Webb. Mar. ret. by R S.—Nov. 8, 1794.

Choice, John. and Jenney Haygood. John Cook, sur.—Feb. .., 1805.

Clark. Christopher, and Elizabeth Hook. Stephen Smith, sur.—Apr. 24, 1790.

Clark. William, and Frances Blades. Francis Blades. sur.—Jan. 21. 1801.

Clay. William, and Lucy Rudy. Consent by Mary Dale. Richard Dale. sur.—Dec. 8, 1793.

Clement. William. and Elizabeth Goard. dau. Wm. Goard—Oct. 7, 1790.

Clower, Jacob, Jr. and Elizabeth Glaspy. John Glaspy, sur.—April 4, 1803.

Clower, John, and Rebecca Harris. Wm. Harris, sur.—May 11, 1796.

Coats, Kinsey, and Jeany Turner. James Turner, sur.—Apr. 13,1789.

Cockran, John, and Susannah Lumsden, dau. John Lumsden.—Jan. 21, 1786.

Cockran, William, and Lucy Milem. Ben!. Davis, sur.—Dec. 12, 1803.

Coffman, Jacob, and Catherine Rudy. Mar. ret. by J. M. 1794-95.

Coger, William, and Elizabeth Kingery, dau. Peter and Mary Kingery.—Sept. 18, 1804.

Coleman, John, and Patsey Arrington, dau. Sam'l Coleman.—Feb. 17, 1792.

Comer, Richard, and Milley Shockley, dau. Levi and Rebeckah Shockley.—Dec. 20, 1790.

Conner, John M., and Margaret Ruble. Mar. ret. by R. H.—Aug. 25, 1795.

Conoway, Edward, and Elizabeth Early. Jasper Franklin, sur.—Feb. 4, 1805.

Cook, John, and Anny Belcher. Francis Belcher, sur—Dec. 14, 1805.

Cook, Joseph, and Sarah Edwards. Arthur Edwards, sur.—Aug. 23, 1788.

Cooley, James, and Patsey Stewart, dau. David Stewart—Oct. 4, 1786.

Cooley, John, and Nancy Brock, dau. Joshua Brock—Sept. 18, 1795.

Coop, David, and Christina Stofer, dau. Henry Stofer—May 12, 1794.

Coop, John, and Sarah Hall, dau. Lane Hall —May 8, 1793.

Cooper, Charles, and Jane Richardson, dau. Green, and Jane Richardson—Mar. 7,1786.

Cooper, Thomas, (son of John Cooper), and Nancy Cornelius, dau. Susannah Cornelius. —Aug. 25, 1797.

Cooper, Edward, and Susannah Cornelius, dau. Susannah Cornelius: James Cornelius, sur.—Mar. 25, 1801.

Cowden, James, and Lucy Rives, dau. Frederick Rives—Jan. 26, 1799.

Cowden, Josiah, and Mully Clay. Wm. Clay sur.—Dec. 31, 1799.

Cowden, William, and Elizabeth Keen, dau. Edw. Keen—Feb. 12, 1802.

Craghead, John, and Elizabeth Hale. John Cemp, sur.—Apr. 3, 1786.

Craghead, Robert, and Nancy Powell. Robt. Powell, sur.—Nov. 18, 1792.

Craghead, Timothy, and Mary Agee. Matthew Agee, sur.—Dec. 6, 1802.

Craghead, William, and Jean Dunns: Thomas Dunns. sur.—Jan. 13, 1800.

Craig, Thomas, and Lucy Bird. Sam'l Bird, sur.—Aug. 17, 1789.

Crawford. James, and Curdilla Richards. Ambrose Raymore, sur.—Nov. 14, 1792.

Crawford, William, and Isabel McClur, dau. David McClur.—Jan. 16, 1788.

Crockett, Tilman, and Elizabeth Dennis, (own cons).—Oct. 27, 1796.

Crowell, Zenns, and Nancy Bartee, dau. Wm. Bartee—Oct. 16, 1794.

Crowl, Davolt. Jr., and Sally Rudy. Dan'l Rudy. sur.—Aug. 15, 1803.

Crowl, Henry, and Elizabeth Cross. Jacob Cross, sur.—Sept. 25, 1801.

Crowl. Jacob, and Polly Allick. John Attick, sur.—Sept. 7, 1801.

Crump. George, and Dyce Haynes. Wm. Haynes, sur.—July 23, 1792 .

Culp, John, and Mary McGuire. John McCuire, sur.—May 18, 1801.

Cundiff, Mishack, and Elizabeth Dale. Richard Dale, sur.—Dec. 27, 1797.

Custer, David, and Zaney Nowlni, dau Elizabeth Campbell—Dec. 9, 1799.

Custard, John, and Elizabeth Hudson, dau. Eliza Beth (Elizabeth?) Hudson.—June 2, 1801.

—D—

Dabney, Garland, and Polly Martin, dau. John Martin—Jan. ...... 1799.

Davenport, John, and Lucy Hall, dau. Isham Hall—Dec. 12, 1791.

David, Abraham, and Rachel Edmond. Wm. Edmonds, sur.—Dec. 5, 1803.

David, Peter, and Elizabeth Hale—Nov.8, 1793

Davis, Isaac, and Jean Bird. Consent signed by John Bird, who states that he is "her nearest living relative."—Apr. 28, 1798.

Davis, Iserael, and Judith Rogers. Elija Brockman, sur.—Oct. 9, 1804.

Davis, James, and Milly James. Jack James, sur.—Sept. 18, 1801.

Davis, Joshua, and Mary Dulaney, dau. Joshua and Mary Dulaney—Feb. 18, 1804.

Davis, William, and Jane Daniel, dau. George Daniel. Lewis Davis, sur.—Apr. 2, 1787.

Davis, William, and Judith Woody (of age). John Davis, sur.—Dec. 19, 1796.

Dearing, John. and Polly Wilks. John Wilks, sur.—Nov. 28, 1801.

Delaney, Samuel, and Polly Griffith. Jonathan Griffith, sur.—Jan. 14, 1806.

Demoss, William, and Pricilla Greer—May 10, 1787.

Dent, John. and Mary Clower. Mar. ret. by R. H.—Oct. 3, 1793.

Dent, Walter, Jr., and Drucilla Wanar: Thos. Prstor, sur.—Nov. 12, 1800.

Devine, Daniel, and Bridget Flood—Oct. 20, 1790.

Dickerson, David, and Jane Martin, dau. John Martin. Bond undated; consent dated—Nov. 16, 1793.

Dillion, Asa, and Elizabeth Greer, dau. Elizabeth Greer: Aquilla Greer, sur.—Aug. 13, 1798.

Dillion, Henry, and Joanna Palvey. Min ret. by John Saunders.— Oct. 15, 1801

Dillion, James, and Martha Belcher, dau. John Belcher—Feb. 2, 1789.

Dillion, Meridith, and Polly Ryherd. Aaron Ryherd, sur.—Feb. 17, 1806.

Dillenham, Peter, and Susannah Rentfro. John England, sur.—Apr. 24, 1793.

Dillon, Squire, and Celia Ward. Benjamin Ward, sur.—Sept. 1, 1806.

Divers, Aquilla, and Nancy Bradly. Archilles Smith, sur.—Apr. 7, 1794.

Divers, Christopher, and Lucy Smith, dau. John Smith—Jan. 27, 1789.

Dixon, John, and Elizabeth Watson. (Own consent). John Witt, sur.—May 11, 1798.

Dodd, Benjamin, and Mary Prosese. William Prosese, sur.—June 16, 1801.

Dodd, John, and Polly Short. Noah Ferguson, sur.—Mar. 26, 1806.

Doggett, Chattin, and Peggy Wilks: Frank Wilks, sur.— Aug. 3, 1801.

Doran, John, and Fanny McCormack. Micajah McCormack, sur.—Apr. 16, 1804.

Doss, Charles, and Sarah Harvey, dau. Thomas Harvey—Jan. 29, 1793.

Douglas, William, and Pricilla Greer. Greenberry Greer, sur.—May 10, 1786.

Douglas, William, and Rachel Davis (Of age) Sam'l Davis, sur.—Feb. 1, 1796.

Dow, Fullard, and Sally Pedoit. John Coalter, sur.—Dec. 29, 1804.

Drake, Braxton, and Patsey Greer, dau. Elizabeth Greer—Apr. 27, 1795.

Drake, Clayton, and Sarah Meadors, dau. Levine Meadors. John Drake, sur.—Aug. 25, 1791.

Drake, Turner, and Polly Graham, dau. Joseph Graham—May 9, 1797.

Dudley, Givin, and Mary Paslay, dau. Robert Paslay—Aug. 17, 1797.

Dudley, James, and Nancy ....Robert Camp, sur.—Sept. 19, 1804.

Dudley, Levi, and Polly Camp, dau. Thomas Camp—Mar. 27, 1802.

Dudley, Thomas, and Nancy Parsley, dau. Robert Parsley—Jan. 16, 1800.

Duese, William, and Sarah Hubble, dau. Jonathan Hubble—Nov. 29, 1789.

Dulaney, William, and Polly Divers, dau. Polly Divers—Jan. 23, 1804.

Dunn, Samuel, and Sally Clarkson, dau. David Clarkson—Dec. 22, 1801.

—E—

Eakenburg, Peter, and Elizabeth Landis. Henry Landis, sur.—Oct. 22, 1791.

Early, John, and Elizabeth Cheatham. Jubal Early, sur.—Feb. 20, 1792.

Edge, Jesse, and Eliza--Childers. Philip Raley, sur.—Mar. 3, 1788.

Edings, Henry, and Abagail Richardson, dau. Martha Richardson........ 1789.

Edmunds, Esom, and Sophia Greer. Isham Hodges, sur.—Nov. 22, 1805.

Edwards, Abdon, and Margaret Storme, dau. Peter Storme—Nov. 29, 1789.

Edwards, William, and Elizabeth Perejoy, dau. Edward Perijoy—Mar. 18, 1793.

Ellkins, John, and Elizabeth Stephens. Mar. ret. by R. H.—Sept. 20, 1794

Eller, David, and Anna Prupecker. John Prupecker, sur. All signatures were in German—Dec. 21, 1802.

Eller, Joseph, and Fanny Woodson, dau. Shadrack Woodson—July 1, 1790.

Eller, Stephen, and Rebecca Lewis. Joseph Lewis, sur.—Apr. 9, 1795.

Ellet, Joseph, and Mary Litterell .. .. .. R. J.—July 12, 1787.
(Mar. bond gives name as Joseph Elliot. Sam'l Litterell, sur.)

Ellis, John, and Mildred Lee, Stephen Lee. sur.—Apr. 6, 1795.

Ellis, Joseph, and Fanny Woodson, Mar. ret. See Eller, Joseph, above.

Ellis, Stephen, and Rebecca Lewis. See Eller above.

Ellison, Amos, and Sarah Price, dau. John Price—Dec. 19, 1797

Ellison, Ezekiel, and Christina Vanover (Of age). John Abshire, sur.—Dec. 6, 1796.

Ellison, John, and Lucy Sharp. (Spelled Leusea Sharp in min. ret.): John Chitwood sur,—Feb. 5, 1788.

Ellison, Joseph, and Aleshey Vanover. Matthew Vanover, sur. Feb. 25, 1791.

Ellison, Lewis, and Betsy Lewis, dau. Thos. and Mary Lewis—Sept. 23, 1790.

England, Titas, and Elizabeth Sewart. James Sewart, sur.—Dec. 26. 1795.

English, Stephen, and Elizabeth Dudley, dau. Gwyn Dudley—Jan. 3, 1791.

Epperson, Anthony, and Ellener Divers, dau. John Divers—............ 1800.

Eperson, Benjamin, and Polly Starkey, dau. Joshua Starkey—Jan 30, 1797 .

Estes, Elisha, and Nancy Harris, dau. Henry Harris—Aug. 29, 1791.

Estes, Jesse, and Elizabeth Nappier, dau Robt. and Elizabeth Nappier—Mar. 14, 1789.

Estes, Joel, and Elizabeth Bradley. Wm. Bradley, sur. June 12, 1801.

Evans, John, and Nancy Eubank. Min. ret by R. H.—July 24, 1793.

Evans, Peter, and Jane Likins, Min. ret by R. H.—July 12, 1791.

—F—

Faris, Amariah, and Elizabeth Beheler, dau. David Beheler—Jan. 10, 1791.

Farley, Archibald, and Jane Farley, dau. Sarah Farley—Dec. 3, 1787.

Farmer, John, and Sarah Wyatt, dau. Alice Wyatt: Matthew Farmer, sur. May 10, 1803.

Farmer, William and Jean Wyatt, dau. Jain Wyatt: Matthew Farmer, sur.—Oct. 21,1799.

Feller, John, and Nancy Jones, dau. Ann Jones—Jan. 31, 1804.

Ferguson, Abediah, and Elizabeth Martin,dau. Sarah Martin. Randolph Martin, sur.—Sept. 9, 1786.

Ferguson, Alexander, and Ann Wood. Min. ret. by T. D.—Apr. 20, 1790.

Ferguson. Daniel, and Jemima Saunders: Pleasant Saunders, sur.—Nov. 28, 1806.

Ferguson, Eli, and Nancy Childress. Robt. Childress. sur.—Mar. 12, 1805.

Ferguson, George, and Polly Crump. Jas. Calloway, sur.—Oct. 25, 1797.

Ferguson, John, and Marv Hill: George Ferguson, sur.—Jan. 21, 1790.

Ferguson. John, and Suky Abshire (Own consent) no date.

Ferguson, Joseph, (son of John. "Underage") and Sarah Hughes—May 2, 1801

Ferguson, Joshua, and Rebecca Toney. Edward Toney, sur.—Aug. 10, 1792.

Ferguson, Joshua, and Jane Johnson: John Johnson, sur.—Dec. 3, 1804.

Ferguson. Noah, and Frances Short, dau. Winnefred Short: Thos. R. Short, sur.—.. .... 1797.

Ferguson, Thomas. and Agnes Chambers,dau. ohn Chambers, Dec. 5, 1796.

Ferguson, Thomas, and Marv Solsbury. Lewis Davis, sur.—Apr. 28, 1802.

Finney, John, and Polly Prunty (?): Robt. Printy, sur.—Jan. 18, 1802.

Finney, John, and Ruth Smith, dau. Mary Smith—Sept. 2, 1805.

Finney, Reiley, and Ellender Sloan. Min. ret. bv R. H.—Mar. 28, 1793.

Fishburn, Peter, and Calah Harger. Aaron B. Wilson, sur.—Apr. 1, 1805.

Fisher, Peter, and Elizabeth Allick. John Allick. sur.— Mar. 12, 1792.

Fitzjarrard, Theodoric, and Sarah Hoff, dau. Philip and Rachel Hoff—June 10, 1793.

Flowers, James, and Jane Moore, dau. Jane Moore—Dec. 13, 1790.

Florow, Abraham, and Nancy Overholt. Consent by her father, signed in German, and undecipherable.—Sept. 11, 1797.

Floro, Samuel, and Elizabeth Dilmon, dau. Jacob and Christinah Dilmon—Apr. 7, 1788.

Folass, Hugh, and Barbary Henley. L. Davis, sur.— Dec....... 1791.

Fortune, Benjamin, and Milley Carter, dau. Barnard Carter—Oct. 13, 1804.

Foster, Charles, and Exiona Turner. Josiah Turner, sur.—Jan. 2, 1804.

Fowler, Thomas, and Molley Spangler, dau. Mary Spangler—Dec. 20, 1790.

Franklin, Aaron, and Millia Richeson, dau. Jonathan Richeson.—Oct. ..., 1799.

Frame, Jesse, and Nancy Abshire, dau. Abraham Abshire—Jan. 10, 1803.

Frame, Paul, and Susanna Hickman. Peter Hickman, sur.—Nov. 20, 1798.

Frame, William (a german), and Nancy Crowl. Devault Crowl, sur.—Sept. 2, 1805.

Frans, Michael, and Rebecca Henry, dau. John Henry. Consent also by Rebeccas' grandfather, Abraham Picard Simons.— Jan. 5, 1798.

French, Richard, and Diney Greer, dau. Mary Greer,—Feb. 22, 1800.

Frith, Joseph, and Littishe Fowler. dau. Susannah Blankenship.—July 23, 1792.

Fuller, Jesse, and Mary Estes, dau. Frances and Lishe Estes.—Jan. 19, 1799.

Furrow, Adam, and Mary Cox. John Ferrow, sur.—July 24, 1788.

Ferrow, Charles, and Deborough Graham. Sarah Ferrow, sur.—Apr. 4, 1796.

Ferrow, John, and Sarah Cox. Jas. Stone, sur.—Nov. 22, 1787.

—G—

Gadd, William, and Dice Young, dau. James Young: Thos. Gadd, sur.—May 21, 1802.

Gallamore, William, and Sarah Grimmitt, dau. John Grimmitt. Absom Gallamore, sur.—Apr. 8, 1787.

Garner, James, and Tibetha Martin. Wm. Griffith, sur.—May 17, 1798.

Garrall (Garsale?), Isham, and Lucy Webb. Mark Rentfro, sur.—Jan. 17, 1790.

Garsale, Isham. See above.

Gearhart, Henry, and Hannah Rentfro, dau. Moses Rentfro.—Dec. 6, 1791.

Geerhart, William, and Elizabeth Wright, dau. John Wright.—Apr. 16, 1804.

Gilbert, ..., and Elener Charter. Min. ret.—May 15, 1798.

Gilbert, James, and Christron Keen. Elisha Keen, sur.—Dec. 3, 1803.

Gilbert, Kement, and Polly Smith. William Smith, sur.—Nov. 4, 1805.

Gilbert, Preston, and Fanny Law, dau. Henry Law—Jan. 11, 1803.

Gillaspy, Evan, and Nancy Lee, dau. Elizabeth Frashier (wife of John Frashier)—Mar. 17, 1789.

Givins, John, and Patty Tally—Aug. 5, 1800.

Goad, Stephen, and Rachel Smith, dau. John John Smith—Mar. 5, 1792.

Gosenell, Dawson, and Rebeckah Frith, "of age",—Sept. .., 1804.

Gossard, Daniel, and Nancy Nofsinger. John Nofsinger, sur.—Mar. 4, 1805.

Gragg, John, and Elizabeth Booth, grand-dau.—John Booth.—Jan. 6, 1800.

Graham, Robert, and Rachel Delaney, dau. Samuel Delaney.—Mar. 2, 1790.

Graves, David, and Nancy Pinckard; Charles Pinkard, sur.—Jan. 27, 1793.

Graves, John, and Nancy Ryan, dau. William Ryan—Dec. 13, 1790.

Graves, Peyton, and Charlotte Pinkard. Nathan Ryan, sur.—Nov. 11, 1788.

Greer, Aquilla, and Elizabeth Smith, dau. John Smith—Aug. .. 1798.

Greer, Asa, and Rebecca Neighbors, dau. Francis Neighbors.—July 20, 1791.

Greer, Barna, and Polly Clarkson, dau. David Clarkson—Dec. .., 1792.

Greer, Benjamin, and Sally Compton, dau. Richard Compton—Jan. 9, 1799.

Greer, Charles, and Agnes Sumpter. Mar. ret. by R. H.—Aug. 1, 1793.

Greer, Charles, and Rebecca Henson. Wm. Curtain, sur.—June 10, 1806.

Greer, George, and Wilmeth Kirby, dau. Francis and Elizabeth Kirby—June 30, 1789.

Greer, George, and Elizabrth Sara Taylor, dau. Sarah Taylor—Aug. 4, 1795.

Greer, James, and Elizabeth Frazer. John Frazer, sur.—Sept. 22, 1800.

Greer, Joseph, and Fanny Lyons. Elisha Lyons, sur.—May 1, 1786.

Greer, Moses, and Charity Salmon. Min. ret. by R. H.—Sept. 8, 1795.

Greer, William, and Elizabeth Harkrider, dau. Conrad Harkrider.—May 1, 1791.

Greybill, Daniel, and Elizabeth Kinzer. Mar. ret. by J. M.—1794-95.

Griffith, Abraham, and Margaret Livesay—July 8, 1789.

Griffith, Alexander, and Rachel Griffith. George Griffith, sur.—Dec. 16, 1806.

Griffith, Isaac, and Peggy Gillaspy. Daniel Gillaspy, sur.—Jan. 12. 1795.

Griffon, Samuel, and Charlotte Hook, dau. John Hook.—Jan. 11. 1800.

Griggs, John, and Christinah Lemons, dau. Mary Lemons—June 30, 1791.

Grimes, Jesse, and Margaret Ray, dau. Moses Ray—June 30, 1790.

Grimmett, Solomon, and Sarah Hale. Min. ret. by R. H.—Sept. 18, 1794.

Grimmett, William, and Delilah Polston. Andrew Polston, sur.—Mar. 17, 1791.

Guillams, John, and Jenn McClary, dau. Richard McClary—Feb. 1, 1796.

Guilliam, William, and Sarah Ferguson. Thos. Gadd, sur.—Dec. 24, 1797.

Guthrey, Benjamin, and Sarah Bradley. Wm. Bradley, sur.—Feb. 22, 1799.

Guthrey, David, and Mary Booth, dau. John Booth—Sept. 15, 1786.

—H—

Hairston, Samuel, and Judith Saunders. Mar. ret.—Feb. 9, 1790.

Hairston, William, and Rachel Hufmon, own consent—Jan. 17, 1804.

Hale, Armstrong, and Elizabeth Ruble, dau. Owen Ruble—Jan. 10, 1789.

Hale, Benjamin, Jr. and Dicey Frankling. Benj. Hale, Sr., sur.—Nov. 13, 1788.

Hale, James, and Jenny Craghead, dau. John Craghead—Oct. 2, 1786.

—11—

Hale, James Lewis, and Ann Crahead, dau.. John Crahead—July 20, 1789.

Hale, John, and Susannah Wade, dau. John Wade—Mar. 17, 1789.

Hale, John, and Doshea Saunders, dau. Peter Saunders—Sept. 12, 1792.

Hale, Joseph, and Sally Turnbull. George Turnbull, sur.—July 20, 1789.

Hale, Joseph, and Elizabeth Turman, dau. Francis Turman—Feb. 13, 1789.

Hale, Maxey, and Dicey Craghead, dau. John Craghead—Oct. 25, 1789.

Hale, Peter, and Sara Morris, dau. Zekel Morris: John Hale, sur.—Mar. 14, 1791.

Hale, Richard. and Tibitha Jones, dau. Robert Jones—Oct. 24, 1788.

Hall, Curry, and Milly Hodges. John Hodges, sur.—Dec. 20, 1792.

Hall. Jonathan, and Joanah Barton. David Barton, sur.—Nov. 9, 1792.

Hammock. Peter, and Nancy Pritty. Macajah Beck, sur.—Jan. 26, 1788.

Hampton, George, and Sally Hodges. John Hodges, sur.—Aug. 2, 1806.

Hancock. Benjamin, and Fanny Holland. Peter Holland, sur.—Jan. 6, 1806.

Hancock, John A., and Sally Ryan—Nov. 3, 1801.

Handy, James, and Hannah Rentfro, dau. Jesse Rentfro—Feb. 11, 1786.

Handy. John, and Grace Grimmett, dau. John Grimmett—Nov. 5, 1792.

Handy, Peter, and Sarah Dixon. Nathaniel Dixon—Apr. 1, 1799.

Handy, William, and Mary Butler. Consent states she is "of lawful age, and without parents living".—Aug. 6, 1792.

Hardwick, Cary, and Cahherine Edwards, dau. Isham Edwards—Oct. 17, 1794.

Hardwick, Cary, and Catherine Saunders. Mar. ret. by R. H. (Same ?)—1794.

Harkrider, John, and Beka Huston, dau. William Huston—Mar. 23, 1801.

Harkrider, David, and Anna Mikesell (of afe). John Fishburn, sur.— .., 1799.

Harkrider, Solomon, and Rachel Huston: Thomas Huston, sur.—Nov. 3, 1800.

Harmon, Robert, and Mary Drake. John Drake, sur.—May 20, 1794.

Harper, Absolum (or Abrohm) and Elizabeth Birchfield, dau. John Birchfield,—July 20, 1790.

Harper, Josiah, and Sarah Parrott: Joseph Parrot, sur.—Dec. 27, 1787.

Harrell, James, and Elizabeth Ellis; Joseph Ellis, sur.—Apr. 3, 1793.

Harrison, Ignatious, and Glicy Farrell. Wm. Harrison, sur.—Sept. 5, 1803.

Harris, Samuel, and Drucilla Huff. by J. H.—Sept. 4, 1793.

Harter, David, and Polly Beckner. George Harter, sur.—Aug. 6, 1804.

Harter, George, and Marv Miller. Tobias Miller, sur.—Feb. 13, 1798.

Harter, Henry, and Elizabeth Young, dau. Joseph Young—Sept. 30, 1799.

Harter, Jacob, and Elizabeth Houts. By J. M.—Mar. 17, 1798.

Harter, John, and Sarah Webb, dau. Mary Webb—Aug. 14, 1797.

Hartzell, Abraham, and Eve Houtz, dau. Christian Houtz—May 23, 1796.

Hatcher, Edmund, and Polly Maxey, dau. Pheby Maxey—Nov. 9, 1803.

Hatcher, Henry, and Sally Greer, dau. Mary Greer—Feb. 4, 1801.

Hatcher, Henry, and Mary Napier, dau. Robert Napier. Champion Napier, sur.—Jan. 7, 1805.

Hatcher, William, and Patty Hale. James Edmundson Hale, sur.—Aug. 8, 1796.

Hayes, Joseph, and Jemima Alley, dau. Joseph Hale—Mar. 31, 1788.

Hayes, Levi, and Anna Adney, dau. Thomas Adney—June 7, 1802.

Haynes, Henry, and Susannah Walker, (of age). Robt. Boulton, sur.—Jan. 16, 1789.

Haynes, Henry W. and Mary Wheat: of age. Stephen Haynes, sur.—July 4, 1797.

Haizlip, Joel, and Drucilla Hazlip. Robert Hazlip, sur.—Apr. 2, 1804.

Hazlip, William, and Polly Roach, dau. Gideon Roach—Apr. 13, 1801.

Heard. Charles, and Sarah Carter. Own consent—Oct. 18, 1795.

Heard, George, and Rhoda Hill. Joshua Rogers, sur.—Feb. 20, 1806.

Heard. John, and Hannah Underwood, dau. Samuel Underwood—Jan. 24, 1788.

Heard, Stephen, and Sarah Marcum, dau. Ogge and Janey Marcum,—Mar. 2, 1790.

Heeth, Timothy, and Mary Ferguson. mar. ret. by R. H.—Dec. 30, 1794.

Helm, Adam, and Conny Webb. dau. Molley Webb—Apr. 25, 1789.

Helm, Jacob, and Nancy Webb. Consent by Conny Helm—Mar. 8. 1806.

Helm, Samuel, and Alian Taylor. Abraham Taylor, sur.—July 12, 1806.

Helm. Thomas, and Molley Webb, dau. Mary Webb. Theoderick Webb, sur.—Aug. 10, 1795.

Henderson, Andrew, and Assenah Harris, dau. Evan Harris—Nov. 3, 1791.

Henderson, Henry, and Assenah Harris. Min. ret. by R. H. (Same as above)—1791.

Henderson, William, and Mary McClure, dau. Mary Henderson: William, son of Samuel Henderson—Mar. 3, 1786.

Henley, Jas. B., and Elizabeth Dodd, dau. Sarah Dodd—June 11, 1804.

Hennes, John, and Rhoda Kendiss? (Candy) Consent by Wm. Candy—Sept. 9, 1787.

Hepenstall, Caleb, and Tege Greer. Thos. Dannoss, sur.—Nov. 7, 1796.

Hepner, Henry, and Mary Heysaw, dau. Mary Hysor—Dec. 30, 1790.

Hewit, Daniel, and Bridget Rowland (of age). —Philmer Whitworth, sur.—Feb. .., 1803.

Hickman, Daniel, and Sally Lane. Mar. ret. bv H. B.—May 4, 1790.

Hickman, David, and Polly Snawffer. Jacob Snawffer, sur.—Feb. 11, 1804.

Hickman, Henry, and Mary Kinzey. Peter Hickman, sur.—Sept. 5, 1803.

Hickman, Nickedemus, and Charlott Edwards, dau. Thomas Edwards: Nicodemus, son of John: both fathers' gave written consent. —Mar. 25, 1792.

Hickman, Jacob, and Mary Overbolt. David Overholt, sur.—May 13, 1793.

Highly, Thomas, and Patty Brown, dau. Lucy Brown—Aug. 22, 1795.

Hill, Francis, and Elizabeth Woods. John Woods, sur.—Feb. 24, 1796.

Hill, John, and Patsey Price. Mar. ret. by R. H.—Apr. 9, 1795.

Hillion, Henry, and Joanna Parsley. Robert Parsley, sur.—Oct. 5, 1801.

Hisaw, John, and Elizabeth Rudy. Dan'l Rudy, sur.—Oct. 10, 1795.

Hix, William, and Rebecca Boles, dau. Jesse Boles—Nov. 18, 1797.
Note: Jesse Boles was anxious for Wm. for a son-in-law: He gave written consent for him to marry both his daughter, Hannah, and Rebecca—same date. In bond, the name of Hannah was first written in, and scratched off, and Rebecca substituted.

Hixon, John, and Polly Phillips. Salter Phillips, sur.—Oct. 7, 1805.

Hodges, Aaron, and Elizabeth Markham. James Markham, sur.—Aug. 13, 1792.

Hodges, Drury, and Dinah Griffith. George Griffith, sur.—June 1, 1800.

Hodges, Joel, and Susannah Hodges; Wm. Hodges, sur.—Nov. 6, 1792.

Hodges, John, and .... obliterated. David Dalton, sur. Aug. 8, 1786.

Hodges, Lewis. See Hoges, Lewis.

Hodges, Robert, and Susannah Hale, dau. Isham Hale—May 18, 1791.

Hodges, William, and Aemy Hall, Wm. Hall, sur.—Mar. 16, 1796.

Hoff, John, and Polly Gearhart. William Kelly, sur.—July 14, 1786.

Hoff, William, and Lydda Miller, dau. Thomas Miller—Feb. 2, 1797.

Hoges, Lewis, and Elizabeth Doss. Abedmiss Hoges, sur.— ...., 1803.

Holland, Mastin, and Polley Bradley, dau. William Bradley—July 20, 1801.

Holland, Meador, and Mary Smith. Peter Holland, sur.—Jan. 2, 1797.

Holland, Thomas, and Sarah Gilbert, dau. Michel and Willmuth Gilbert—Dec. 27, 1790.

Holliday, Jeremiah, and Margaret Marten, dau. James Marten—Aug. 15, 1788.

Holt, Ambrose, and Lucy Richardson. John Burgis, sur.—Sept. 9, 1788.

Horsley, William, and Elizabeth Patton, dau. Lewis Patton—Aug. 27, 1802.

Hough, Daniel, and Hannah Hale, dau. John Hale—Aug. 30, 1790.

Howell, David, and Susanna Helton. Elijah Helton, sur.—Oct. .., 1789.

Hubbler, Isham, and Catey Hughes. Consent by .., Johnson, "and wife",—May 3, 1789.

Hubble, Itamer, and Damorise Lewis, dau. Thomas Lewis—Mar. 12, 1787.

Huddleston, Abraham, and Martha Pate, dau. Anthony Pate—Jan. 8, 1790.

Huff. (See Hoff)

Huff, William, and Lydia Miller, Mar. ret. by I. R.—Feb. 10, 1791.

Hughes, David, and Sussannah Hammond. James Vest, sur.—Apr. 7, 1786.

Hughes, Reese, and Polly Lyon. Jos. Greer. sur.—Aug. 2, 1801.

Hunter, John, and Sarah Price. Joseph L. Price, sur.—Aug. 7, 1786.

Hunter, Robert, and Sally Martin, dau. John Martin—Feb. 23, 1798.

Hurd, Stephen, and Sarah Marcum—Apr. .., 1790.

Hurt, Colby, and Polley Ballard. Stephen Stone, sur.—Mar. 5, 1788.

Huston, Samuel, and Elizabeth Brown, dau. Richard Brown—Dec. 31, 1790.

Huston, Samuel, and Jenny Abshire. Sherod Abshire, sur.—Apr. 16, 1802.

Huston, Thomas, and Tabitha Wright, dau. John Wright—June 8, 1799.

Hutcheson, William, and Catherine Cook. Jesse Pruntz, sur.—Sept. 30, 1796.

—I—

Ikenberry, Peter, and Elizabeth Landers. Mar. ret. by R. H.—Oct. 28, 1791.

—J—

Jacoby, John, and Anny Dalton— ...., 1790.

James, Daniel, and Polly Harmon, dau. Levicey and John Drake—Aug. 5, 1801.

James, Jamey, and Elizabeth Huston, dau. Thomas Hutson—Feb 21, 1789.

James, John, and Hanney Estes, dau. Franny Estes: Elisha Estes, sur.—Jan. 22, 1798.

James, Nicholas, and Elizabeth Phillips, dau. Sally Phillips.—Dec. 2, 1805.

James, Samuel, and Pa†sey Snead, dau. John Snead—Apr. 7, 1791.

Jameson, Sam'l & Winney Bird. John Bird, sur.—Dec. 9, 1806.

Janel, Isham, and Lucy Webb. Mar. ret. by R. H.—Jan. 21. 1790.

Janney, Moses, and Peggy Dixon. Nathaniel Dixon, sur.—Apr. 28, 1802.

Jaques, James, and Nancy Harger. George Harger, sur.—May 23, 1806.

Jarrett, Allen, and Polley Spangler—Oct. 15, 1805.

Jefferson, Field Jr., and Elizabeth Beasley, dau. Elizabeth Beasley—Sept 7, 1789.

Jefferson, Field, and Elizabeth Bushby—Apr. 4, 1790.

Jefferson, Field, and Lucy Johnson. Daniel Low, sur.—Sept. 5, 1806.

Johnson, Jacob, and Nancy Hall, dau. Martha Hall—Jan. 30, 1790.

Johnson, John, and Elizabeth Wattson. I. Rentfro, sur.—Sept. 4. 1786.

Johnson, Silas, and Polly Woody. Martin Woody, sur.—Dec. 23, 1806.

Johnson, William, and Edith Wattson. Alexander, and Elizabeth Wattson, sur.—Sept. .., 1786.

Johnson, William, and Mary Maynor, dau. John Maynor—May 19, 1790.

Jones, Ansilom, and Lener Noles, dau. Joshua Noles—Dec. 21, 1799.

Jones, Barnet, and Sesley Blankenship. Mar. ret. by J. F.—Oct. 23. 1795.

Jones, Edward, and Betsev Hodges, dau. Robert Hodges—July 25, 1805.

Jones, Elijah, and Rebecca McCutcaan, dau. James McCutchan—Feb. 13, 1789.

Jones, James Martin, and Elizabeth Blankenship, dau. Nancy Blankenship,—Mar. ...., 1792.

Jones, Jesse, and Hannah Hale, dau. John Hale. Robt. Jones, sur.—Sept. 2, 1788.

Jones, Jeremiah, and Susannah Agee, dau. Matthew Agee (Susannah had brother, Jesse.) Obediah Jones, sur.—Oct. 2, 1800.

Jones, John, and Sarah Sumpter, dau. George Sumpter—July 5, 1790.

Jones, Jonathan, and Sarah Barton. David Barton, sur.—Nov. 7, 1803.

Jones, Robert, and Violet Barton. David Barton, sur.—Feb. 1, 1796.

—K—

Kailer, John, and Selmy Kinsey. Henry Kinsey, sur.—June 14, 1792.

Keen, Anderson, and Polly Rollins—Aug. 20 1804.
Keen, John, and Elizabeth Redman —......
...... 8, 1786.
Keen, John, and Nancy Shockley, dau. Levi Shockley—Mar. 22, 1802.
Keep, Matthew, Jr., and Lucy Bowls. George Bowls, Jr., sur.—Jan. 19,1806.
Keester (Koster), Lodewick, and Mary Boon, dau. Jacob Boon—Aug. 1, 1789.
Kelly, John, and Frances McIllwane. William Kelly, sur.—Nov. 8, 1798.
Kelly, Wiliam, and Martha Richeson. Mar. ret. by R. H.—Nov. 29, 1792.
Kelly, William, and Hannah Richards. Ambroas Raines, sur.—Nov. 26, 1792.
Kemp, Jorden, and Peggy Mattox. Richard Robinson, sur.—Dec. 1, 1795.
Kenze, Jacob, and Elizabeth Hartzell. Philip Hartzell, sur.—Sept. 11, 1798.
Kersey, Edmund, and Martha Wade. Castleton Wade, sur.— Feb. 8, 1806.
Key, John, and Pheby Akers. Nathaniel Akers, sur.—Sept. 12, 1806.
Key, Thomas, and Ester Brammer, dau. John Brammer—Nov. 17, 1802.
Key, Worley, and Susannah Akers. William Akers, sur.—Sept. 3, 1804.
Kidd, George, and Lidia Chiles—Apr. 17,1805.
Kimmons, Robert, and Lydia Reese. James Reese, Jr., sur.—Jan. 7, 1798.
King, Samuel, and Mary Richardson, dau. Frances and Stanhope Richardson—Sept. 29, 1790.
King, Thomas, and Christina Stockton. Richard Stockton, sur.—Nov. 7, 1803.
King, William, and Lidda Edwards, dau. Isham Edwards—Mar. 22, 1803.
Kingery, Kingary, Kingry. Kingsey.
Kingery, Christian, and Jenny Hudson, dau. Abraham Abshire.—Nov. 9, 1800.
Kingery, Daniel, and Elizabeth Perry. George Perry, sur.—May 5, 1795.
Kingery, Jacob, and Leah Kelly, dau. Wm. and Rachel Kelly—Jan. 7, 1799.
Kingery, John, and Anny Richardson, dau. Caty.............—May 15, 1800.
Kingery, Joseph, and Caty Kelly. William Kelly, sur.—June 27, 1796.
Kingery, Joseph, and Eva Ritter. Jacob Miller sur.—Aug. 12, 1794.
Kingery, Peter, and Sarah Davis, dau.Joseph Davis—Dec. 20, 1800 or 1806.
Kingery, Samuel, (son of Jacob), and Sally Hickman, dau. Barabra Hickman.—Apr. 4 1803.
Kinsey, John, and Barbara Hickman, dau. Barbara Hickman, Sr.—Sept. 3, 1804.
Kirby, George, and Elinor Jameson, dau. Hannah Jameson—Oct. 10, 1795.
Kirby, Joel, and Mary Brammer, dau. John Brammer—June 4, 1804.
Kirby, John, and Anna Dalton, dau. James and Elizabeth Dalton—Mar. 1, 1790.
Kirby, Samuel, and Mary Spangler. Bartlet Wade, sur.—Mar. 22, 1788.
Knafe, Daniel, and Polly Logan. William Knape, sur.—Sept. 28, 1795.
Knape, Jonathan, and Catherine Hoss. Jos. Flora, sur.—Aug. 31, 1795.
Knave, Isaac, and Barbary Mayer, dau. Kohor Boon—June 1, 1789.
Knave, Joseph, and Mary Magdeline Barnhart, dau. Conrad Barnhart—Mar. 7, 1796.

Knight, John, and Jane Ferguson. Isham Ferguson, sur.—Sept. 6, 1802.
Knowles-Knoles.
Knoles, John, and Susanna Reel. Matthew Knoles, sur.—Feb. 23, 1791.
Knowles, Matthew, and Jane Smith, dau. Elizabeth Smith—Feb. 27, 1792.
Kymes, Abraham, and Mary Hare. Valentine Kymes, sur.—Nov. 9, 1804.

—L—

Lacy, John, and Sally Brown, John Napier, sur.—July 20, 1799.
Landers, David, and Betsy Pickelsimer, dau. Jacob Picklesimer—May 31, 1800.
Landes, Abraham, and Polly Hockmon. Daniel Nofsinger, sur.—Nov. 16, 1803.
Lapwell, Moses, and Susannah Brook, dau. George Brook—Jan. 4, 1792.
Lark, Dennis, and Sally Lovel. Markham Lovel, sur.—Oct. 21, 1802.
Lavender, Robert, and Nancy Willis—Feb. 27, 1794.
Lavender, Robert, and Milly Willis. John Highly, sur.—Sept. 30, 1795.
Lavender, Thomas, and Margaret Kel-y. Mar. ret. by R. H.—May 28, 1795.
Law, Burwell, and Elizabeth Wood. Stephen Wood, sur.—Dec. 24, 1788.
Law, Coleman, and Susannah Sutherland. Sam'l Sutherland, sur.—Apr. 3, 1805.
Law, Daniel, and Biddy Tyre. William Law. sur.—May 10, 1791.
Law, David, and Nancy Bell, dau. Frances Bell. Burwell Law, sur.—Mar. 1, 1802.
Law, Jesse, and Sally Hopkins. Benjamin Hopkins, sur.—Oct. 8, 1805.
Law, John, and Sarah Maxey, dau Jeremiah Maxey—Sept. 5, 1796.
Law, William, tnd Letty Cockran, dau. Susanna Cockran—Jan. 7, 1799.
Lebart, Charles, and Catherine Lemon—Mar. 2, 1787.
Lee, Braxton, and Elizabeth Hatcher, dau. Archibald Hatcher—Feb. 1, 1790.
Lee, David, and Susannah Barber. William Boid—Oct. 9, 1792.
Lee, John, and Rachel Richards. Benjamin Richards, sur.—Jan. 16, 1802.
Lee, William, and Sarah John. John John sur.—Jan. 13, 1801.
Lee, William, and Sara Coger. Joseph Wier, sur.—Dec. 4, 1797.
Lehmon, Daniel, and Fanny Ruday. Dan'l Ruday, sur.(All Germans)—Feb. 18, 1791.
Lemon, Isaac, and Vina Richardson. David Jones, sur.—May 1, 1786.
Lepew, Elias, and Rebecca Quigley, dau. Thomas Quigley—June 28, 1802.
Lewis, Edward, and Polly Wright, dau. Tabithy and Wintfield Wright—Dec. 25, 1792.
Lewis, Jesse, and Rhoda Bell, dau. John Bell —Sept. 24, 1790.
Lewis, Joseph, and Sarah Bell, dau. John and Sarah Bell—Sept. 3, 1787.
Lewis, Joseph, and Nancy Griffin, dau. Hannah and Wm. Griffin—Mar. 20, 1792.
Lianberry, Henry, and Mary Landis. Min. ret. by J. M.—............1794.
Light, James, and Hannah Hathaway ,dau. Leanord and Susannah Hathaway—Oct. 3, 1791.
Likins, William, and Margaret Ritter. Min. ret. by R. H.—Jan. 2, 1790.

—14—

Littleberry, Atkins, and Nancy Hedge. Min. ret. by R. H. June 22, 1790.

Lloyd, John, and Ann Roberts, own consent —Nov. 5, 1805.

Lloyd, Robert, and ....(Name not written in)—April .... 1804.

Loader, James, and Susannah Gipson. William Gipson, sur.—Sept. 15, 1795.

Long, Edward, and Milla Boulton, dau. Thomas and Femyah Boulton—Sept. 26, 1803.

Long, Isaac, and Nancy Boulton, dau Thomas Boulton—Nov. 18, 1799.

Long, James, and Pricilla Losefield, dau. Jacob Losefield—May 12, 1790.

Love, James (son of Philip), and Polly Mays. Stephen Mays, sur.—Dec. 15, 1787.

Lovin, Henry, and Sally Aday. Walter Aday, sur—Nov. 8, 1786.

Lowe, James, and Sarah Napier, dau. Robert Napier—Aug. 12, 1794.

Lumsden, Dudley, and Sally Chitwood. Mar. ret. by J. S.—June 15, 1802.

Lumsdale, Charles, and Polly Reaves. Jeremiah Lumsden, sur.—Mar. 16, 1787.

Lumsdale, Elijah, and Rachel Greer, dau. Benjamin Greer—Feb. 7, 1787.

Luney, Peter, and Judith Robinson, dau. Thomas Robinson—Mar. 10, 1786.

Lutteril, John, and Sarah Elliott. Mar. ret. by T. D.—Nov. 13, 1786.

Lutteril, Richard, and Susannah Walker. Sam'l Lutteril, sur—Sept. 17, 1788.

Lykins, David, and Jemima Willis, dau. Isiah Willis—Dec. 22, 1797.

Lykins, William, and Margaret Ritter, dau. Susannah Ritter—Jan 13, 1790.

Lyons, John, and Lydia Arrington, dau. Sam'l Arrington—Nov. 25, 1800.

Lyons, William, and Celia Brown, dau. Jinnians (?) Brown—Aug. 11, 1795.

—M—

Maddox, Michael, and Polly Fraley, dau. Frederick Frailey—Sept. 19, 1795.

Maddox, Wilson, and Elizabeth Richards, dau. Edward Richards—Apr. 11, 1796.

Maddox-See Mattox.

Magers(?), Roland, and Elizabeth Stanley. Mar. ret. by J. F.—Oct. 29, 1795.

Mainer, Richard Tucker, and Nancy Davis, dau. Martha Davis.Jan. 15, 1793.

Malloy, James, and Zeanith Richeson, dau. Jonathan Richeson—June 3, 1804.

Mannin, Meridith, and Catey Burnet, dau. Charles Burnet—Mar. 7, 1796

Mannin, Samuel, and Patsy Brock, dau. Lucy and Jushua Brock—Aug. 6, 1804.

Marcum, Barnet, and Lacy Belcher. John Tyre, sur.—June 6, 1791.

Marcum, John, and Dicey Greer. Thomas Demoss, sur.—Dec. 18, 1789.

Markham, Beverley, and Elizabeth Ward, dau. Betsy and Daniel Ward—Oct. 8, 1792.

Mares, Benjamin, and Margaret Saunders, dau. Samuel and Catherine Saunders—Feb. 24, 1804.

Marrs, Hercules, and Betty Chavers. Jesse Chavers, sur.—Feb. 11, 1806.

Martin, Absolom, and Senah Henderson. Mar. ret. by R. H.—May 14, 1794.

Martin, Benjamin, and Judith Walker. Edw. Beard. sur.—Mar. 17, 1792.

Martin, George, and Judith Willis, dau. David Willis—Oct. 8, 1804.

Martin, James, and Margarett Beuman—Dec. 16, 1794.

Martin, James, and Doria Mullins. Thos. Roberts, sur.—June 6, 1803.

Martin, James, Sr., and Mary McGee (of age). Hugh Martin, sur.—Aug. 22, 1805.

Martin, John, and Meley Meadow. Mar. ret. by J. F.—Jan. 13, 1795.

Martin, John, and Sally Huston, dau. William Houston—May 30, 1803.

Martin, Joseph, and Anne Langdon, dau. John Langdon—Sept. 12, 1786.

Martin, Robert, and Susanna Ray. Own consent—Feb. 13, 1798.

Martin, Robert, and Susannah Robinson, dau. William Robinson—Dec. 16, 1799.

Martin, William, and Anny Craig, sur.—Jan. 7, 1805.

Marshall, Lewis, and Martha Jameson. Wm. Jameson, sur.—Jan. 11, 1798.

Marshall, Robert, and Susanna Dodd, dau. Sally Dodd—Dec. 9, 1800.

Mason, Nathan, and Hannah Aden. Swinefield Hill, sur. July 21, 1789.

Mattox, David, and Sally Hail. Henry Page White, sur.—Dec. 1, 1806.

Mattox, John, and Fanny Parrott. Joseph Parrott, sur.—Sept. 3, 1787.

Mattox, William, and Catherine Tennis, dau. William Tennis—Nov. 1, 1795.

Mattox-See Maddox.

Mavity, John, and Dorotha Reel. Mar. ret. by J. J.—June 25, 1795.

Maxey, Jabez, and Betsey Soursbury, dau Jeremiah Soursbury—Feb. 4, 1799.

Maxey, James, and Sally Agnu. Matthew Agnu, sur.—Jan. 4 1796.

Maxey, John, and Sarah Greer. Thos. Demoss, sur.—July 21, 1794.

Mayvey, James, and Martha Richeson. Mar. ret. by J. M.—May 20, 1798.

McCall, John, and Phebe Smith. Wm. McCall, sur.—Jan. 24, 1805.

McCall, William, and Milley Holland. Peter Holland, sur.—Nov. 11, 1799.

McCallister, George, and Agnes Stewart. Wm. Dillenham, sur.—Aug. 24. 1796.

McCan, Edward, and Mary Clowser. Wm. Bernard. sur.—June 19, 1793.

McCarroll, Samuel, and Polly Menifee. George Menifee, sur.—Dec. 8, 1806.

McCelwain, Thomas, and Susannah Vanson, dau. Chas. & Susannah Vanson—Oct. 7, 1799

McConnell, John, and Ferriby Barnerd: a widow of John Barnerd (who was son of Peter Barnerd, sur. on this bond)—Aug....1803.

McConner, John, and Margaret Ruble, dau. Owen Ruble—Aug. 17, 1795.

McCormack, Richard, and Mary Roberson. dau. William Roberson—Dec. 1, 1798.

McCutchen, Samuel, and Phoeby Carter. Bailey Carter, sur.—Feb. 25, 1796.

McGuire, Elijah, and Sary Robertson (23 years old). Ephriam Thomas, sur.—Mar. 11, 1791.

McGuire, John, and Nancy Hembrick, dau. Joseph Hambrick—Oct. 1, 1803.

McHenry, Thomas, and Nancy Martin, dau. Hugh Martin—Mar. 25, 1800.

McMullins, Samuel, and Elizabeth Weaver, dau. Jacob Weaver—Jan. 27, 1803.

McNanny, Archibald, and Chloe Cutle. M. Stone, sur.—Mar. 29, 1796.

McNeal, John, and Rebecca Griffith. Jonathan Griffith, sur.—Aug. 5, 1805.

Mc. New, William, and Elizabeth Jones. Mar. ret. by J. S.—Oct. 23, 1801.

McVey, James, and Martha Richardson, dau. Martha Kelly, wife of Wm. Kelly—Mar. 5, 1798.

Meador, Meadow, Meadors.

Meador, James, and Mary Divers. John Divers sur.—Sept. 13, 1797.

Meador, Jesse, and Mary Mann. Joel Meador, sur.—Feb. 23, 1789.

Meador, Joel, and Edith Clebourn. John Clebourn, sur.—Dec. 27, 1798.

Meador, Job, and Millev Simmons, dau. Charles Simmons—Sept. 29, 1806.

Meador, John, and Nancy Clark, dau Susannah Clark—Dec. 2, 1805.

Medley, George, and Sarah Johnson, dau. William Johnson—Sept. 7, 1787.

Mellon, John and Amelia Guarner (of age). Jas. Welch, sur.—Feb. 7, 1803.

Miles, Enos, and Anna Buchanan. Moses Beck, sur.—July 25, 1789.

Miles, Evan, and Mary Christy. James Christy sur.—Aug 4, 1800.

Miles, Isaac, and Mary Jones, dau. John and Mary Jones—Jan. 24, 1787.

Miles, James, and Catey Miksel. John Miksel sur.—Feb. 3, 1799.

Miller, Abraham, and Mary Peary, dau. George Peary, (Germans)—July 21, 1791.

Miller, Henry, and Mary Hemlick. Andrew Hemlick, sur.—Aug. 31, 1799.

Miller, Isaac, and Hannah Webb, dau. James and Lucy Webb—Aug. 18, 1800.

Miller, Jacob, and Susannah Peary, dau. George Peary—Dec. 10. 1800.

Miller, James W. C., and Dicey Chitwood. Wm. Chitwood, sur.—Dec. 18, 1797.

Miller, John, and Margaret Turpin, dau. Mary Turpin—Sept. 1, 1789 .

Miller, John, and Susannah Scott. Daniel Bainhart, sur.—Dec. 7, 1789.

Miller, John, and Phebe McCleur. Consent by Samuel and Mary Henderson—July 14, 1792.

Miller, John, and Hester Brown. Christian Brown, sur.—Nov. 20, 1798.

Miller, Pierson, and Nancy Hoof, dau. Philip Hoof. Thos. Miller, sur.—Dec. 4, 1797.

Miller, Tobias, and Sally Henderson, dau. Mary and Samuel Henderson—May 9, 1799.

Mills, Arthur, and Nancy West, dau. Jenny West. Peter Abshire, sur.—Aug. 17, 1800.

Mills, James, and Nancy Frame. Wm. Brown, sur.—May 3, 1799.

Mills, William, and Elizabeth Abshire, dau. Abraham Abshire—Feb. 29, 1796.

Mikesell, David, and Molly Harter. Christian Harter, sur,—Feb. 7, 1803.

Mikesell, Peter, and Mary Troup, dau. Mary Troup. Henry Troup, sur.—Aug. 14, 1797.

Minnix, Charles, Jr., and Fanny Rickmond—July 17, 1798.

Mitchell, James, and Elizabeth Niblett.Thomas Niblett, sur.—May 5, 1806.

Mitchell, William, and Mary Jackson, dau. Thomas Jackson—Jan. 31, 1803.

Mixell, George, and Catey Harter, Christian Harter, sur.—Feb. 4, 1804.

Montgomery, Samuel, and Elizabeth Bowman. Peter Bowman, sur.—Sept. 3, 1805.

Moody, George, and Rachel Mitchell, dau. John and Ann Mitchell—Feb. 13, 1797.

Moody, John, (son of Thomas), and Polly Lilley, dau. Robert Lilley—Jan. 7, 1786.

Moody, Moses, and Polly Beeby (Bigley?). Mar. ret. by H. B.—May 21, 1798.

Moor, John, and Elizabeth Davis. Joseph Davis. sur.— May 19, 1793.

Moor, Samuel, and Elizabeth Stuard. David Thompson, sur.—Mar. 26, 1793.

Moor, William, and Sarah Grammett. Mar. ret. by R. J.—.........1787.

Morgin, Morgan, and Elizabeth Blades. Francis Blades, sur.—May 6, 1796.

Morton, Absolum, and Sarah Henderson. D'nl Barnhart, sur.—May 12, 1794.

Moyer, John, and Catherine Nafe, dau. Elizabeth Nafe—Feb. 7, 1797.

Mullenden, Jacob, and Catherine Hartzell. (Germans)—Oct. 20, 1794.

Muller, (Above written Muller in min. ret.)

Mullins, Bowker, and Judith Stanley. Joseph Stanley, sur.—May 12, 1803.

Mullins, John, and Lucy Bohanon. Wm. Bohanon, sur.—Sept. 3, 1787.

Mullins, Nehemiah, and Elizabeth Doss. (age 21, Feb. 7, 1804).—Feb. 21, 1804.

Mullins, William, and Judith Stanley. Richard Stanley, sur.—Mar. 23, 1803.

Murrill, William and Caroline Binnion. Wm. Binnion, sur.—Oct. 20, 1795.

Musgrove, Henry, and Nancy Burdet. William Burdet, sur.—Jan. 4, 1798.

Muse. Peter, and Jenny Smith. Consent by William Camp—Aug. 6, 1804.

—N—

Nafe, David, and Polly Brower. Jacob Brower, sur.—Nov. 14, 1803.

Nafe, Jacob, and Polly Rentfro, dau. Moses Rentfro—June 24, 1795.

Nape, Daniel, and Polly Logan. William Logan, sur.—Sept. 28, 1795.

Nape, See Knape.

Napier, John, and Elizabeth Henson. Mary Henson, sur.—Oct. 29, 1799.

Napier, John, and Lucy Cook, dau. Mary Cook—Mar. 15, 1804.

Napier, Robert, Jr., and Catherine Napier. Ashford Napier, sur.—Dec. 19, 1789.

Napier, Skelton, and Elizabeth Throusall (?)—Feb. 13, 1789.

Napier, Tarlton, and Susannah Smith. John M. Holland, sur.—Oct. 6, 1806.

Nemo, Robert, and Lydda Holland. Peter Holland. sur.—Jan. 18, 1800.

New, William, and Elizabeth Jones, dau. William Jones—Oct. 27, 1801.

Newlin, William, and Nancy Booth. Richard Booth, sur.—Feb. 4, 1806.

Nicholls, Gilbert, and Elener Carter. Min. ret. by H. B.—.............1798.

Nickols, Nehemiah, and Eliza Dlades. dau. Francis Blades—Mar. 11, 1791.

Norris, William, and Jane Craig. Williamson Davis, sur.—Apr. 1, 1805.

Nowles, Matthew, and Sarah Smith. Wm. Smith, sur.—Sept. 21, 1805.

Nowlin, Robert, and Froney Taylor, dau. John and Jane Taylor—Feb. ...... 1796.

Nunn, Joseph, and Patty Stone. Stephen Stone, sur.—Oct. 19, 1798.

—O—

O'Brian, Dennis, and Ruth Marus. Richard I. Marus, sur.—Dec. 5, 1792.

Ogle, Hercules, Jr., and Margaret Griffith. Wm. Griffith, sur.—Jan. 15, 1798.

O'Neal, Hugh, and Nancy Sheridon. Wm. Campbell, sur.—July 3, 1797.

Osborne, John, and Sarah Hill, dau. Thomas Hill, sur.— Aug. 16, 1804.

Otenneal, Thomas, and Polly Tuning, dau. George Tuning—Aug 10, 1804.

Overholts, Abraham, and Catherine Gossett. Daniel Gossett, sur. (All Germans)—Feb. 3, 1800.

Overholt, David, and Elizabeth Kailer. Mar. ret by J. M.—1794-95.

Overties, Conrad, and Peggy Haister. Anthony Pate, sur.— Nov. 7, 1788.

Owens, Anthony, and Elizabeth Young. John Young, sur.—May 17, 1791.

Oyer, Valentine, and Caty (surname omitted) Joseph Wysong, sur.—May 17, 1806.

Ozley, Joseph, and Mary Bridgett. James Bridgett, sur.—Dec. 24, 1789.

—P—

Packwood, William, and Elinor Anderson, dau. John and Mary Anderson—Mar. 1, 1802

Packwood-See Parkwood.

Pagan, David, and Mary Harmon. Mar. ret. by J. F.—Oct. 8, 1795.

Pane, Thomas, and Fanny Powell, dau. Robert Powell—Jan. 11, 1799.

Pane-See Payne.

Parker, Henry, and Elizabeth Dorryby. John Jones, sur.—July 7 ,1791.

Parker, John, and Rhoda Rentfro. Jesse Rentfro. sur.—Oct. 17, 1786.

Parker, John, and Susannah Webb, dau. Smith Webb—Apr. 5, 1802.

Parkwood, Samuel, and Judith Sneed. John Sneed, sur.—May 6, 1800.

Parrott, Joseph, and Susannah Thompson— Apr. 2, 1793.

Parrott, Thorp, and Elizabeth Sutherland. James Roberts, sur.—May 15, 1793.

Pate, John,(and Rhoda Doran. dau. Hartmon Doran—Dec. 2, 1794.

Pate, Stephen, and Sucky Martin, dau William Martin—Feb. 12, 1792.

Patterson, James, and Margaret M. Innes (of age). Benj. Cook, sur.—Oct. 12, 1796.

Paulwen, John, and Citziah Belcher, dau. Phebe Belcher—Apr. 5, 1790.

Payne, Daniel, and Susannah Carter, dau. Barnet Carter—Mar. 13, 1802.

Payne, George, and Milla Young, dau Joseph Young—Nov. 20, 1802.

Payne, John, and Lucy Clarkson, (of age), dau. David ClarksonOct. 7, 1806.

Payne-See Pane.

Peak, Abel, and Lydia Jones. Mar. ret. by R. H.—May 8, 1794.

Peak, Jacob, and Polley Jones, Abe. Peak, sur.—Jan. 5, 1789.

Peckner, Abram, and Lena Hickman ,dau Barbary Hickman—Aug 12, 1796.

Pedige, Abel, and Susannah Ross—Sept. 17, 1792.

Pedigay, Henry, and Leah Cochrum. Mar. ret. by R. H.—Nov 23, 1790.

Penn, Flayle ,and Elizabeth Pollard, dau. Elizobeth Tony—Oct. 13, 1800.

Penegoy ,Henry, and Leah Cockrand. Edward Cockrand, rsu.—(See Pedigay).

Perdue, Daniel, and Happy (Hassy?) Ward, dau. Daniel Ward—Sept. 24, 1792.

Perdue, Daniel, and Preudnce Ward, dau. Daniel Ward—Feb. 27, 1804.

Perdue, William, and Nancy Smith, dau. John Smith—Oct. 6, 1806.

Perdue, Zachariah, and Elizabeth Coon. Henry Coon, sur.—Oct. 24, 1803.

Pergran, David, and Susannah Brumley. A. Ritter, sur.—May 3, 1799.

Perkins, William, and Sisley Moss. Thos. Prunty, sur.Nov. 20, 1786.

Pepple, Daniel, (of Maryland), and Elizabeth Lewis, dau. Thomas and Elizabeth Lewis. —May 18, 1789.

Peters, Chrisley, and Mary Nofsinger. John Nofsinger. sur.— Feb. 20, 1796.

Peters, Jacob, and Susannah Bowman. John Bowman, sur.—Jan. 7, 1805.

Pettison, Samuel, and Jean Pincard. Dan'l Jett, sur.—Mar. 22, 1788.

Pharis, Amariah, and Elizabeth Beheler. Mar. ret. by R. H. Jan. 27, 1791.

Phelps, John, and Polly Ferguson. John Ferguson, sur.—Feb. 16, 1804.

Phillips, George, and Sally Smith. Wm. Kemp sur.—Aug. 6, 1806.

Philpot, Samuel, and Frances Kesterson. Macajah Stone. sur.—Oct. 21, 1803.

Picklesimer, Pickelsimer, Picklesymer. etc.

Picklesimer, Abraham. and Polly Kingary, dau. Peter Kingary—Oct. 28, 1790.

Picklesimer, David, and Sarah Moore, dau. Sarah Moore—June 14, 1802.

Picklesimer, Joseph, and Susannah Trout, dau. Joseph Trout—July 27, 1797.

Picklesimer, Joseph, and Christinah Lezenah. Melcher Waggoner, sur.—Mar .18, 1793.

Picklesimer, Samuel, and Catren Logan, dau. William and Marget Logan—Mar. 18, 1793.

Plaster, Thomas, and Mary Carter. dau. Ann Carter. Thomas, son Michael and Charitie Plaster—May 9, 1791.

Plaster, William, and Elizabeth Griffith. Wm. Griffith, sur.—Feb. 1, 1795.

Pollard, Chatten. and Molley Greer, dau. Moses Greer.—Sept. 13, 1790.

Polson, Absolom, and Delelah Davis, dau. Joseph Davis—Sept. 30, 1799.

Porter, David, and Abagall Howell, dau. Joshua Howell—Dec. 29, 1788.

Porter, Thomas, and Rachel Hale. dau. Joseph Hale—Oct. 23, 1789.

Poteet, James, and Sarah Arthur. John Arthur. sur.—Dec. 4, 1796.

Potter, Elias, and Sarah Roach, dau. Gideon Roach. Elias, son of Benjamin Portter— Nov. 26, 1794.

Potter, Elisha, and Judah Dalton, dau. James and Elizabeth Dalton—June 24, 1791.

Potter, Lewis, and Nancy Hickerson, dau. Thomas Hickerman—Aug. 8, 1786.

Potter, Moses, and Frances Kirby, dau. Dicey Bartee—July 14, 1789.

Potter, Thomas, and Susannah Shockley, dau. Levy and Rebeckah Shockley—Jan. 5, 1801.

Powell. Robert, and Polly Sutherland, dau. Philemon Sutherland—Jan. 7, 1803.

Powell, William, and Sophia Hancock, dau. Lew Hancock—Dec. 26, 1804.

Preebracker, Henry, and Elizabeth Florah. Joseph Florah, sur.—Mar. 19, 1795.

Pressel, Daniel, and Mac'lin Rudd. Daniel Rudd, sur.—Mar. 25, 1792.

Preston, Bowker, and Catherine Hook, dau. John Hook—July 27, 1802.
Preston, John, and Elizabeth Barrott, dau. George Barrott—July 13, 1795.
Price, David, and Mary Parker, dau. Thomas Parker. David, son of John Price—Sept. 17, 1796.
Price, David, and Sally Hill, dau. John Hill —Nov. 6, 1797.
Price, Jonathan, and Polly Hill, Swinfield Hill, sur.—Jan. 7, 1806.
Price, Joseph, and Nancy Webster, dau. Samuel Webster—Jan. 2, 1797.
Prillemon, Christopher, and Elizabeth Wright dau. Molly Wright. Jacob Prillomon, sur. —June 18. 1796.
Prim. David, and Nelly Parker—Sept. 26, 1795.
Primty (?), James, and Martha Wimmer. Mar. ret. by R. H.—June 26, 1794.
Prunty, Jesse, and Nancy Finney. John Finney, sur.—Mar. 18, 1802.
Prunty, Thomas, and Sally Rives, dau. Burwell Rives—Aug. 4, 1804.
Prupecker, Henry, and Elizabeth Flora. Mar. ret. by J. M.—1794-95.
Prupecker, Jacob, and Hannah Peters. Stephen Peters, sur.—Mar. 29, 1802.
Prupecker. John. and Phebe Harter. Christian Harter, sur.—Jan. 30, 1798.
Pyrtle. Joseph, and Rebecca Miller. Joseph Miller, sur.—Sept. 22, 1803.

—Q—

Quarles, William, and Elizabeth Rives, dau. Frederick Rives—Jan. 12, 1802.
Quigley, James. and Charity Bybee. Sherwood Bybee, sur.—May 20, 1797.

—R—

Radford. George, and Catherine Woodcock, dau. Henry Woodcock.—Oct. 29, 1789.
Radford, John, and Nancy Crawford, dau. Rachel Crawford—May 25, 1799.
Radford, John, and Garbry Trumon, dau. Mary and William Trumon—Oct. 17, 1794.
Ragland, William, and Phebe Clebourn, dau. Elizabeth Clebourn—Nov. 21, 1796.
Ramsey, Hailey S., and Esther Zigler, dau. Jacob Zigler—Feb. 22, 1803.
Ramsey, John, and Elizabeth Ann Martin. James Martin, sur.—Dec. 2, 1799.
Ramsey, Thomas, and Winny (?) Litteral. Wm. Hodges, sur.—Nov. 9, 1791.
Ramsey, Thomas, and Nancy Stewart, dau. David Stewart—July 2, 1792.
Rasor (Rason?)? George, and Elizabeth Hudson, dau. John and Elizabeth Hudson—Nov. 5, 1804.
Ratcliff, Ruben, and Pheby Ratcliff, dau. Silus and Elizabeth Ratcliff—July 1, 1786.
Ray, James, and Susannah Chambers, dau. John Chambers—Jan. 13, 1803.
Read, George, and Peggy Griffith. Jonathan Griffith, sur.—Feb. 10, 1806.
Read, John, and Susannah Young, dau. William Young—Feb. 23, 1790.
Read, William, and Sarah Delany, dau. Samuel and Mary Dulany—Feb. 3, 1790.

Reagan, Benjamin, and Polly Price, dau. Jonathan Price—Jan. 24, 1802.
Real, Andrew, and Mary Dirst, dau. Mary Dirst. Tobias Miller, sur.—Feb. 15, 1796.
Real, George, and Hannah Greer, dau. William Greer—Mar. 22, 1787.
Real, Henry, and Pattey Akers, dau. William Akers,—Apr. 29, 1790.
Realey, Charles, and Ann Burris Goodwin, dau. John Henry Goodwin—Oct. 21, 1802.
Reas, William, and Mary Smith Booth, dau. Richard Booth—Nov. 17, 1797.
Reese, Samuel, and Sophia Booth, dau. Richard Booth—Dec. 31, 1803.
Reges, Townley, and Charity Guilliams (of age). John Guilliams, sur.—Feb. 7, 1797.
Renne, Brummit, and Mary Estes. Mar. ret. by T. D.— ...., 1790.
Rentfro, Jesse, and Lucy Bates. William Rentfro, sur.—July 26, 1787.
Rentfro, Turpen, and Sarah Troupe. Moses Rentfro, sur.—Apr. 7, 1792.
Reynolds, Joseph, and Mary Ross. Mar. ret. by R. H.—Mar. 5, 1795.
Rich, David, and Sally Pridy, dau. Nancy Pridy—Dec. 29, 1789.
Richards, Benjamin, and Polly Williams, dau. ....adrid Williams—Dec. .., 1804.
Richards, Edmund, and Sally Warren, dau. Zacheriah Warren—Mar. 22, 1802.
Richards, Isiah, and Hannah Gearhart, dau. Peter Gearhart—Aug. 26, 1798.
Richards, Waitman, and Sally Hodges, dau. Robert Hodges—Jan. 1, 1797.
Richardson, Aaron, and Sally Bennett (Bonnett?). William Bennett, sur.—Oct. 6, 1788.
Richardson, Benjamin, and Elinor Holt, dau. Ambrose Holt—Dec. 19, 1789.
Richardson, Benjamin, and Celia Basham. Wm. Basham, sur.—June 17, 1800.
Richardson, Edmond, and Elizabeth Cooper, dau. Arthur Cooper—Dec. 16, 1799.
Richardson, Richard, and Salah Hubble. David Duease, sur.—Feb. 24, 1789.
Richardson, William, and Mary Adney, dau. Thomas Adney—Feb. 18, 1800.
Richeson, Richard, and Rachel Kelley. William Kellev, sur.—Jan. 30. 1797.
Richeson, William, and Nancy Wright. Joseph Wright, sur.—Mar. 24, 1806.
Rickeson, David, and Marah Tully (Tally?). dau. Happy Tully—Sept. 7, 1797.
Rigney, William, and Americah Potter. Benjamin Potter, sur.—Sept. 19, 1791.
Rinehart, Jacob, and Susannah Brower. Enock Brower, sur.—Jan. 6, 1805.
Rippito, William, and Fanny Jones. Joshua Rentfro, sur.—Mar. 6, 1792.
Ritter, Abraham, and Catherine Kelley, dau. William Kelley—Mar. 11, 1791.
Ritter, John, and Eve Miller. Wm. Kelley, sur.—Aug. 7, 1787.
Ritter, John, and Delelah Willson, dau. John and Elizabeth Willson,—Mar. 18, 1793.
Ritter, Joseph, and Mary Kelley. Wm. Rentfro, sur.—May 27, 1787.
Roason, William, and Elizabeth Webster. Edward Toney, sur.—Aug. 8, 1792.
Roason,-see Rasor.
Robbins, Absolum, and Mary Ogle. Mar. ret. by R. J.— ...., 1787.
Robbins, Daniel, and Keziah Allee, dau. Nicholas Allee—Feb. 21, 1788.

—18—

Robbins, Jacob, and Rachel Robins. Consent to marriage signed by Jacob and Mary Robbins and Nathaniel and Ann Robbins —Nov. 15, 1790.

Robinson, John, and Sarah Bold. Abraham Harris, sur.—Nov. 23, 1799.

Robinson, William, and Nancy Skinner Duvall: dau. Benjamin Duvall—Aug. 19, 1786.

Roberts, Absolom, and Mary Ogle. Hercules Ogle, sur.—This mar. bond was written Robins, but was signed "Absolom Roberts". Min. ret. was also Robbins. See Absolum Robbins, above—Mar. 13, 1787.

Roberts, James, and Nancy Underwood, dau. Samuel Underwood.—Dec. 27, 1790.

Roberts, John, and Elizabeth Mitchell. James Mitchell, sur.—June 3, 1805.

Robertson, David, and Mary Hunter. John Hunter, sur.—June 6, 1803.

Robertson, Edward, and Mary Coger, dau. Peter Coger—Oct. 13, 1803.

Robertson, George, and Susannah Woody. Martin Woody, sur.—Nov. .., 1798.

Robertson, Henry, and Martha Arnold. Elisha Arnold, sur.—Mar. 6, 1802.

Robertson, John, and Hannah Smith. John Smith, sur.—Sept. 3, 1804.

Robertson, Littlebury, and Nancy Watts. Benjamin Watts, sur.—Nov. 28, 1805.

Robertson, Thomas, and Naomi Wade, dau. Fanny Wade—Feb. 7, 1803.

Rodgers, Andrew, and Polly Starkey. John Rodgers, sur.—Oct. 23, 1806.

Rodgers, Benjamin, and Pricilla Doss. Joshua Doss, sur.—Dec. 21, 1795.

Rodgers, Josiah, and Martha Clack, dau. Spencer Clack—Jan. 22, 1786.

Rodgers, Josiah, and Chloe Hill. Wm. Armstrong, sur.—Apr. 16, 1806.

Ross, David, and Mary Wood (Mar. ret. by R. H. has "Mary Dodd"), Stephen Wood, sur.—Sept. 7, 1795.

Ross, David, and Sally Anderson, dau. John Anderson—Oct. 20, 1802.

Rowland, Andrew, and Margaret Hartzell. Philip Hartzell, sur.—Jan. 25, 1793.

Ruble, Swinfield, and Polly Staton. Mar. ret. by R. H.—July 11, 1793.

Ruble, Thomas, and Elizabeth Ross, dau. Daniel Ross—Oct. 17, 1786.

Ruble, Thomas, and Alley Wade. Owen Ruble, sur.—Dec. 24, 1801.

Rudy, Samuel, and Sally McGivin, dau. Sally McGuire. No date on bond, but consent dated—Sept. 21, 1795.

Running, Adam, and Rachel Wright, dau. Isaac Wright—Sept. 20, 1788.

Ryan, Adam, and Catey Stover, dau. Jaramis Stover, "and wife"—Dec. 25, 1785. In mar. ret. it is written 'Adam Ryner'.

Ryherd, Jacob, and Peggy Dehaven. Abraham Dehaven sur.—Mar. 7, 1803.

Ryner—see Ryan.

—S—

Salmon, Roland, and Frankey Carter. Mar. ret. by R. H.—Mar. 12, 1795.

Sammons, William, and Elizabeth Griffith. Benjamin Griffith, sur.—Dec. 27, 1798.

Sample, John, and Elizabeth Turnbull. George Turnbull, sur.—Jan. 1, 1803.

Saul, John, and Ann Luke. Faithful Luke, sur.—Sept. 15, 1804.

Saunders, John, and Catey Meador, dau. John Meador—Feb. 24, 1801.

Saunders, Philip, and Jemima Greer. Elisha Lions, sur.—Nov. 23, 1786.

Scott, Hugh, and Martha Parrott. John Mattox, sur.—Jan. 4, 1792.

Scruggs, John, and Amelia Menefee. William Menefee, sur.—Mar. 14, 1786.

Seabrough, Robert, and Catherine Beheler. Mar. ret. by R. H.—Aug. 29, 1793.

Sebert, Charles, and Cahherine Lemon. Daniel Spangler, sur.—Mar. 2, 1789.

Sellers, Samuel, and Ellener Duease, dau. Wilburn Duease.—Oct. 3, 1789.

Sellers, Thomas, and Elizabeth Harry, dau. Evan and Abagail Harry. Bond, undated: consent dated—Dec. 3, 1787.

Sence, Adam, and Sally Simmons. William Simmons, sur.—Sept. 23, 1797.

Sephens, John, and Sarah Musgrove. Consent by Nicholas Allen—Oct. 3, 1791.

Sevenney, Joseph, and Pheba Belcher. Benjamin Cock, sur.—July 4, 1791.

Shastain, Valentine, and Mary Robins, dau. Zach and Mary Robins: Valentine, son of William and Sary—Sept. 24, 1791.

Shattain, George, and Rebeccah Statton, dau. George Statton—Aug. 13, 1791.

Shavers, Jesse, and Rebecca Beverly. Harold Beverley, sur.—Dec. 16, 1805.

Shaver, Michal, and Hannah Miller. Tobias Millar, sur. (Germans)—June 21, 1791.

Shelton. William. see Skelton.

Sherwood, Thomas, and Elizabeth Davis, dau. Jonathan Davis—Nov. 28, 1789.

Sherwood, William, and Jenny Davis. Jonathan Davis, sur.—Mar. 27, 1786.

Shilling, Jacob, and Rosanna Shockley. John King, sur.—Dec. 2, 1787.

Shoemaker, Isaac, and Nancy Louney. Peter Louney, sur.—Apr. 6, 1806.

Showalter, Abraham, and Frances M'Cormack. William M'Cormack, sur.—Jan. 12, 1802.

Showalter, Henry, and Catherine Gosel. Joseph Gosel, sur.—Dec. 25, 1806.

Simmons, Elijah, (son of Charles), and Rhoda Anderson, dau. Charles Anderson—Jan. 14, 1805.

Simmons, Ezekiel, and Patty Cooper, dau. Nathaniel Cooper—July 28, 1797.

Simmons, Moses, and Aggy Meadows. Jesse Meadows, sur.—June 2, 1797.

Simpkins, Garrat, and Susannah Roberts, dau. Anne Roberts.—Aug. 20, 1786.

Siner, Jesse, and Sithey Barton. Wm. M'Cormack, sur.—May 1, 1799.

Sink, Henry, and Betsy Snider. John Snider, sur.—Apr. 15, 1805.

Skelton, William H., and Elner Greer. Moses Greer, sur.—Jan. 9, 1797.

Slaughter, John, and Mary Handy. Mar. ret. by R. H.—Feb. 10, 1787.

Sleator, Edmond Smith, and Susannah Dishon. Drury Hodges, sur.—June 22, 1799.

Sleator, John, and Mary Handy. John Handy, sur.—Feb. 7, 1787.

Sloan, William, Jr. and Rhoda Doran, dau. Halmon Doran—July 26, 1792.

Sloy, John, and Mary Miller. Moses Greer, Jr., sur.—Nov. 4, 1805.

Smith, Abenezer, and Sarah Knowles, dau. Joshua Knoles—June 14, 1793.

Smith, Benjamin, and Elizabeth Drake. John Drake. sur.—July 2, 1786.
Smith, Benjamin, and Nancy Sutherland, dau. Philemon Sutherland—Nov. 23, 1801.
Smith, Charles (son of Peyton), and Jane Pinkard, dau. Jane Patterson—Nov. 8, 1790.
Smith, Daniel, and Ruth Hickson. Daniel Hickson. sur.—Jan. 7, 1789.
Smith, Guy, and Aberella Rickeson, dau. Jonathan Rickeson—Jan. 20, 1793.
Smith, Guy, and Hannah Hill, dau. Swinfield Hill—Oct. 28, 1795.
Smith, George, and Mary Boulton, dau. Thomas Boulton. Consent witnessed by Susannah Boulton—Jan. 11, 1800.
Smith, George Anderson, and Milly Jones, dau. Rachel Jones.—Mar. 6, 1787.
Smith, Henry, and Nancy Young. David Young. sur.—Dec. 13, 1806.
Smith, Henry, and Elizabeth Powell, dau. Robert Powell.—May 10, 1796.
Smith, Henry, and Polly Wright. William Wright, sur.—Aug. 4, 1800.
Smith, Isaac, and Nancy Johnson. George Johnson, sur.—Sept. 26, 1798.
Smith, James, and Elizabeth Clarkson. David Clarkson, sur.—Feb. 2, 1802.
Smith, James and Eltha Bolle (own consent, signes Coyles).—Sept. 4, 1790.
Smith. John, and Frances Hatcher, dau. Benjamin Hatcher—Jan. 4, 1790.
Smith, John, and Rosanna Bolf. John Webster, sur.—Dec. .., 1806.
Smith, Leroy, and Milly Guttery. Penlope Guttery, sur.—Mar. 25, 1792.
Smith, Peter, and Hannah Richardson, dau. James and Martha Richardson— ...., 1789.
Smith, Peyton, and Polly James. Fielden James, sur.—Jan. 17, 1805.
Smith, Philemon, and Nancy Abshire, dau. Luke Abshire—Feb. 10, 1795.
Smith, Stephen, and Elizabeth White, dau. Henry Page White—Feb. 23, 1799.
Smith, William, and Ann Preston, dau. Ann Robertson—Oct. .., 1796.
Smith, William, and Sally Law, dau. John Law—Jan. 3, 1799.
Sneed. Richard, and Patsey Adams, dau. William Adams—Mar. 5, 1792.
Sneed, Richard, and Siney Turner—Dec. 29, 1801.
Sneed, William, and Elizabeth Adams, dau. William Adams—Nov. 5, 1792.
Snider, David, and Susannah Gearhart, dau. Margaret Gearhart—Aug. 1, 1803.
Solsbury, Thomas, and Lucy Maxey, dau. Phebe Maxey—Jan. 7, 1801.
Souter, Jacob, and Ann Prillemon, dau. Jacob and Pricilla Prillomon—June 18, 1788.
Sowel, Pleasant, and Caty Stone. Patrick Stone, sur.—May 15, 1798.
Spalden, Flemin, and Mary Fears, dau. Athanations Fears—Feb. 2, 1793.
Spangle, George, and Elizabeth Langdon, dau. John D. Langdon—Feb. 9, 1786.
Spangle, John, and Christina Myers. Flay Nickols, sur.—Feb. 5, 1787.
Sparks, Samuel, and Susannah Jones. John Jones, sur.—Dec. 6, 1798.
Spiller, Michael. and Polly Peters, dau. Michael Peters—Aug. 25, 1802.
Spoon, John, and Polly Crowl, dau. Mary Bolf. Michael Crowl, sur.—Jan. 8, 1806.

Standfer, Luke, and Maryann Price, dau. Toxes Showers Price—June 15, 1787.
Standley, James, and Aley Standley, dau. William Standley—Nov. 12, 1805.
Standley, Joseph, and Polly Mullins. William Mullins, sur.—Aug. 25, 1806.
Standley, Moses, and Jenny Warren. Benjamin Warren, sur.—Mar. 29, 1806.
Standley, Thomas, and Delilah Hill. Wm. Mullins, sur.—Apr. 27, 1801.
Starkey, Bryant, and Permelia Blankenship. Elijah Starkey, sur.—Feb. 28, 1805.
Starkey, John, and Polly Plybon. James Calloway, Jr., sur.—Oct. .., 1799.
Starkey, Josiah, and Susannah Fellows, dau. Peter and Caty Feller: John Starkey, sur. —Mar. 22, 1798.
Starkey, William, and Elizabeth Webb, dau. Samuel and Rebeckah Webb—Apr. 7, 1788.
Starter, John—see John Sleater.
Staten, George, and Jane Handy. John Handy, sur.—Nov. 6, 1797.
Staton, Ruben, and Martha Smith, dau. Elizabeth Smith—Dec. 20, 1795.
Steagall, William, and Mary Hodges (written Chloe in consent), dau. Abednego Hodges —Nov. 24, 1804.
Stephenson, Benjamin, and Ruth Shey. Patrick Sloan, sur.—May 26, 1792.
Stephens, Edward, and Mary Noles. John Noles, sur.—Apr. 2, 1809.
Stevens, Gilbert and Hannah Poteet, dau. Wm. and Keziah Poteet,—June 6, 1791.
Stephens, John, Derben, and Polly Bates. Isaac Bates, sur.—Dec. 24, 1804.
Stewart, James, and Phebe Jones, dau. Robert Jones. (James the son of James Sr.) —Feb. 24, 1804.
Stewart, John, and Agnes Warren, dau. Zacheriah Warren—Apr. 15, 1805.
Stewart, Joshua, and Elizabeth Stewart— Apr. 2, 1787.
Still, Murphy, and Phebe Rives. A. Dehaven, sur.—July 23, 1795.
Stinnett, John, and Betsy Justice, dau. John Justice—Jan. 2, 1788.
Stinnett, William, and Nancy Carter, dau. Betsy Carter—July 13, 1789.
Stokes, William, and Isebel Hale. Mar. ret. by H. B.—Nov. 20, 1798.
Stone, Clifford, and Peggy Doram. Thomas Stone, sur.—July 31, 1789.
Stone, Jesse, and Deborah Thomas, dau. David Thomas—June 5, 1790.
This note with above bond: "This is to certify that the marriage intended between Jesse Stone, and Deborah Thomas, has the approperation of all their friends". Signed, Wm. Thomas, Deborah Thomas, John Stephenson, and Nicholas Call.
Stone, Reuben, and Polly McGrady, dau. Lorthem M'Grady. Patrick Stone, sur.—Sept. 24, 1789.
Stone, Thomas, and Sarah Griffith. Geo. Griffith, sur.—Aug. 22, 1805.
Stone, William, and Mary Ann Turner. John Turner, sur.—Nov. 18, 1806.
Stover, Jacob, and Sally McGahee. Holderell McGhee, sur.—Mar. 16, 1788.
Stuart, Bruce, and Polly Hodges, dau. Robert Hodges—Jan. 30, 1798.
Stuart, Robert, and Polly Goff. Asa Dillion, sur.—Dec. 13, 1806.

Stuart, William, and Caty Short. John Starkey, sur.—Sept. 3, 1806.

Sullivant, Walter, and Martha Craghead. Consent by John and Polly Camp. Thomas Camp, sur.—Dec. 18, 1797.

Sullivant, Samuel, and Sarah Bell, dau. James Bell—Dec. 17, 1792.

Sumnsden (?), Dudley, and Sally Chitwood. John Chitwood, sur.—June 7, 1802.

Sumpter, Edmond, and Elizabeth Kingrey. Jacob Kingery, sur.—Mar. 16, 1795.

Sumpter, Richard, and Mary Kingery, Jacob Kingery, sur.—Nov. 12, 1801.

Swanson, Gabriel, and Malinda Arnold, dau. Maryan Arnold—Oct. 20, 1802.

—T—

Taswell, Peter, and Abagail Sherwood, dau. Robert Sherwood—Apr. 3, 1789.

Taylor, Obediah, and Mary Choice, dau. Anne Choice. Silas Choice, sur.—Oct. 10, 1791.

Taylor, Samuel, and Elizabeth Conner. William Conner, sur.—Feb. 29, 1792.

Teal, Adam, and Caty Baker, dau. George Baker.—Nov. 19, 1790.

Teal, George, and Catey Showalter. John Showalter, sur.—Feb. 7, 1801.

Teel, Peter, and Jemima Ray. James Ray, sur.—Oct. 6, 1800.

Terry, Champ, and Judith Cook—Dec. 27, 1790.

Thomas, David, and Sarah McGuire. James Stone, sur.—Sept. 8, 1797.

Thomas, Ephriam, and Caty Teal, dau. Adam, and Mary Teal—Jan. 19, 1791.

Thomas, Pleasant, and Polly Kenneday. James Kennaday, sur.—Mar. 6, 1800.

Thomason, David, and Elizabeth Pridy, dau. Nancy Pridy—July 25, 1789.

Thompson, Dickerson, and Susannah Darety, dau. Elizabeth Parker—June 21, 1797.

Thompson, John, and Rhoda Bowls. George Bowls, sur.—Feb. 8, 1803.

Thompson, Joseph, and Elizabeth Hedge. Mar. ret. by R. H.—June 18, 1790.

Thompson, Samuel, and Sarah Greer, Jas. Calloway, sur.—Nov. 20, 1797.

Thompson, William, and Frances Boales. Stophel Smith, sur.—May 11, 1791.

Thompson, Woody, and Catherina Jones, dau. Spencer Jones—Sept. 2, 1799.

Thornton, Allen, and Elizabeth Warren. Starlen Thornton, sur.—Apr. .., 1799.

Thornton, Starling, and Sally Mosley. David Richeson, sur.—Aug. 29, 1803.

Tinsley, Willis, and (womans' name not written in). Reuben Tinsley, sur.—Sept. 4, 1809.

Toney, Carey, and Betsy Isom, dau. Harkmon Isom—Aug. 27, 1789.

Toney, Edward, and Linny Chasteen. James Toney, sur.—Feb. 6, 1795.

Toney, Poindexter, and Mary Rawson, dau. Charles Rawson—Dec. 28, 1788.

Troup, Henry, and Dolly Wade. Mar. ret. by R. H.—Jan. 8, 1794.

Trout, David, and Nancy Murphy. Butler Murphy, sur.—Mar. 13, 1802.

Trout, Joseph, and Sarah Jones, dau. David and Sarah Jones—Oct. 3, 1798.

Truman, Anderson, and Sally Hancock, dau Lew Hancock—Dec. 31, 1804.

Turnbull, Lewis, and Abiah Taylor. Henry Taylor, sur.—Oct. 5, 1801.

Turnbull, William, and Ruth Hairston, dau. Ruth Hairston—Nov. 4, 1792.

Turner, George, and Elizabeth Greer. Joseph Greer, sur.—Dec. 2, 1805.

Turner, Isham, and Elizabeth Young, dau. Catherine and Allen Redley Young—Mar. 16, 1792.

Turner, Isiah, and Elizabeth Candy. Jas. Prunty, sur.—Dec. 9, 1797.

Turner, James, and Elizabeth Brown, Mar. ret. by J. J.—Jan. 4, 1791.

Turner, James, and Mary Mailery, dau. Richard Mailery—Dec. 21, 1790.

Turner, James, and Lydda Rentfro, dau. Joseph Rentfro—Jan. 13, 1787.

Turner, Jeremiah, and Rachel Ross, dau. Daniel Ross—Apr. 21, 1792.

Turner, John, and Betty Price, dau. Joseph Price—June 23, 1787.

Turner, Jonas, and Rebecca M'Clary, dau. Richard M'Crory—Dec. 25, 1792.

Turner, Stephen, and Lucy Snead. Richard Snead, sur.—Feb. 15, 1803.

Turpin, Thomas, and Sally Charter, dau. Thomas Charter—Oct. 10, 1806.

Turtle, John, and Sally Easly, dau. William Easly. Joseph Parrott, sur.—Mar. 5, 1788. This bond contained the following note: "Sir: As it has happened you have licensed my daughter to be married to a man without my consent, or my wife's; who was under age, much to her ruin, and my dissatisfaction. Therefore, might I inform you that I intend for to take the advantage of the law, unless you have a mind to compromise without trouble. Please to inform me, by my son, in a few lines, what you mean to do, and oblige, yours humbly, Wm. Easley."

—U—

Underwood, John, and Sarah Lemon. Samuel Underwood, sur.—Nov. 22, 1795.

Underwood, Joseph, and Ellin Jestin, dau. John Jestin—Nov. 3, 1789.

Underwood, Seth, and Sarah Wirley, dau. John Worley—Jan. 13, 1797.

—V—

Vancel, Samuel, and Mary Picklesimer. Malcolm Waggoner, sur.—Feb. 2, 1791.

Vanover, Cornelius, and Nancy Moody. Edmund Moody, sur.—Oct. 10, 1795.

Vest, Littlebury, and Polly Moore. James Moore, sur.—Jan. 7, 1805.

Vier, David, and Nancy King, dau. Lida King —Apr. 28, 1804.

Vier, James, and Sarah Hale. Thomas Hale sur.—Nov. 4, 1803.

Vier, Josiah, and Rachel Hale, dau. Benjamin Hale. John Vier, sur.—Jan. 2, 1800.

Vinson, Charles, and Sarah McClivain, dau. Nancy McClewain.—Apr. 22, 1799.

Vinson, Francis, and Mary New. Mar. ret. by H. B.—Nov. 9, 1798.

Vinson, John, and Nancy McKelwain, dau. John and Franky Kelly—Feb. 2, 1799.

Vinson, Thomas, and Mary New. John New. sur. (See Francis).—Nov. 9, 1798.

—W—

Wade, John, and Hannah Jones, dau. Henry Jones,—Jan. 30, 1792.

Wade, Reuben, and Lucy Martin, dau. High Martin—Jan. 30, 1804.

Wade, Royal, and Rachel Jones. John Hale sur.—Feb. 24, 1791.

Waggoner, Melcher, and Elizabeth Picklesimer, dau. John Picklesimer.—Mar. 21, 1789

Walker, Burwell, and Susannah Walker. Joel Walker, sur.—Jan. 13, 1806.

Walker, Danday, and Judy Greer. Esom Edmons, sur.—Oct. 26, 1806.

Walker, James, and Phebe Estes, dau. Bolton Estes—Feb. 11, 1803.

Walker, John, and Elizabeth Sailor. Joseph Davis, sur.—Jan. 15, 1802.

Walker, William, and Mary Hartman, dau. Mary Hartman—Sept. 13, 1794.

Walton, William, and Nancy Griffith. Benjamin Griffith, sur.—Sept. 29, 1800.

Ward, Benjamin, and Elizabeth Perdue. Mistick Perdue, sur.—Sept. 15, 1804.

Ward, Jesse, and Anna Greer. Philip Sanders, sur.—Sept. 30, 1799.

Warden, David, and Theodothe Hardwick. Jos. Dyche, sur.—Apr. 26, 1791.

Warner, Joseph, and Sarah Allen, (Of age)—Nov. 25, 1805.

Warren, Elijah, and Sarah Mason, dau. Robert Mason—Feb. 27, 1787.

Warren, Jesse, and Rhoda Richards. Elijah Warren, sur.—Feb. 15, 1790.

Warren, Langston, and Drucilla Preator, dau. Thomas Preator: Jesse Warren sur.—Oct 5, 1791.

Warren, Thomas, and Mary M. Williams, dau. Hugh Mack Williams—Dec. 21, 1786.

Warwick, Wiatt, and Polly Belcher. Isham Belcher, sur.—Nov. 15, 1805.

Watson, James, and Lydda Willis, dau. John and Phebe Willis—July 2, 1789.

Watson, James, and Mary Lyon—Aug. 29, 1792.

Watson, John, and Elinor Martin. James Martin, sur.—Mar. 7, 1796.

Weaver, Jacob, and Elizabeth Sink. Stephen Sink, sur.—Jan. 3, 1803.

Weaver, John, and Matilda Murray—Dec. 30, 1805.

Webb, Aaron A., and Lidia Quisenberry. Henry Gatewood, sur.—Aug. 11, 1806.

Webb, Adron, and Lucy Fitzgerald. Mar. ret. by R. H.—June 27, 1793.

Webb, Cuthbert, and Mary Jarrel (Janel?), dau. Elizabeth Webb: Theodrick Webb, sur. —Mar. 2, 1791.

Webb, Daniel, and Mary Burton. John Robertson, sur.—Dec. 24, 1803.

Webb, Jacob, and Elizabeth Webb. Cuthbert Webb, sur.—Apr. 4, 1791.

Webb, Jacob, and Elizabeth Fitzgerald. Theodoric Webb, sur.—June 4, 1789.

Webb, Jacob, and Hannah Jones, dau. Thomas Jones—Oct. 3, 1805.

Webb, James, and Elizabeth Billups, dau. Ed ...... Billups,—Feb. 12, 1802.

Webb, John, and Levice Wilson. John Wilson, sur.—Sept. 15, 1798.

Webb, Joseph, and Barbary Thompson. Andrew Thompson, sur.—Oct. 4, 1790.

Webb, Littlebury, and Suckey Webb, dau. Adam and Conny Helm—Nov. 5, 1800.

Webb, Smith, and Nancy Clower. Jacob Clower, sur.—July 4, 1797.

Webb, Theodorick, and Permelia Webster, dau. John Webster—Feb. 17, 1792.

Webb, Theodorick, and Christly Copeland. Richard Copeland, sur.—Oct. 24, 1789.

Webster, Daniel, and Rhoda Arthur, dau. John Arthur: George Webster, sur.—Jan. 25, 1803.

Webster, Henry, and Elizabeth Webster, dau Samuel and Susannah Webster: James Webster, sur.—Aug. 12, 1800.

Webster, Jacob, and Fanny Walker Woodson. Shadrack Woodson, sur.—May 3,1803.

Webster, James, and Elizabeth M. Kinzey. James Kinzey, sur.—Oct. 29, 1801.

Webster, John, and Jane Webster. Mar. ret by R. H.—Mar. 20, 1794.

Webster, Samuel, and Sarah Billups, dau. Edward Billups—Feb. 4, 1801.

Welch, James, and Rhoda Willis, dau. Josiah Willis—Dec. 31, 1792.

West, John,and Hester Wright- own consent —Oct. 11, 1798.

West, Thomas, Esq., and Margaret Hook, dau. John Hook—Feb. 11, 1801.

Wheat, John, and Sarah Hudson—Sept. 2, 1800.

White, Benjamin, and Suckey Bartee. William Bartee, sur.—Oct. 8, 1786.

White, Obediah, and Lucy Akers. William Akers, sur.—Apr. 28, 1806.

White, William, and Elizabeth Pratt. Obediah White, sur.—Aug. 4, 1806.

Whiteneck, Benjamin, and Martha Wimmer. Jacob Wimmer, sur.—July 17, 1794. (Spelled Whitenought in min. ret.)

Whitworth, Philmon, and Rebecca Woody, dau. Henry Woody—Feb. 13, 1801.

Wilks, Gilbert, and Eleanor Charter. Jonathan Charter, sur.—Apr. 2, 1798.

Wilks, James, and Susannah Ross, dau. Mourning Ross—Sept. 18, 1801.

Wilks, Jesse, and Juda Pratt, dau. Mary Pratt—Aug. 3, 1801.

Wilks, Minor, and Lucy Waller. Wm. Estisan, sur.—June 23, 1797.

Williams, John, and Polly Richards. Isaac Richards, sur.—Sept. .., 1804.

Williams, Lewellen, and Winnefer Lovel Markham Lovel, sur.—Nov. 17, 1803.

Williamson, Jonathan, and Nancy Jackson. Mar. ret. by J. M.—Nov. 7, 1797.

Willis, Mark, and Lucy Garrell. John Highly, sur.—Feb. 23, 1803.

Willis, William, and Rozzy Pigg, dau. James Pigg—May 21, 1788.

Willson, Samuel, and Elizabeth Croxall, dau. Richard Croxall—Feb. 2, 1791.

Willson, Thomas, and Milley Smith. John Smith, sur.—Sept. 7, 1795.

Wimmer, Jacob, Elizabeth Copper. William Key, sur.—Oct. 30, 1794.

Wimmer, Jacob, and Margaret Caper, dau of Elizabeth Wimmer: Thos. Caper, sur—Nov. 23, 1799.

Wimmer, John and Hannah Lemon. Mar. ret. by R. H.—Sept. 19, 1793.

Winters, Lewis, and Anne Prillemon, dau Jacob Prillemon—Feb. 16. 1799.

Woods, John, and Anny Hairston—Oct. 12, 1792.

Wood, Thomas, and Sally Parsley, dau. Rob-Parsley—Dec. 17, 1802.

Woodall, Willis, and Cary Johnson. Wm. H. Shelton, sur.—Apr. 16, 1804.

—22—

Woodcock, Mark, and Sussannah Simmons, dau. Thomas Simmons: Thomas Woodcock, sur.—Mar. 5, 1803.

Woodcock, Thomas, and Mary Standifer. Isreal Standifer, sur.—July 3, 1786.

Woodcock, William, and Rhoda Simmons, dau. Charles Simmons—May 16, 1804.

Woodson, David, and Margaret Ritter. Abraham Ritter, sur.—Oct. 7, 1795.

Woody, Wyatt, and Polly Robertson. Own consent witnessed by Edward Robertson, Martin Woody, sur.—Aug. 21, 1799.

Wolf, Jacob, and Hannah Kingery. Henry Kingery, sur.—Mar. 2, 1801.

Woosley, David, and Elizabeth Butler, of age —Aug. 3, 1801.

Wooten, Jooseph, and Sarah Wilson, dau. John Wilson—Dec. 25, 1905.

Worley, Finch, and Elizabeth Cunningham—Dec. .... 1804.

Wray, Benjamin, and Patsey Goode. David Goode, sur.—Mar. 5, 1806.

Wray, Elias, and Polly Thurman. John Thurman, sur.—Mar. 25, 1806.

Wray, Isaac, and Mary Carlton. Own consent —Apr. 5, 1805.

Wray, John, and Susannah Kinsey. John Wright, sur.—Feb. 4, 1805.

Wray, Staphen, and Susannah Harter. Mar ret. by R. H.—June 1, 1794.

Wright, George, and Polly Abshire, dau. Luke Abshire—June 9, 1792.

Wright, James, and Peggy Young. David Morgan, sur.—Oct. 9, 1786.

Wright, Jesse, and Elizabeth Crawford, dau. Rachel Crawford: George Wright, sur.—Mar. 21, 1799.

Wright, John, and Elizabeth Abshire. Lodowick Abshire, sur.—Feb. 8, 1800.

Wright, John, and Eligabeth Kelly. John Vincent, sur.—Sept. 2, 1805.

Wright, Josiah, and Peggy Ferguson. Nelson Chapman, sur.—Nov. 20, 1797.

Wright, William, and Ellener Johnson, dau. George Johnson. Feb. 18, 1803.

Wyatt, John, and Susannah Law, dau. John Law. Jr.—Aug. 9, 1802.

Wyatt, Soloman, and Hannah Reese. Edward Wyatt, sur.—June 12, 1797.

Wyatt, Thomas, and Mary Reese. John Reese sur.—Dec. 4, 1797.

Wysong, Jacob, and Mymy Catteral, dau Mymy and James Catterel—Feb. 24, 1801.

Wysong, Valentine, and Mary Allick. John Allick, sur.—Dec. 21, 1798.

—Y—

Yates, William, and Milly Board. Own consent—Nov. 30, 1798.

Young, Isaac (son of Peter), and Mary Walker, dau. Joel—Nov. 19. 1809.

Young, Joshua, and Nancy Walker. John Walker, sur.—Nov. 14, 1798.

Young, Milen, and Polly Brock, dau. John Brock—Oct. 14, 1798.

Young, Robert. and Chloe Kinzey, dau. Cloe A. Kinzey—Mar. 7, 1789.

—Z—

Zegler, John, and Mary Ann Brook. No date. James Monroe, Gov. 1799-01.

In these Franklin county marriage records

where the record is from a minister's return, only the initials of the minister are used. Below are the names of these ministers'.

Burns, Horatio.	Jones, Robert.
Douglas, Thomas.	Miller, Jacob.
Fears, Jesse.	Rentfro, Isaac.
Hall, Randolph.	Saunders, Joseph.
Jones, Jesse.	Stockton, Robert.

GRAYSON COUNTY

—A—

Alderman, Jonathan, and .... (name omitted)—May 23, 1833.

Alexander, Elisha, and Polly Pool—May 3, 1835.

Alley, Ishom, and Polly Taylor—Sept. 25. 1821.

Alley, Thomas, and Lena Sexton—May 9, 1824.

Anderson, David. and Amey Reed—Sept. 20 1820.

Anderson, Howery, and Keziah Holloway—Nov. 16, 1826.

Anderson, Isaac, and Matilda Prichard—Feb. 14, 1836.

Anderson, Jesse (?), and Nancy Harper—Mar. 30, 1815.

Anderson, John, and Ferraday Cornett—Dec. 4, 1813.

Anderson, Joseph, and Mary Shuler—Dec. 30, 1819.

Anderson, Sam, and Lydia Rankin—Mar 22, 1817.

Anderson, Stephen, and Sarah Perkins—Dec. 29, 1825.

Anverson(?), Andrew, and Gintey Sleen—May 29, 1834.

Ashworth, Joel. and Elizabeth Edwards—April 28, 1836.

Atkins, Ambrose, and Lucy Byrd—Apr. 7, 1831.

Atkins, James, and Polly Hall—Oct. 31, 1822.

Atkins, Parker, and Matilda Shockley—July 14, 1831.

Amburn, Amos, and Ann Burcham—June 21, 1832.

—B—

Bailey, Zacheriah, and Hetty Amburn—Mar. 29, 1821

Bailey, Zach, and Rachel Glandon—June 14, 1834.

Barker, John, and Jane Porter—Nov. 27, 1793.

Baldwin, Jeremiah, and Hannah Thornberry Oct. 25, 1806.

Baldwin, Thomas, and Elizabeth Brazendine —June 11, 1820.

Baldwin, Thomas, and Nancy Brizendine—July 25, 1822.

Ballard, Anthony, and Elinor Massah (?)—July 28, 1808.

Ballard, Charles, and Usury Fitzpatrick—Nov. 23, 1815.

Bartley, John and Alsha McNight—Dec. 22, 1836.

Barton, John, and Betsy Raves—April 16, 1822

Bedsaul, David, and Sally Ward—Dec. 29 1831.

Bedsaul, Isaac, and Jane Davis—Dec. 6, 1833.

Bedsaul, John, and Delilah Carrico—July 30 1818.

Bedwell, James, and Jane Wells—July 6, 1797
Bedwell, John, and Patsy Pool—Dec. 20, 1820.
Bedwell, The., and Barbary Catron—May 7, 1807.
Bedwell, Wilson, and Patsy Pool—Dec. 6, 1822.
Beller, Elias, and Nancy Wills—Feb. 7, 1822
Beller, John, and Mary Coulson—Apr. 20, 1820.
Bird, Richard, and Sally Rudy—Sept. ..1835.
Blackard, Thomas, an dElley Sutphin—Aug. 20, 1822.
Blakely, James, and Pricilla Greer—Nov. 30, 1804.
Blevins, James, and Charity Isom—Nov. 1, 1833.
Bobbitt, James, and Rosanna Bobbit—Feb. 16, 1799.
Bobbitt. William, and Celia Jennings—March 3, 1836.
Bolt, Elias, and Penelope Cock—March 7 1833.
Bolt, Isaac, and Elizabeth Alderman—March 14, 1833.
Bolt, James, and Elizabeth M'Gahey March 6, 1825.
Bonds, Joseph, and Nancy Gallimore—March 7, 1827.
Bond, Nathan, and Nancy Dickens—June 1, 1808.
Bonds, Stephen, and Polly G. Whitshell—Nov. 11, 1824.
Bonham, Joseph, and Tibatha Russell—Aug. 29, 1822.
Bourn, George, and Nancy Vaughan—Sept. 6, 1821.
Bourn, Stephen, and Milly Martin—Jan 24, 1820.
Bourn, William, and Hannah Boyer—Nov. 3, 1825.
Bottomley, Jonathan, and Ann Ward—Oct. 27, 1835.
Bowers, William, and Rebecca Porter—Aug 22, 1833.
Boyer, Jacob, and Caty Wyatt—July 28, 1805.
Boyer, John, and Jane Fielder—Dec. 20, 1836.
Branscome, Edmond, and Nancy Huff—Dec. 20, 1820.
Brewer, James, and Polly Hall—June 11, 1822.
Brewer, Lewis, and Susanna Bedwell—March 9, 1820.
Brizendine, Brooks, and Joanna Webb—Oct 21, 1824.
Browder, Richard, and Betsy Vaughan—March 25, 1815.
Brown, Abraham, and Sarah Holloway—Feb. 2, 1834.
Brown, Abram, and Patty Harden—May 15, 1821.
Brown, Jesse, and Sally Dixon—May 3, 1806.
Brown, John, and Grace Harrigan—Dec. 5 1822
Brown, Sam, and Elizabeth Bedsaul—March 12, 1818.
Brown, Sam, and (name omitted)—May 3 1806.
Brown, William, and Polly Bird—Agu. 8, 1818.
Brown, William, and Hannah Sutphin—Sept. 18, 1825.
Bryant, Benjamin, and Peggy Willis—Nov. 2 1801.
Bryant, Isiah, and Polly Frost—Jan. 30, 1836.
Bryant, Joseph, and Sarah Hall—May , 1824.

Bryant, William, and Sally Samleth—July 9 1836.
Bullan (Pullam?), James, and Katura Wilson —October 10, 1833.
Burcham, Allen, and Fanny Spence—May 15, 1823.
Byrd, James, and Katty Wheeler—Nov. 12, 1818.
Byrd, Samuel, and Milly Whader—Nov. 12, 1818.
Byrd, William, and Sally Martin—Aug. 5, 1813.

—C—

Cain, David, and Deborah Hackler—Nov. 28, 1815.
Carder, Jake, and Mary Swaney—Jan. 8, 1807.
Carlan, John, and Jane Coulson—Feb. 4, 1907.
Carnoy, John, and Eve Hackler—July 15, 1833.
Carrico, Abel, and Peggy Wells—Oct. 11, 1804.
Carrico, Alexander, and Martha Edwards,—July 19, 1821.
Carrico, James, and Elizabeth Shuler—Feb. 23, 1836.
Carrico, John W., and Matilda Cooley—June 8, 1823.
Catron, Chris, and Fanny Jones—Sept. 14, 1801.
Chance, (Chancl?), Lewis, and Elizabeth Plasson—Dec. 9, 1806.
Clark, James, and Polly M'Clain—Dec. 24, 1806.
Clark, Jeffry, and Betsy Ward—Aug 13, 1818.
Clonch, (Clouch?), Doneal, and Fanny Wilks —Jan. 14, 1808.
Clark, James, and Elizabeth Sexton—Sept.— 17, 1800.
Cole, James, and Lydia Howell—Mar. 1, 1826.
Cole, John, and Franky Bowman—Oct. 14, 1824.
Cole, Isiah, and Aner Howell—Nov. 6, 1804.
Collier, Henry, and Sally Hays—Oct. 5, 1805.
Collier, Shadraok, and Lucy Bobbitt—...... 1803.
Collins, John, and Jane Collins—Mar. 24, 1796.
Collins, John, and Celia Rainey—Mar. 11, 1832.
Collins, Joseph, and Nancy Collins—Mar. 24, 1796.
Collins, Isaac, and Catey Willits—Nov. 3, 1821.
Collins, Maheon, and Effey Hays—May 8, 1824.
Collins, Randolph, and Celia Hayes—Mar 14, 1833.
Comer, John, and Sall Holland—Jan. 27, 1801
Conley, Joel, and Effie Pennington—May 20 1806.
Conner, John, and Tempy Pool—Oct. 3, 1835
Connute, David, and Phede Sutherland—Feb. 2, 1826.
Connute, James, and Polly Rankins—Dec. 4, 1814.
Connute, Ivan, and Mourning Bedwell—June 23, 1814.
Connute, William, and May Hatfield—June 2, 1795.
Cook,e, John and Anne Baker—Oct. 20, 1814.
Cooley, Benjamin, and Jane Dickey—Oct. 1, 1805.
Cooley, Peter, and Mary Hanks—May 29, 1806.
Cooley, Tucker, and Martha Thompson—July 24, 1831.

Couch, Daniel, and Susannah Delp—Feb. 21, 1822.
Coulson, George, and Catherine Lineberry—Dec. 11, 1824.
Cox, Braxton, and Nancy Phillips—Dec. 21, 1826.
Cox, Edward, and Violet Hampton—Oct. 15, 1833.
Cox, Harden, and Jane Osborne—Oct. 5, 1819.
Cox, Isom, and Jane Phipps—Feb. 25, 1836.
Cox, James, and Sally Fielder—Jan. 4, 1815.
Cox, Jeremiah, and Eady Davis—Dec. 1, 1825.
Cox, John, and Nellie Ward—Sept. 13, 1821.
Cox, John, and Charity Howell—Oct. 24, 1833.
Cress, David, and Deborah Kester—Nov. 28 1815.
Cross, Benson, and Lydia Baldwin—May 29, 1823.
Crowder, Balam, and Elizabeth Hiett—Mar. 7, 1806.
Cunningham, John, and Judah Ballard—July 2, 1804.

—D—

Dalton, John, and Pricilla Webb—Sept. 29, 1825.
Dalton, Marin, and Kezia Hill—Dec. 5, 1833
Daniels, Eli, and Jane Bedwell—Oct. 8, 1832.
Daniels, William, and Clory George—Aug. 29, 1833.
Davis, David, and Lucinda Hanks—Oct. 1 1835.
Davis, Hugh, andw Margaret Davis—Feb. 25, 1832,
Davis, Isaac, and Sally Halsey—Jan. 24. 1819
Davis, James, and Lydia Simcock—May 16, 1822.
Davis, John, and Mary Freeman—Mar. 25, 1806.
Davis, Joshua, and Frances Williams—Feb. 26, 1824.
Divis, Peter, and Sally Halsey—May 1, 1825.
Davis, Sampson, and Milly Murphy—Oct. 15, 1835.
Davis, William, and Ruth Fields—Jan. .., 1820.
Dean, Abner, and Susanna Johnson—Apr. 18, 1833.
Dean, Howell, and Mary Beamer—Sept. 17, 1800.
Dean, John, and Matilda Johnston—Jan. 14, 1824.
Delp, Daniel, and Peggy Couch—June 13, 1813.
Delp, George, and Polly Baker—July 28, 1814.
Delp, Jacob, and Elizabeth Sage—Feb. 14, 1836.
Delp, Peter, and Sarah Rudy—May 12, 1823.
Delp, Philip, and Jeney Wright—Dec. 5, 1822.
Delp, William, and R. A. Tigner—July 24, 1821.
Demford, Josiah, and Alice Randall—Jan. 10, 1825.
Dennis, Archibald, and Sally Taylor—Jan. 21, 1833.
Dickens, Jesse, and Susanna Webb,—Sept. 19, 1824.
Dickey, James, and Elizabeth Bourn, (dau. Stephen, and Elizabeth Bourn)—Dec. 5, 1822.

Dillard, Abel, and Polly Pogue,—Mar. 1, 1832.
Dilman, Samuel, and Ann Gropbles—Oct. 25, 1832.
Dixon, Henery, and F........ Farmer—Sept. 17, 1800.
Dixon, William, and Rachel Hobson—Sept. 21, 1820.
Doss, James, and Mary Slaughter—Oct. 24, 1824.
Dunkin, Henry, and Mary Dalton,—Nov. 3, 1835.
Durnel, Levi, and Anne Lundy—Feb. 12, 1807.

—E—

Edwards, Allen, and Nancy Landrith,—June 16, 1822.
Edwards, Augustine, and Polly Lineberry—Apr. 2, 1836.
Edwards, Isaac, and Polly Beamer—Mar. 7, 1821.
Edwards, Isaac, and Nancy..........—Oct. 7, 1835.
Edwards, Jonathan, and Elizabeth Tuit,—Apr. 8, 1807.
Edwards, John, and Polly Hogue—June 13, 1816.
Edwards, John, and Elizabeth Worrell—July —6, 1820.
Edwards, Martin, and Polly Ward—Mar. 28, 1832.
Edwards, Nathan, and Jane Phelps—Mar. 20, 1823.
Edwards, William, and Martha Coley—Oct. 7, 1835.
Eleir, Frederick, and Elizabeth Pierce—June 17, 1822.
Eller, Frederick, and Margaret Long—June 2, 1795.
Elliot, William, and Betsy Patton—Jan. 1, 1822.
Evans, Joshua, and Patsey Leonard—June 12, 1831.
Evans, William, and Betsy Harmon—Oct. 5 1806.

—F—

Farmer, Howell, and Catherine Hoza—July 10, 1833.
Farmer, Isaac, and Nancy Early,—Mar. 8, 1832.
Farmer, John, and Elizabeth Blakely,—Sept. 10, 1801.
Farmer, John, and Tabitha Kee,—Apr. 27, 1821.
Farmer, John, and Nancy Shockley,—June 1, 1826.
Farmer, William, and Polly Durham,—Sept. 17, 1800.
Fielder, Dennis, and Dealy Wheeler—Mar. 2, 1806.
Fielder, Enos, and Elizabeth Byrd—July 4, 1808.
Fielder, Matthew, and Dorcas Isom—Jan. 27, 1824.
Fielder, Thomas, and Polly Canoy—Feb. 7, 1836.
Finley, Thomas, and Polly Rickman—July 24, 1823.
Fisher, John W., and Ann Delp—Dec. 11, 1832.
Fitzpatrick, James, and Mary Poole,—Aug. 9, 1825.
Foley, Spencer, and Nancy Rector—Jan. 29, 1807.

Fortner, Micajah, and Ellenor Phipps,—Sept. 2, 1834.

Fostor, John, and Polly Simpson,—Aug. 28, 1806.

Fowler, Samuel, and Peggy Stoots,—Feb. 11, 1821.

Franklin, H., and Charlotte Worrell,—Dec. 31, 1835.

Franklin, John, and Phebe Gallimore,—Dec. 5, 1822.

Franklin, Robert, and Lydia Brown—Nov. 9, 1820.

Frost, Stephen, and Mary Hill—Nov. 13, 1806.

Fulks, John, and Sally Carrico—Apr. 3, 1822.

Fulton, Thomas, and Peggy Fulton—Dec. 19, 1812.

Fultner, Samuel, and Betsy Stoneman—Dec. 27, 1823.

Funk, Isaac, and Sally Vaught—Sept. 18, 1834.

Funk, John, and Polly Vaughn—Nov. 16 1824.

—G—

Gallemore, James, and Patience Dalton,—Nov. 14, 1835.

Gallemore, Jesse, and Jane Quessenberry,—Feb. 29, 1824.

Gallemore, William, and Nancy Largin—June 12, 1834.

Ganoway, William, and Lucy Stone—Oct. 15 1807.

Gardner, John, and Rachel Horton—Dec. 26, 1822.

Garntson, Isaac, and Susannah Jones—Mar. 5, 1796.

George, Henry, and Peggy Farmer—Nov. 26, 1824.

Goad, Aaron, and Ellin Cock—Sept. 24, 1835.

Goad, Reuben, and Celeste Cock—Sept. 24, 1835.

Goose, Adam, and Polly Canwell—Apr. 10, 1796.

Greer, Aquilla, and Polly Fielder—May 19, 1814.

Greer, Enoch, and Rachel Stoots—Nov. 24, 1824.

Greer, Jacob, and Mary Kinder—Aug. 28, 1825.

Greer, Shadrack, and Ceely Thomas—Nov. 8, 1821.

Grev, Nathan, and Jane Hutton—July 25, 1802.

Griggin, George, and Sally Davis—March 7, 1833.

Grev, Samson, and Sarah Jessop,—Sept. 21, 1806.

Grimes, John, and Mary Cook,—Sept. 26 1826.

Gwinn, James, and Jane Dickenson—Mar. 1 1825.

—H—

Hackler, George, and Evy Wisear,—Feb. 1, 1796.

Hackler, George, and Polly Hampon,—Apr. 18, 1820.

Hackler, James, and Elizabeth Delp—Sept 27, 1826.

Hackler, John, and Catherine Delp—March 11, 1796.

Hackler, John, and Polly Parker—Feb. 15, 1822.

Hackler, Peter, and Darbars Sutherland—Feb. 12, 1823.

Hackler, Peter, and I........ McGrady—June 26, 1823.

Haga, David, and Peggy Delp—Sept. 18, 1806.

Haga, Henry, and Elizabeth Cooper—Sept. 24, 1825.

Haga, Jacob, and Celia Cooper—May 22 1836.

Hale (Hail), Absolom, and Mary McCloud,—Apr. 4, 1822.

Hale, Preston, and Elizabeth Comary (Canoy?),—Oct. 17, 1816.

Hale, Rufus, and Nancy Hail—Aug. 16, 1835.

Hale, Stephen, and Charlotte Dickerson—Aug. 4, 1814.

Hale, Stephen and Rosamond Bourne—Jan. 9, 1834.

Hale, Thomas, and Sally Sutherland—July 4, 1817.

Hale, W. B., and Matilda Jones—Jan. 31, 1833.

Hale, Wicks, and Peggy Bryant—June 6, 1822.

Hall, (Hill?) Arthur, and Nancy Patton—Feb. 20, 1820.

Hall, Benjamin, and Nancy Light—Aug. 21, 1825.

Hall, John, and Polly Sage—Oct. 30, 1804.

Hall, John, and Sally Bedwell—Aug. 16, 1821

Hamilton, Thomas, and Eliza Jennings—Oct 19, 1803.

Hammons, George, and Esther Phelps,—Oct. 9, 1821.

Hampton, Alix, and Justin Fulton—Mar. 27 1834.

Hampton, Wade, and Betsy Barber—Dec. 8, 1825.

Hancock, Aaron, and Bulah Bryant—Feb. 17, 1801.

Hanks, Richard, and James Bryant—Sept 2 1824.

Hanks, William, and Nancy Carrico—Jan. 2, 1820.

Hardy, Henry, and Rachel Beasley—Jan. 17, 1822.

Hardy, John, and Martha Allin—Feb. 19, 1822.

Harmon, Patrick, and Polly Melton—Dec. 26, 1822.

Harper, George, and Mary Wright—Oct. 20 1796.

Harris, Charles, and Janes Kigas (?),—Nov 7, 1833.

Hart, Mark, and Barbary Kirk—Sept. 17, 1800.

Hart, Stephen, and Sarah Bradford—May 30 1805.

Hash, Andrew, and Nancy Hart—Feb. 25 1805.

Hash, William, and Nancy Anderson—Dec. 12, 1796.

Hash, William, and Hannah Buchanan—Sept. 14, 1817.

Hash, William, and Jane Bonham—Oct. 18, 1833.

Haslip, William, and Inda Peek—Apr. 27, 1817.

Hawks, Felix, and Amy Swift—Oct. 20, 1795.

Helton, Henry, and Sally Starr—Sept. 20, 1821.

Helton, Hiram, and Milly Boothe—Feb. 29 1824.

—26—

Helton, Jesse, and Martha Montgomery—Nov. 18, 1824.

Helton, John, and Louise Helton—July 29, 1824.

Helton, John, and Elizabeth Smith—Jan. 23, 1823.

Helton, Samuel, and Marget Clement—Feb. 18, 1805.

Hera, William, and Elizabeth Hatton—Oct. 14, 1824.

Hiatt (Hiett), Jehu (John?), and Rebeckah Payne—Oct. 27, 1801.

Hiatt, Jehu, and Hannah Hogan—Aug. 8, 1807.

Hiatt, Zacheriah, and Anne Coffin—Sept. 17, 1803.

Hill, (Hall?), Arthur, and Nancy Patton—Feb. 20, 1820.

Hill, James, and Sally Edwards,—March 21, 1821.

Hill, Spencer, and Mary Jones—Dec. 28, 1805

Hilyard, Chris, and Elizabeth Jones—Sept 14, 1807.

Hoge, Math, and Charity Pope—Nov. 30, 1826.

Holdway, David, and Mary Hash—Feb. 15, 1821.

Holsey, William, and Polly Cress—Nov. 11, 1834.

Hoover, William, and Lilly Connutte—Mar. 31, 1796.

Horn, John, and Christinah Vaught—Oct. 25, 1825.

Horton, Benjamin, and Mary Largen—Oct 13, 1825.

Houson, John, and Elizabeth Smith—Dec. 5, 1822.

Howell, Calvin, and Barbary Rudy—Dec. 24, 1804.

Howell, George, and Ruth Cooley—Sept. 4, 1825.

Hudson, William, and Uley Catron—July 2, 1801.

Huff, Peter, and Mary Gallimore—March 18, 1821.

Huffman, James, and Malvina Lundy—Aug 9, 1836.

Hylton, Elisha, and Elizabeth Harris—Mar 15, 1832.

—I—

Isom, Ivan, and Rebeekah Cole—Sept. 17, 1800.

Isom, Jack, and Sarah Lawson—June 3, 1824.

Isom, John, and Sally Jones—Oct. 22, 1835.

—J—

Jackson, James, and Elizabeth Collins—Dec. 5, 1822.

James, Joshua, and Sarah Trump, and May 29, 1825.

James, Spencer B., and Nancy Bourne—Dec. 22, 1835.

James, William, and Rhoda Trump—April 5, 1824.

Jennings, Andrew, and Jane Collier,—Dec. 20, 1825.

Jennings, Clifton, and Catherine Dalton—June 16 ,1831.

Jennings, Jeremiah, and Peggy Robinson—Sept. 5, 1826.

Jennings, Jonathan, and Nancy Hanson..) —........, 1803.

Jennings, Lacy, and Mary Lawson—May 15, 1831.

Jennings, Thomas, and Elizabeth Ogles—Apr. 4, 1822.

Jennings, Wisley, and Sarah Bond—Apr. 12, 1836.

Jessop, Timothy, and Catron Stanley—June 14, 1804.

Johnson, David, and Beauty Anderson—Dec. 11, 1832.

Johnson, William, and Lucinda Feare—June 12, 1833.

Johnston, Jonathan, and Micah (?) Bedwell—Aug. 30, 1807.

Jones, Churchwell, and Julia Jones—Dec. 5, 1811.

Jones, Daniel, and Elizabeth Flors—June 17, 1819.

Jones, Gordon, and Martha Anderson—Aug. 31, 1823.

Jones, Levi, and Nancy Dickey—Dec. 5, 1822.

Jones, Naish, and Sarah Jones—May 18, 1797.

Jones, Sam'l and Amy Williams—Sept. 17, 1800.

Jones, Thomas, and Elizabeth Severy—Nov. 29, 1804.

Jones, Thomas, and Jane Phipps—Sept. 27, 1826.

Jones, William, and Agnes Keith—July 17, 1805.

Joyce, John C., and Gezyah Stuart—Dec. 11, 1824.

—K—

Keith, George Jr., and Betsy Pitts—July 5, 1796.

Keith, John, and Leah Earle—May 8, 1823.

Kester, Peter, and Hannah Davis—Mar. 25, 1806.

Kester, Richard, and Phebe Brown—Apr. 3, 1799.

Kirk, George, and Polly Staley—May 27, 1801.

Kirk, Jacob, and Sarah Wright—July 29, 1800.

—L—

Landreth, Benjamin, and Elizabeth Farmer —Jan. 31, 1822.

Landreth, Benjamin, and Pricilla Wilkerson —Jan. 10, 1836.

Landreth, John, and Rebekah Ward—Jan. 26, 1826.

Larew, Jesse, and Mary Cole—Nov. 12, 1818.

Larew, Lewis, and Mary Stoneman—Sept 10, 1818.

Largen, Anson, and Mary Quesenberry—Oct. 15, 1835.

Leonard. Greenbury, and Eleanor Ballard—Apr. 28, 1832.

Leonard, Obediah, and Hannah Cooley—Dec. 26, 1805.

Leiter, Joseph, and Eve Mill (?)—Sept. 20, 1825.

Lineberry, Francis, and Elizabeth Wilkenson —Nov. 4, 1824.

Linesay (Livesay?), George, and Margaret Hackler—Aug. 8, 1826.

Livesley, Andrew, and Nancy Anderson—Feb. 28, 1822.

Literal, Lewis, and Sally Jones—Aug. 3, 1826.

Long, John, and Celia Delp—May 8, 1833.

Long, Samuel, and Molly Cornutte—Sept 12, 1811.

Longwith, Burges, and Kezia Davis—Aug. 5, 1821.
Love, Joseph, and Susanna Stone—Sept. 21, 1804.
Lougher, Edward, and Milly Cornutt—May 20, 1806.
Lovin, James, and Sarah Staples—June 21, 1826.
Lundy, Aaron, and Mahala Segar—Jan. 15, 1807.
Lundy, George, and Sally Thomas—Sept. 10, 1836.
Lundy, John, and Martha South—Feb. 1, 1827.
Lundy, Nathan, and Aimv Pichell—Apr. 13, 1801.

—M—

Maberry, Samuel, and Tabitha Branscome—Nov. 20, 1823.
Mallory, Henry, and Kezia Hanks—June 29, 1826.
Mallory, Joel, and Sally Carrico—Sept. 23, 1824.
Mallory, Thomas, and Polly Byrd—Oct. 6, 1836.
Mainor, Vincent, and Rachel Hampton—Oct. 21, 1804.
Marshall, Abraham, and Mary Bond—Aug. 8, 1835.
Marshall, Elijah, and S........ Stanley,—June 23, 1826.
Marshall, Joseph, and Elizabeth Bond—Sept. 13, 1834.
Martin, Ryol, and Betsy Vaughan—Nov. 4, 1824.
Martin, Smith, and Nancy Livesay—Dec. 12, 1824.
Mash (Wash?), Jehu, and Polly Jones—Jan. 3, 1805.
Matthews, Thomas C., and Kezia Spruel—Apr. 17, 1821.
McClain, Wm., and Phebe Newman—Feb. 11, 1807.
McClarin, Lace, and Nancy Hoge—April 7, 1814.
McCluer, Samuel, and Sarah Balwin—Apr. 3, 1799.
McCluer, Williams, and Rosanna Worrell—June 15, 1820.
McCraw, Thomas, and Elizabeth Perry—Oct. 21. 1835.
McElea, John, and Betsy ...., —Oct. 5, 1793.
McKendre, Alexander, and Mary Evans—Sent. 5, 1822.
McMillon. Abram, and Elizabeth Morris—Sept. 16, 1832.
McNight, Sam'l, and Nancy Welch—Aug. 29, 1821.
McPeak, Archeleus, and Cathrin Sutphin—March 13, 1825.
Meek, James, and Jestianna Dickenson—July 4, 1822.
Melton, Amos, and Charity Williams—Feb. 27, 1816.
Melton, Stephen, and Elizabeth Bryant—Sept. 29, 1836.
Melton, William, and Sally Bedsal—May 27, 1823.
Mitchell, Stephen N., and Nancy Davis—Oct. 8, 1836.

Mooney, John, and Sarah Stoneman—Oct. 26, 1801.
Mooney, William, and Asenith Lundy—Jan. 25, 1827.
Moore, Adam, and Susannah Philips,—Aug. 13, 1835.
Moore, Benjamin, and Susanna Barbour—Sept. 6, 1821.
Moore, Daniel, and Patsey Hampton—Dec. 29, 1822.
Moore, Enoch, and Rhoda Hanks—Mar. 4, 1819.
Moore, John, and Polly Pope—Oct. 25, 1835.
Moore, Ruben, and Elenor Carson—Aug. 19, 1824.
Moore, Sam'l, and Polly Murphy—June 9, 1836.
Moore, Thomas, and Jane Bobbitt—Jan. 6, 1825.
Moore, Thomas, and Huldah Carrico—Feb. 22, 1827.
Montgomery, George, and Nancy Turman—Mar. 13, 1834.
Montgomery, Hiatt, and Elizabeth Maberry—Sept. 25, 1823.
Montgomery, Irvin, and Betsy Davis—Nov. 6, 1833.
Montgomery, Kelly, and Zelphia Cock—Dec. 24, 1835.
Montgomery, Martin, and Elizabeth Turman June 26, 1834.
Montgomery, Robert, and Rebecca Turman—May 22, 1834.
Montgomery, William, and Nancy Sutphin—May 15, 1831.
Morgan, William, and Elizabeth Bobbitt—Feb. 16, 1799.
Murphy, John, and Rebeckah Payne—Oct. 27, 1801.
Murphy, Joseph, and Margaret Lenton—Sept. 11, 1834.

—N—

Nebbitt, Abraham, and Elizabeth Nuckolls—Jan. 3, 1824.
Nebbitt, Dave, and Sally Denny—Sept. 29, 1805.
Nelson, Allen, and Eliza Vaught—Feb. 15, 1834.
Nester, Daniel, and Elizabeth Huett—June 21, 1824.
Nester, Joshua, and Rebecca Cock—Oct. 9. 1823.
Newman, Arthur, and Margaret Farmer—May 2, 1834.
Newman, Byrd, and Rebeckah Farmer—Sept. 28, 1815.
Night, Robert, and Sarah Taylor—Nov. 10, 1805.
Nuckolls, Ezra, and Lucinda Hail—Apr. 10, 1823.
Nuckolls, Lorenza, and Catherine Fulton—July 27, 1833.
Nuckolls, Robert, and Peggy Swift—Feb. 28, 1805.
Nugen, Jacob, and Rhoda Harrold—Mar. 11, 1823.

—O—

Ogles, David, and Sarah Jennings—Nov. 6, 1823.
Ogles, Hiram, and Sarah Richardson—July 28, 1801.

Ogles, James, and Catherine Golden—Jan. 25, 1823.
Ogles, Jonathan, Agnes Wells—Sept. 24, 1796.
Ogles, Reeve, and Mary Young—May 19, 1835.
Ogles, Solomon, and Hannah Cox—Feb. 14, 1822.

—P—

Painter, Alexander, and Polly Eller—Sept. 21, 1831.
Parker, Joseph, and Elizabeth Denny—Sept. 17, 1800.
Parker, Joseph, and Elizabeth Rector—Sept. 17, 1800.
Parsons, Isaac, and Susannah Pugh—Dec. 25, 1835.
Parsons, John, and Polly Roberts—April 21, 1821.
Parsons, Ruben, and Mary Richeson—Aug. 13, 1799.
Patton, Hosea, and Elizabeth Hill—Feb. 14, 1822.
Patton, Thomas, and Nancy Patton—April 26, 1826.
Patterson, John, and Rachel South—Oct. 21, 1832.
Payne, Nathaniel, and Betsy Hazlewood—Mar. 9, 1801.
Pearson, Isaac, and .... Whittey—Sept. 21, 1806.
Pennington, James, and Susannah Chambers—Sept. 7, 1824.
Perkins, Alexander, and Malinda Well—Oct. 12, 1826.
Perkins, Philip, and Rebeckah Grady—Oct. 17, 1825.
Perkins, Samuel, and Caroline Woods—Mar. 31, 1825.
Perkins, Stephen, and Margaret Hannah Woods,—Jan. 29, 1818.
Perkins, William, and Catherine Mitchell—July 8, 1819.
Perry, Joseph, and Sally Frost—Oct. 4, 1836.
Phelps, John, and Alisey Love,—Mar. 23, 1833.
Phelps, William, and Amelia Burnet—Jan. 21, 1820.
Phillips, James, and Elizabeth Mallory—Feb. 12, 1824.
Phillips, Jehee, and Feby Durnill—Oct. 6, 1825.
Phillips, Randolph, and Mary Cox—Dec. 26, 1822.
Phillips, Thomas, and Polly Moore—Sept. 4, 1834.
Phillips, William, and Jenny Smith—Dec. 16, 1824.
Phipps, Larkin, and Charity Barton—Mar. 15, 1834.
Pickle, James, and Margaret Robinson—May 19, 1835.
Pitts, Mayson, and Barbary Hackler—June 13, 1805.
Poff, Jacob, and Elizabeth Chappell—Jan. 8, 1814.
Pool, David, and Mamy Horton—June 14, 1814.
Pool, David, and Patsy Pope—Dec. 4, 1823.
Pool, Jonathan, and Ann Conoy, June 18, 1821.
Pool, John, and Evy Hawk—Aug. 6, 1797.
Pool, Minetrea, and Polly Hail—Nov. 13, 1823.
Pool, William, and Lester Roberts, Mar. 4, —1819.

Porter, James, and Rachel Daniel— Aug. 24, 1823.
Porter, William and Patsy Hudson—Sept. 5, 1805.
Porter, William, and Franky Jones—Jan. .. .. 1822.
Powers, Fetty, and Elizabeth Stealey—Sept. 14, 1800.
Prichard, Thomas, and Betsy Mays—Aug 2', 1804.
Puckett, George, and Ruth Arthur—Apr. 3, 1823.
Puckett, George, and Sarah Puckett—Apr. 14, 1831.
Pugh, John, and Cynthia Bourn—Apr. 25, 1822.
Pugh, Robert, and Mary Thomas—Jan. 3, 1817.
Pugh, William, and Lucy Anderson—Apr. 14, 1820.
Quesenberry, Amos, and Usley Goad—Aug. 28, 1832.
Quesenberry, Frederick, and Mary Huff—July 3, 1836.
Quesenberry, Frederick, and Nancy Banks—Oct. 15, 1835.
Quesenberry, George, and Matilda Jennings—Apr. 20, 1836.
Quesenberry, George, and Joanna Webb—Feb. 1, 1836.
Quesenberry, Tober, and Isabell Goad—Dec. 15, 1831.

—R—

Rankin, John, and Olive Wallace—Nov. 7, 1822.
Rankin, William, and Nancy Mullin—Sept. 25, 1811.
Rankin, William, and Isabella Patton—July 27, 1823.
Rathbone, Andrew, and Ruth Ayers—June 26, 1807.
Rathbone, Andrew, and Sarah Britt—Nov. 8, 1804.
Redas, F......... and Lucy Oglesby—Feb. 27, 1816.
Redas, Joel, and Caty English, Nov. 25, 1815.
Reedy, Andrew, and Hiley Anderson—Jan. 19, 1836.
Reedy, David, and Sally Quillin—Dec. 17, 1824.
Reedy, Frederick, and Ruth Davis—Mar. 22, 1825
Reese, Abraham, and Sarah Bond, Dec. 15, 1836.
Reese, Thomas, and Claretty Hill, Nov. 29, 1803.
Reeves, John H., and Nancy Horton, Nov. 24, 1796.
Richardson (Richeson, Richerdson).
Richardson, John, and Elizabeth Wright, Apr. 9, 1807.
Richardson, John, and Fanny Hufman, Mar. 9, 1801.
Richardson, Joshua, and Anne Myers, Apr. 6, 1820.
Richardson, Joshua, and Polly Cock, Sept, 17, 1800.
Richardson, Joseph, and Rebecca Ferriss, Dec. 24, 1835.
Richardson, William, and Neoma Boham, Sept. 16, 1824.

Ring, Martin, and Hester South, Dec. 12, 1833.

Roberts, Fountain, and Peggy Moore, Oct. 30, 1823.

Roberts, Jacob, and Olive Stoots, Sept. 17, 1800.

Roberts, John W., and Bency Shinault, Apr. 21, 1825.

Roberts, Michael, and Patty Farmer, May 19, 1823.

Roberts, William, and Lydia Lewis, Oct. 30, 1806.

Roberts, William, and Susannah Wright, Oct. 1822.

Robinson, Ezekill, and Hannah Crouch, Sept. 2, 1806.

Robinson, Preston, and Polly Dunfors,—Nov. 5, 1810.

Rogers, James, and Juda Sexton—June 2, 1795.

Rogers, Russell, and Keziah M. Hale—Mar. 7, 1836.

Ross, Archibald, and Mary Cross—Sept. 25, 1824.

Ross, Stephen, and Elizabeth Anderson—Mar. 12, 1818.

Ross, Wilborn, and Adah Perkins—July 3, 1825.

Ross, William, and Millie Anderson—Apr. 29, 1624.

Rouse, Jesse, and Cleo Pearl (?),—Feb. 12, 1807.

Routrof, Peter, and Levice Sage,—Mar. 23, 1812.

Rowark, Charles, and Polly Reed—Sept. 17, 1800.

Rowark, Moses, and Evey Stealey—Sept. 17, 1800.

Rudd, Archibald, and Nancy Woosley—Dec. 27, 1822.

Rudy, Washington, and Amey Comer—Sept. 24, 1835.

Runer, Balser, and Catherine Eller—Nov. 16, 1823.

Russell, Philip, and Rebeckah Russell—Mar. 30, 1797.

Russell, William, and Anna Bonham—Apr. 29, 1822.

Rutherford, John and Nancy Philips—Mar. 13, 1823.

Rutherford, William, and Sealy Hale—Feb. 12, 1822.

—S—

Sage, Martin, and Susanna Wright—May 5, 1824.

Sass (Sap?), Nathan, and Susanna Hale—July 12, 1821.

Schooley, James, and Polly Ogles—Sept. 28, 1815.

Scott, William, and Mary James—July 27, 1834.

Semones, Seconiah, and Polly Eaton—Mar. 19, 1812.

Sexton, Benjamin, and Nancy Taylor—Aug. 22, 1806.

Sexton, Thomas, and Charlotte Forkner—Nov. 1, 1832.

Sexton, William, and Elizabeth Cock—Sept. 17, 18u0.

Sexton, William, and Polly Cock—Sept. 17, 1800.

Sexton, William, and Betsy Hoge—Nov. 11, 1824.

Shockley, Amos, and Jemima ....,—Jan. 16, 1823.

Shockley, Esau, and Elizabeth Farmer—Oct. 31, 1822.

Shockley, Meridith, and Drucilla Dehaven—May 6, 1824.

Shively, David, and Sealy Cannoy—Sept. 9, 1824.

Short, David, and Nancy Cuddy—Dec. 9, 1821.

Shoop, Henry, and Hetty A? Gullion,—June 25, 1825.

Shoop, Peter, and Sally Wright—Dec. 22, 1814.

Shupe, Andrew, and Malinda Williams—Sept. 22, 1836.

Shuler, Daniel, and Elizabeth Eller—Dec. 17, 1818.

Shuler, John, and Sarah Cornutt,—Dec. 1, 1825.

Simcock, Thomas, and Susanna South—May 29, 1823.

Smade, Simon, and Rebeckah Failey—July 22, 1806.

Smith, Hezekiah, and Nancy Cooley—Mar. 22, 1835.

Smith, James, and Nancy Allison—Mar. 18, 1834.

Smith, Stephen, and Polly Cooley—Sept 23, 1832.

Smith, William F., and Rachel Rankin—July 7, 1836.

Snow, Bird, and Eliza Harris—Mar. 15, 1832.

South, Huel, and Rachel Swanson—Sept. 17, 1800.

South, John, and Bety Wilson—Sept. 16, 1824.

South, Stephen, and Matilda Wilkinson—Mar. 11, 1834.

Spence, Burwell, and Nancy Thomas—July 7, 1831.

Spence, John, and Mary Woolsey—Oct. 30, 1823.

Spencer, Isaac, and Phebe Anderson—Dec. 11, 1835.

Spinling, William, and Martha Stanbury—Dec. 25, 1835.

Stafford, James, and Lueretia Reins,—Mar. 29, 1837.

Stamper, Hiram, and Anna Hackler—May 2, 1833.

Stealey, Frederick, and Mar. . Kirk—Apr. 6, 1797.

Steele, Edward, and Rebeckah Beard—Sept. 17, 1800.

Stone, John, and Sally Leonard—July 31, 1823.

Stone, John, and Nancy Fielder—Mar. 10, 1824.

Stone, Philip, and Deborah Peaks—July 24, 1831.

Stone, William, and Louisa Lundy—Sept. 10, 1835.

Stuart, Joel, and Millay Rdan—Apr. 5, 1821.

Suit, Samuel, and Nancy Snow—June 4, 1824.

Sullivin, James, and Elizabeth Baldwin—May 18, 1822.

Sumner, Miah (?), and Polly Baton—Mar. 19, 1812.

Surratt, Joseph, and Malinda Carter—Sept. 26, 1835.

Sutherland, John, and Deedma Cornutt—Feb. 12, 1807.

Sutherland, Joseph, and Susanna Robinson June 25, 1807.

Sutphin, Elijah, and Drucilla Nuckolls—Nov. 3, 1825.

Swaney, James, and Betsy Byrd—Nov. 5, 1807.

Swift, Thomas, and Polly Catron—Nov. 6, 1804.

Swindle, Joseph, and Beeca Nobbett—Nov. 23, 1826.

—T—

Taylor, Edmond, and Jane Durham—Jan. 12, 1826.

Taylor, Rawson, and Sally Faddis—Sept. 8, 1836.

Taylor, William, and Sally Collins—Apr. 20, 1834.

Terry, John, and Usa West,—Nov. 16, 1825.

Thomas, Grogg, and Nancy Crider—Dec. 17, 1833.

Thomas, Jonathan, and Seney Harker—Sept. 19, 1824.

Thomas, Martin, and Sally Wilkerson—Mar. 21, 1837.

Thomas, Nathan, and Rebecca Pool—Dec. 1, 1796.

Thomas, William, and Mary Sutherland—Dec. 16, 1819.

Thompson, George, and Malin.. Sancreth—May 2, 1834.

Thompson, Nathan, and Rhoda Branscom—Nov. 6, 1831.

Tolbert, John, and Sally McCluer—May 3, 1806.

Tolbert, John, and Alley Cock—Dec. 17, 1834.

Tolliver, George, and Margaret Blevins—Apr. 13, 1834.

Tolliver, William, and Betsy Long—May 24 1814.

Trocksal, Jacob, and Sarah Bowan—Dec. 4, 1824.

Trout, Philip, and Caty Kirk—June 2, 1795.

—V—

Vannoy, Nathaniel, and Mary Halsay—Dec. 21, 1819.

Vaughan, Alexander, and Polly Landreth—Nov. 20, 1834.

Vaughan, Jefferson, and Earbary Phillips—Dec. 11, 1832.

Vaughan, Meridith, and Polly Shupe—Apr. 12, 1836.

Vaughan, Peyton, and Jane Picket—Aug. 25, 1836.

Vaughan, Samuel, and Martha Roberts—Aug. 23, 1836.

Vaughan, William, and Elizabeth Himes—Sept. 7, 1836.

Vaught, John, and Eliza Fuller—Feb. 15, 1834.

—W—

Wade, Garland, and Rebeckah Williams—June 17, 1806.

Wade, Nathan, and Delphia Cox—June 15, 1826.

Ward, Benjamin, and Jane Cox,—June 3, 1820.

Ward, Charlie, and Anne South—Jan. 29, 1807.

Ward, Elijah, and Polly Collins—Sept 17, 1800.

Ward, Ezekiel, and Pheebe Screech—Jan. 14, 1836.

Ward, Lewis, and Maryann Hash—Apr. 3, 1823.

Ward, Stephen, and Jane Hash—Apr. 26, 1833.

Ward, William, and Elizabeth Wilson—Sept. 17, 1800.

Ward, William T. and Nancy Carrico—Feb. 27, 1835.

Ward, Zacheriah, and Tabitha Hash—Jan. 29, 1818.

Warwick, James, and Sukey Conoy—Mar. 12, 1812.

Warwick, John, and Betsy Roberts—Oct. 17, 1805.

Warwick, Robert, and Polly Conoy—Dec. 22, 1814.

Warwick, William, and Eliza Vanover—Sept. 5, 1805.

Webb, Culbert, and Sarah Nester—Dec. 30, 1824.

Webb, Henry, and Nancy Bobbitt—Oct. 23, 1823.

Webb, Jacob, and Hester Dickerson—Aug. 20, 1822.

Webb, John Jr., and Elizabeth Dickerson—July 10, 1823.

Webb, Robert, and Elizabeth Nester—July 28, 1825.

Webb, William, and Catherine Dickerson—Dec. 22, 1825.

Wells, John, and Phebe Beller—Jan. 10, 1822.

West, John, and Melinda Roberts—Sept. 8, 1824.

White, David, and Sarah Tipton—Sept. 8, 1835.

White, John, and Anne Fulton—July 12, 1797.

Whip, (Whiss?), Joan, and Love Grindly—July 4, 1817.

Wilkerson, Martin, and Surany Lineberry—Sept. 27, 1807.

Williams, Abodiah, and Susanna Short—Nov. 30, 1807.

Williams, Garrett, and Charity Beemer—Mar. 7, 1822.

Williams, Henry, and Sally Keneocritty—Dec. 5, 1804.

Williams, James, and Susannah Harvey—June 1, 1826.

Williams, Jonathan, and Elizabeth Bobbitt—Sept. 13, 1821.

Williams, John, and Nancy Hays—Nov. 3 1807.

Wilson, Cyrus, and Matilda Bartell—July 13, 1834.

Wilson, Henery, and Rebecca Bartell—Apr. 2, 1833.

Wilson, John, and Catha Isom—Nov. 27, 1832.

Winsett, I ....and Hannah Williams—Jan. 7, 1836.

Wiste, Michael, and Rebeckah Boyer—Mar. 28, 1797.

Woods, Joseph W. and Suranda Perkins,—Nov. 20, 1833.

Woosley, William, and Elizabeth Puckett—Jan. 3, 1823.

Worrell, Amos, and Mary Shinault—Jan. 10, 1825.

Worrell, Esau, and Nancy Bobbitt—Oct. 20, 1785.

Worrell, Esau, and Nancy Edwards—Oct. 29, 1837.

Worrell, James, and Olive Houson—Aug. 27, 1821.

Worrell, Jesse, and Rebecca Cooley—Feb. 4, 1840.
Worrell, John Jr., and Elizabeth Shinault—Nov. 2, 1826.
Worrell, William, and Patsy Wilson—Nov. 9, 1826.
Wright, Abner, and Christinah Vaught—Feb. 7, 1836.
Wright, Andrew, and Susanna Cornwell—Oct. 11, 1812.
Wright, F........, and Elizabeth Harper—June 2, 1795.
Wright, Fletcher, and Matilda Fulton—May 5, 1836.
Wright, Harrison, and Polly Vaught—Jan. 24, 1827.
Wright, Jacob, and Rebecca Porter—Mar. 2, 1806.
Wright, Jeremiah, and Muornen Fielder—Jan. 21, 1808.
Wright, Richard, and Seney Butten—Sept. 17, 1800.
Wright, Stephen, and Marvet Kelly—Aug. 23 1822.
Wright, William, and Mary Screse—Dec. 25, 1812.

—Y—

Yonce, Peter, and Barbary Kenson—Apr. 29, 1832.
Young, Joseph, and Jane Phipps,—Aug. 11, 1825.
Youns (Yonce), Frederick, and Elizabeth Rimer—Dec. 30, 1824.

PULASKI COUNTY

The following marriage records are from ministers returns; the marriage bonds, as well as almost all of the ministers returns, prior to 1854, having been destroyed by fire.

Anderson, Tolbert, and E. Fizer—June 2, 1843.
Barger, Isaac, and Mary Dick—Jan. 1, 1840.
Beekner, George W., and Rachel Husk—Sept. 16, 1840.
Bell, Crockett, and Elizabeth Arnacot—Feb. 27, 1844.
Bell, David, and Harriet Snow—May 21, 1840.
Booth, William H., and Catherine Smith—Feb. 8, 1844.
Bradshaw, William, and Edie Honaker—Jan. 6, 1842.
Bratton, Thomas, and Polly Cecil—Dec. 1, 1842.
Brookman, Samuel, and Mary Blankenship—Jan. 1, 1840.
Bowden, Jack, and Jane Mullen—Sept. 17, 1840.
Carper, Isaac, and Hannah Godey—May .., 1840.
Cecil, John H., and Mary Trinkle—June 9 1842.
Clark, Andrew J., and Margaret Raines—June 1, 1840.
Cooper, Alexander, and Ann Farmer—Feb. 5, 1840.
Cooper, Oljlestan and Amanda Odill—Mar 12, 1840.
Covey, Joseph, and Mary Ann Elliot—Sept 17, 1840.
Dawson, Alexander, and Christina Minix—June 13, 1839.

Dawson, Hiram, and Sarah Fortune—Oct. 13, 1840.
Dudley, Jonathan, and Rachel Steel—May 25, 1843.
Durst, Thomas, and Margaret Miller—Dec. 19, 1839.
Farmer, Allanson, and Charlotte Graham—Nov. 21, 1839.
Fortner, William, and Jane Williams—Sept. 24, 1842.
Fortune, Benjamin, and Nancy Davis—Jan. 3, 1842.
Hail, Thomas, and Paulina Hedge—May 7, 1840.
Haines, William L., and Nancy Kelly—Apr. 2, 1841.
Harris, Jacob, and Mariah Stewart—May 12, 1841.
Hayse, William, and Sarah Showalter—Oct. 27, 1842.
Hetherton, John, and Rhoda Bratton—Oct. 27 1842.
Hickman, Rev. William P., and Margaret R. Hoge—July 18, 1844.
Hill, Harvy, and Lucinda Odel—Aug. 18, 1844.
Honaker, Henery, and Elizabeth Coobough—Feb. 10, 1840.
Hurst, Jesse, and Mary Fugate—Oct. 1, 1840.
Hurst, Samuel, and Virginia Bruding—Nov. 17, 1740.
Hurst, William, and Phebee Odell—Jan. 1, 1840.
Jones, William F., and Anne Cooper—Feb. 27, 1841.
Kibler, Philip, and Lucy Dudley—Oct. 20, 1842.
Leay, Marshall, and Rachel Bushby—Apr. 17, 1843.
Longer, John, and Martha 2ruster—Apr. 16 1840.
Miller, Samuel, and Mary G. Early—Sept. 17, 1840.
Miller, Thomas, and E. Crawford—Nov. 16, 1843.
Mitchell, William, and L. Michael—Oct. 1 1843.
Muncey, Jacob, and Martha Dillimore—Sept. 1, 1842.
Nester, Jonathan, and Matilda Hurst—Aug 21, 1845.
Newby, Joseph, and Martha Smith—Apr. 14 1842.
Nuingold, Jonathan, and Mary Ann Michean Mar. 12, 1840.
Parker, Willson, and L. Cook—Jan. 8, 1841.
Quesenberry, Crockett, and Elizabeth Moore —Dec. 12, 1843.
Quesenberry, Jan. and Euphenia Breeding—Jan. 24, 1840.
Racy, James, and Polly Russell—Dec. 1, 1842
Richardson, Joseph, and Eliza Hall—Feb. 18 1844.
Robinson, Henry, and Phebe Simpkins—Sept. 2, 1841.
Robinson, Isaac, and Ann Brookman—Feb 18, 1841.
Robinson, Thomas, and Louisa Peck—Jan. 10, 1840.
Ronk, Daniel, and Mary Diddle—Sept. 4, 1841.
Runnion, James, and Lucinda Smith—Jan. 22, 1839.

Rupe, Lewis, and Jane Worsham—Nov. 10, 1842.

Rutter, G. W., and Rebecca Runyan—Jan. 5, 1845.

Scott, John, and Sally Jones—Mar. 2, 1843.

Showalter, Elijah, and Catherine Showalter —Apr. 19, 1841.

Showalter, William, and Malvina Farmer— Apr. 21, 1842.

Sifford, Samuel, and Barbra Songer—Jan. 31 1842.

Simpkins, James, and Malinda Willson—July 27, 1839.

Simpkins, James, and Catherine Fink—Apr. 3, 1843.

Slusser, Joseph, and Nancy Farmer—Nov. 3, 1843.

Stewart, William, and Margaret Moyers— Jan. 5, 1843.

Stone, James, and Rhoda Hurst—Aug. 18, 1840.

Stuart, John B., and Ellin C. Cecil—Nov. 6, 1843.

Thornton, Thomas, and Rebecca Shepherd— Sept. 2, 1841.

Trinkle, William H., and Nancy H. Thompson—Mar. 7, 1844.

Trollinger, John, and Mary Wygal—Oct. 3, 1839.

Umbarger, Abraham, and Mariah Miller— Apr. 13, 1841.

Vickers, Harrison, and Zerilda Bateman— June 9, 1842.

Warden, Thomas, and Sarah McLanel—May 12, 1842.

Warnacot, Kennerly, and Margaret Bell— Feb. 27, 1844.

Yost, James, and Nancy E. Wygal—Oct. 29, 1840.

ROANOKE COUNTY

Abbott, Thomas, and J. S. Smith—Sept. 20, 1840.

Barnes, Jefferson, and Esther Hubbard—May 17, 1841.

Barnhart, Joel, and Margaret U. Steller— Jan.19, 1843.

Basham, Solomon, and Clarinda Mungold— Dec. 14, 1840.

Beemer, George W., and E .A. Roof—Sept. 10, 1840.

Blankenship, Marquis, and Lucinda Shartzer —Aug. 28, 1838.

Brewbaker, Benjamin, and Mary Garst— Nov. 12, 1839.

Brickey, Samuel, and Mahala Brickey—Jan. 1841.

Brown, David S., and Leana Trayner—Feb. 20, 1841.

Brown, Joshua R. C., and Mary J. Williams June 11, 1840.

Brown, Philip, and Elizabeth Garst—Oct. 10, 1838.

Bucey, Thomas H., and Sarah N. Fox,—Sept. 23, 1841.

Butt, Henry, and Eliza Coffman—Oct. 15, 1840.

Putt, Martin, and Salome Coffman—Oct. 22, 1839.

Caldwell, John, and Adeline Smith—Sept. 30, 1840.

Carper, Casewell C., and Mary T. Evans— Mar. 20, 1841.

Carper, Isaac, and Rebecca Dodd—Feb. 13, 1840.

Carper, Valentine, and Malinda Shawver— Jan. 1842.

Coleman, John D., and Martha Goodwin— June 30, 1841.

Cook, William M., and Mary L. Walton—Jan. 27, 1841.

Crawford, Floyd, and Martha Willet—June 12, 1838.

Day, Mordicah, and Sarah Webster—Aug. 2, 1838.

Damewood, Eraser (?), and Sarah Abbott— Mar. 20, 1840.

Deaton, John C., and Eliza B. Elam—June 24, 1841.

Deaton, Joseph, and Susan Bow—Dec. 20. 1841.

Dodd, James and Aggy Smith—Feb. 13, 1840.

Edmundson, Henry, and Mary A. Lewis— Jan. 7, 1840.

Elkins, Levi, and Eliza Glenn—Dec. 31, 1840.

Elyson, Peyton, and Magdalene Lavender— May 16, 1840.

Faris, Benjamin, and Mary Garwood—Mar. 4, 1840.

Ferguson, James, and Harriet Hays—Oct. 15, 1840.

Ferguson, McDonald, and Catherine Griffith —Sept. 4, 1838.

Furrow, James M., and Lucy A. Brickey— May 26, 1841.

Garrett, William, and Eliza Ann Circle—Dec. 29, 1842.

Garst, Jacob, and Catherine Wright—July 10, 1838.

Garst, Thomas, and E. Brubaker—Nov. 11, 1841.

Gray, Jackson, and Elizabeth Willet,—Dec. 24, 1840.

Harris, William, and Sarah E. Muse—Feb. 16, 1843.

Hartman, George B., and Blanche Crow, (Coon?)—Sept. 11, 1838.

Hartman, George W., and Elizabeth Jordon —Nov. 28, 1838.

Hawley, Edwin and Catherine Henry—Jan. 6, 1842.

Henry, Stephen, and Elizabeth Webster— Oct. 6, 1840.

Huffman Isaac, and Margaret Eply—July 23. 1840.

Jennings, Pascal, and Elizabeth Stover—Oct. 8, 1838.

Jones, James, and Charity Richeson—Dec. 20, 1839.

Jones, Peter, and Mary Angle—July 31, 1838.

Kipler, Christian, and Mary A. Smith—June 14, 1843.

Lea, Cassell, and Elizabeth Johnston—Sept. 23, 1839.

Leffler, Richard, and Lidia Bradley—May 26, 1841.

Light, Henry, and Magdalene Henry—Dec. 24, 1840.

Mason, Jonathan, and Sophia W. Hix—Nov. 18, 1841.

McClanahan, Elisha B., and Frances C. Jeter —Mar. 16, 1841.

McCray, William, and Nancy Blankenship— June 30, 1840.

McCrary, Fulton, and Martha Harvey—Mar. 7, 1841.

McFalls, James, and Elizabeth Farrer—Jan. 16, 1840.

Melon, James, and Mary Harmon—Dec. 21, 1841.

Miller, Jacob, and Eliza Thomason—Nov. 16, 1842.

Moody, Jacob, and Susannah A. Baker—Nov. 26, 1840.

Moomaw, Mark B., and Mary A. Gish—Nov. 18, 1841.

Moore, Enoch, and Mary Garst—Jan. 24, 1839.

Moses, Jacob, and Neomi Coffman—Dec. 31, 1840.

Niday, Joseph, and Sarah Carper—Feb. 14, 1843.

Nininger, David, and Catherine Philips—Nov. 8, 1838.

Owens, William, and Lucy Brandy—Nov. 14, 1839.

Painter, John, and Mary Abbott—Nov. 23, 1841.

Pate, Absolom, and Caroline Anderson—Oct. 15, 1839.

Petitit, William, and Catherine Winger—Mar. 15, 1842.

Peyton, John R., and Catherine White—Aug. 20, 1840.

Phlegar, Isaac, and Catherine Rutherford—Oct. 23, 1838.

Poage, William, and Elizabeth Crow (?),—Sept. 12, 1838.

Pobst, Henry G., and Sarah P. Stover—Sept. 15, 1840.

Renn, Isaac, and Eliza A. Gish—Dec. 18, 1839.

Reynolds, Andrew, and Sarah Martin—Mar. 15, 1840.

Richards, William M., and Sarah M. Harvey—Oct. 15, 1839.

Riffey, James, and Anna Rhodes—Nov. 23, 1841.

Robinson, Madison, and Sarah Richardson—Feb. 24, 1842.

Ronk, Jacob, and M. Beath—Sept. 27, 1840.

Ronk, John, and Salome Showalter—June 6, 1841.

Rutherford, Reuben S., and Martha J. Stewart—June 25, 1839.

Sarver, George, and Catherine Huffman—Feb. 3, 1842.

Shartzer, Andrew, and Emmeline Goad—July 16, 1838.

Showalter, Henry, and Rutha Robinson—June 30, 1842.

Shirey. John, and Leanna M. Miller—May 27, 1842.

Sisson, John, and Hannah Wilson—Jan. 5, 1843.

Smetzer, Jacob, and Evaline Blankenship—Oct. 13, 1838.

Smith, Absolom, and America Smith—Sept. 20, 1839.

Smith, Henry, and Martha A. Gordon—Jan. 1840.

Smith, William, and Mary Ann McFalls

Steele, John, and Elizabeth Fowler—Apr. 24, 1839.

Stratton, Wyley, and Paulina White—Mar. 27, 1839.

Thurman, James S., and Frances Farrer—Jan. 12, 1843.

Trout, David, and Pricilla Goodwyn—June 1842.

Wertz, W. S., and Mary M. Thomason—Sept. 17, 1843.

Willett, James, and Lucy Webster—Feb. 13, 1840.

Winger, Elias, and Eliza Jane Smith—Apr. 19, 1842.

Wright, George, and Ann Shaver—Sept. 14, 1843.

Wright, John E., and Magadaline Hymelick—Dec. 21, 1841.

Wrightman, Samuel, and Anna Wertz—Oct. 23, 1838.

Yopp, William N., and Barbara Neighbors—Sept. 3, 1840.

Zirkle, William, and Mary Jenkins—June 1842.

Brief of Wills, Bedford County
1763 - 1803

Adams, John. Will pro. Jan, 1797. Names Peggy Pullem, and Elizabeth Hunt; relationship not stated.

Akins, William. dec. Apraisment of estate returned—May, 1768.

Alford, Silvator. Will pro. Nov., 1777. Names children, William, Judith Vest, Leney Vest, Mary Mulins, Milicent Broms (?), and Elizabeth Edds.

Allen. Reynolds. Will pro. Oct., 1779. Names wife, Mary; and ch. Ann Thomas. Elizabeth Broagan, Mary Edward, William, Thomas, John, James, and Milley.

Allen, Robert. Will pro. Mar., 1773. Names ch. Reynolds, Betty, Anny, Lucy, and son-in-law, William Handy.

Anderson, Elizabeth. Will pro. April, 1799. Names son, John.

Anderson, George. Will pro. May, 1778. Names ch. Jacob, George, Pattey, Duley, Elizabeth Underwood, Anna Beazly. Sarah Early. His wifes' son, Thomas Cofer.

Anthony. John. Will pro. Nov., 1760. Names wife, Elizabeth: and ch. John, Lucy Jones, Elizabeth Irvine, and Sarah Talbot. Ex. wife. and Wm. Irvine, ohn Talbot.

Arnold, William. dec. Apr. of estate returned Sept. 1776. (Note: wife was Sarah, and had ch. Benjamin, Anderson, William, Nancy, Mary, and John).

Ayres, James. Will pro. July, 1797. Names wife, Hannah: and ch. James, Samuel, Dinah, Nancy, and Rachel.

Baber, Geroge, dec. Inv. returned March, 1771.

Badiker, William. Will pro. Feb., 1770. Names William James and "his spouse, Margaret". Relationship not stated.

Ballard, William. Will pro. June, 1792. Names ch. Byron. Frances Wilson, Mary McKinney, and Delphiah Caldwell.

Banister, Isaac. Will pro. Jan., 1803. Names wife, Mary, and brother, James Banister; nephews William and James Banister.

Banister, William. Will pro. April, 1767. Names ch. Isaac and James.

Banks, Thomas, Will pro. Aug. 1755. Names ch. Thomas, Mary, Frances, Elizabeth, Jane, Milly, and William.

Bates, John. Will pro. Dec. 1777. Names wife, Mary, and son, William.

Baugahns, Samuel, dec. Apr. returned Jan., 1777.

Beard, Adam. Will pro. Mar. 1778. Names wife, Elizabeth; and ch. David, Rachel Dickson, Samuel, and Adam.

Beard, Adam. Will pro. Feb., 1788. Names wife, Margaret, and ch. Elizabeth, and Mary Enls.

Beard, Elizabeth. Will pro. March, 1778. ch. David, Rachel Dickson, and Samuel.

Beard, John. Will pro. Nov., 1780. Names wife, Elizabeth; and child, Elizabeth Campbell (and HER dau. Elizabeth.) Granch. Samuel and Adam Beard, Esabel

Boze, Rosanna Russell, William and Jean Rutherford (ch. of William Rutherford), and Rachel Dixon. A former son-in-law, Edward Phavi.

Bennett, Peter. Will pro. May, 1778. Names wife, Frances; and ch. William, Mary Lawson. Reuben, Elizabeth Pevry, Micajah, Rachel, Abner, and Richard.

Best. Thomas, dec. Apr. of estate ret.—June, 1780.

Board, John. Will pro. Sept., 1787. Names wife, Jeremima; and ch. Steven, Absolom, James, William, and Mary Hicks.

Bobbitt, Lucy. Will pro 1788. ch. Randolph, William. and Francis.

Bowker, Archilles, dec. Apr. returned, Feb, 1779.

Bowyer, Frederick. Will pro. Dec. 1777. Names wife, Mary; and ch. unnamed-minors.

Boyd, William. Will pro. Mar., 1761 Names wife, Elizabeth; and ch. John, James, Robert. Francis, Joseph, Lettice, Elizabeth, Rhoda and Martha.

Boyd, William. Will pro. Jan., 1794. Names ch. Martha Patterson. Nancy Oliver, Jenny Dooley, Elizabeth Milam, and Mary Dooley.

Bramlett, James. Will pro. Nov. 1759. Names wife, Winefred, and sister, Nancv.

Bramlett, William. Will pro. Aug., 1779. Names wife, Anna; and ch. James, and others, names or numbers not given. Ex. Wm. Calloway, and Wm. Buford.

Brander. John. Will pro. July, 1778. Names nephews, John Brander. of Bedford; James, Alexander, and Andrew Shaws of shire of Elgin. North Brittian; sisters, Margaret Carmichael (and her ch. Elspeth and Wm.), and Marjery Brander.

Brickey, Garrett. Will pro. Oct. 1790. Names wife, Elizabeth; and ch. Patsy. Christopher, Nancy, Milley, John, and Peter.

Bright, Edward. Will pro.—Oct., 1784. Names wife, Mary Ann; and ch. Charles, Mary Gaddy, Rebecca Woodward. Sarah Woodward, Mildred Watts. Elenor M'Kinney. Grandson, Charles Bright.

Brooks, Elizabeth. Will pro. Feb. 1802. Names brother, Humphrey and Robert. a sister, Lucy.

Brown, Daniel. Will pro. Feb. 1797. ch. William and Daniel. Leaves estate to Anney Hastens (rel. not given). and at her death to son, Wm.

Brown, James. Will pro. July 1780. Names sons, Thomas, David, and John.

Brown, John. Will pro. Mar., 1778. Names wife, Margaret, his "dutiful daughter. Anne. Says when Anne reaches age of eight she is to have three years at school.

Brown, Joseph. Will pro. Oct., 1795. Names wife, Elizabeth; and ch. Jesse Dent, Rhodham, Joseph, Hezekiah, Orpah, Sarah, Margaret.

Bryan, William. Will pro. Feb. 1764. Names wife, Mary; and ch. Elijah, William, and others, unnamed or number not given.

Buford, Thomas. Will pro. Nov., 1774. Wife, Ann; and ch. John, William, and Nancy.

Bunch, James. Will pro. Feb., 1798. Names wife, Mary; and ch. Elizabeth, Sukey Coil, Sally Scott, Martha Harris, Precilla Scott, Margery Harris, Molley Gentry, Nancy, and James.

Burgess. William. Will pro. July, 1778. Names wife, Susannah; and ch. Edward, John, William (Land in Fluvanna county to these three), Thomas (land in Bedford), Isabel, Mary, Franky, Betty, and Susannah. Land in Fluvanna to Watt Johnson (a son-in-law).

Burks, John Partree, dec. Inv. returned, Apr., 1775.

Burwell, George. Will pro. Nov. 1781. Names wife, Mary; and ch. Robert, Sarah, Ann, George, Elizabeth, Joseph, James, Joshua, Mary, and Jane.

Bush, John. Will pro. Jan. 1774. Names wife, Martha; and ch. Marget Jackson, Mary, Frances, Elizabeth, Milley, Philip, Darkish, Ann, and Susannah.

Butler, Philip, dec. Apr. returned, Apr. 1776.

Butler, William. Will pro. July, 1774. Estate to Wm. Little, "a boy living with me.".

Calloway, George. Will pro. Jan., 1773. Wife, Milly; and dau. Betty.

Campbell, Moses. Will pro. Apr. 1792. Names wife, Jene, and ch. Moses, James, Aaron, and Henry.

Campbell, William. Will pro. Jan. 1781. Names wife, Rebekah; and ch. Samuel, Thomas, William, and John.

Canada. William. Will pro. Feb., 1791. Names ch. William, Mary Cassey, Elizabeth Martin Isabella, and Sarah Huddleston.

Candler, Daniel. Will pro May, 1766. Names wife, Hannah, and ch. John, William, Elizabeth Cophry, Elloner Ballard, and Frederick.

Cantrel, Sarah. Will pro. Mar., 1784. Names ch. John Edwards; Mary (wife Christopher Taylor); Sarah Chitwood; Stephen; Delilah Nowland.

Carson, John. Will pro. May, 1762. Names wife-name not given-, and ch. Ezekiel (land in Buckingham Co.); John; Thomas and others, names or number not given.

Chiles, Henry. Will pro. Apr. 1755. Names mother, Ann Chiles (Halifax Co.); brother John (Prince Edward Co.), and sister, Anne Ward of Halifax county.

Chinault, Stephen, dec., Apr. of estate, Apr. 1770.

Condof, Richard, dec. Apr. returned Nov. 1774.

Cooper, William, dec. Apr. returned, Jan., 1778.

Couke, Andrew, dec. Inv of estate returned, Aug. 1778.

Cowan, Robert. Will pro. Apr. 1803. Names wife, Elizabeth; and ch. Peggy Penn; and Grace Freeland. A brother, William Irvine

Credell, Humphrew. Will pro May, 1780. Names wife, Mildred, and ch. no. or names not given.

Creel, Ann, dec. Apr. of estate returned June, 1775.

Creesey, Thomas. Will pro. July, 1803. Names ch. William, Elliner, Pleasant, Owen, Franklin, Lucy Clayburn, Bethena, George Mary, Thomas, and Annis.

Dabney, Cornelius. Vill pro, Oct. 1792. Names wife, Mary, and son, Goerge.

Dale, Francis. Will pro. July, 1777. Names ch. Richard, William, and Elizabeth Mason.

Daugherty, Hugh, Will pro. Sept. 1788. Names grandch. John, Margaret, Sarah, and Mary Daugherty.

Daulton, Timothy. Will pro. Apr. 1775. Names ch. James, and others, names or numbers not given. Wife living, but name omitted.

Davis, Benjamin, dec. Apr. returned, Feb. 1764.

Davis, Samuel. Will pro. Feb. 1798. Names wife, Anna; and son, William.

Davis, Zachary, dec. Will pro. June, 1792. Names wife, Margaret.

Dixon, Thomas. Will pro. Feb., 1770. Names wife, Ann, and ch. Mary McCain; John; George; Jane Bellon Mariag (?) and James Jane Bellon Mariag (?); and James.

Dooly, Thomas. Will pro. June, 1778. Names wife, Rebekah; and ch. Stephen, Henry, John, Obediah, Jemimah, Rachel, Martha, Keziah, and Katey.

Dowell, George, dc. Apr. of est. returned, July, 1772.

Downing, John. pro. Dec., 1777. Names ch. William, John, Andrew, James, Ezekiel, Martha Margaret M'Farland, and Mary Yoakum.

Eakins, Walter, dec. Executors settlement, May, 1772.

Early, Jeremiah. Will pro. Sept, 1779. Names wife, Mary; and ch. Elizabeth Calloway, Jenny, Jeffrey, Sarah, Abner, Jacobus, Joseph, John, Jubell, Jeremiah, and Judith Calloway.

Edwards, William. Will pro. May, 1757. Names wife...., and ch. William, Mary, Elizabeth, Richard, Agnes, Hana, and John. Executors "my trusty sons, Major Weatherford, and William."

Egar, George. Will pro. Oct. 1765. Names wife, Elizabeth; and ch. John, Jenet, Agnes Eagar ("alias McDavid), James, George, Mary and Thomas.

Embree, Moses. Will pro. Apr. 1795. Names ch. Moses and John.

English, Stephen. Will pro. Mar, 1783. Names wife, Dinah; and ch. Henry, Stephen, William, Parmenas, James, George Lewis, Charles Frederick.

Eskhold, John. Will pro. May, 1795. Names wife, Mary; and niece, Rebekah, dau. or Joseph and Alphah Eskhold.

Ewing, Charles. Will pro. July, 1770. Names wife, Martha; and ch. Charles, William, Robert, Samuel George, David, Caleb, Mary, and Martha.

Ewing, Robert. Will pro. June, 1787. Names wife, Mary; and ch. Tenis, Betey, Urbin, Robert, Baker, Rhuben, Chatten, Young, John, Pety Wills, and Sidney Linns.

Ferguson, John. Will pro. Sept. 1786. Names wife, Mary, and Ch. Jerry; Pleasant, William; Isom; King, and John.

Ferrell, William. Will pro. Oct., 1780. Names wife, Martha; and ch. William, and others, no. or names not given.

Fields, John. Will pro, July, 1778. Names wife

Sarah; and ch. Thomas and John.
Finley, James, dec. Apr. of estate, Oct. 1785.
Franklin, Lewis, dec. Inv. of estate Apr. 1770.
Fuqua, John. Will pro. Sept, 1796. Names wife, Ann; and child, Edy Milam, and her son, John.
Fuqua, Ralph. Will pro. July 1770. Names ch. Joseph (youngest); John, Mary Robinson, Martha, Ann, Elizabeth Stovall, William, Thomas, Susannah Richardson, Ralph, Henry, Isom, and Martha.
Gaddy, George. Will pro, Sept. 1785, Names wife, Anna; and ch. William, George, Elijah Barthlemew, Francis, Benjamin, Mary Parish, and Anna.
Gibson, James. Will pro. Feb. 1765. Names ch. James; Randall; Elizabeth Candler; Catherene Hale; Hanner Cook; Joseph; and the heirs of his dec. son, John, and Archibald.
Gibson, William. Will pro. Aug, 1792. Names wife, Mary; and ch. Nancy; John; Pattv; Elizabeth; Polly; Sally, and William.
Gilbert, Samuel. Will pro. Mar. 1776. Names wife, Martha; and ch. Benjamin, Samuel. Names Wm. Clements-relationship not stated.
Gilliam, Richard. Will pro. Apr., 1799. Names wife; Mary; a son, Richard, and grand-daughters, Polly and Elizabeth Gilliam.
Goad, John. Will pro. July, 1771. Names wife, Ann; and ch. Joanah Seviar; Elizabeth Cox; Hannah Bennett; Ann Risden; William (and his son, John); Abraham (and his son James); Robert; John (and his son Thomas).
Goff, Leonard, dec. Apr. of estate returned, Aug. 1773.
Goggin, Stephen, dec. Ex. settlement, Aug. 1761.
Goode, John. Will pro. July 1775. Names ch. Thomas, John, Sarah, Judith, and Nancy Fowler. Grandch. Samuel Martin Allen, and James Martin Allen, both ch. of Nancy Fowler.
Gouldman, Edward. Will pro. Dec. ,774. Names bros. Robert, Francis, Thomas; To Francis Davis's son, Edward; to Sally, Clary and Mark Davis, ch. of Samuel Davis.
Gray, John. Will pro. Mar. 1785. Names wife, Sarah; and ch. Mary; Rhoda; John Putman; Burkett; William; James; Thomas; Obed; Alexander.
Gray, Sarah. Will pro. Sept. 1802. Names ch. Mary Crump; Rhoda Crump, and William.
Graves, Isham, dec. Apr. of estate returned Mar. 1775.
Green, John. Will pro. July, 1775. Names wife Betty; and ch. James, Barbus, and Tabitha.
Greer, Joseph. Will pro May, 1781. Names wife, Annie; and ch. Thomas, and others unhamed, or numbers not given.
Haile, Francis. Will pro. Aug., 1780. Names wife, Adara; and ch. Richard, Stephen, Lewis, Elizabeth, Mary, Ruth, Ushely, and Mourning.
Halle, Richard. Will pro. June, 1784. Names wife, Elizabeth; and ch. Sarah Hatcher; John, Elizabeth; James; Martha; Richard; Frank; Powel; Molly, and Lewis.
Hall, Charles. Will pro. Jan. 1804. Names wife, Mary; and ch. Ann; Elizabeth; Lace; Nathan: David, Jonah; Jacob; Mary; Rebecca, and Levi.

Hall, John. Pro. May, 1794. Names wife, Magdalene; and ch. Mathew, William, Elisha, Jesse, Hezekiah, John, Tabitha.
Hall, William, dec. Inv. of estate ret. Dec., 1758.
Halley, Henry. Will pro. July, 1799. wife, (name not given); and ch. Timothy, Charles, Judy, Jane (or June), Samuel, Betsy, John, Giles, Henry, and grand-dau, Earles.
Halley, John, Will pro. Dec., 1802. Names wife, Judah; and ch. Benjamin, Mary, William, Sarah, John, Joshua, and Susanna.
Hamilton, Thomas. Will pro. Sept. 1772. Names wife, Esther: and ch. Richard and Thomas.
Hancock, George. Will pro. Jan. 1783. Names wife, Rachel; and ch. Mary Rairford, Judith, Hannah, Elizabeth Hancok.
Hancock, Simon. Will pro. Jan. 1791. Names sons, Edward, and Samuel; grand-children, Simon, Jean, and Anna Jackson.
Hardwick, Robert. Will pro. June 1794. Names wife, Elizabeth; and ch. Patty M'Car, Elizabeth, Sally, Frankie, Nancy Arnold, Richard, Pleasant, Robert, John, and Nellesy.
Hatcher, Edward, Will pro. Jan. 1782. Names wife, Sarah; and ch. Lucy, Elijah, Edward, Josiah, Wiliam, Rhody, and Elizabeth.
Hatcher, Ruben. Will pro. Aug. 1789. Names brothers, Farley and Edward.
Hayth, William. Will pro. Apr. 1775. Names ch. Thomas, Jane Lane, Elizabeth Manley, Elinor Burgess, Mary Christian, and Sarah Cunningham.
Haynes, William. Will pro. June 1781. Names ch. John, Frances Smith, Elizabeth Leftwich, William, Mildred (wife Stephen Sanders), Mary Long. Henry, and Ann Ferrel (and her ch. Mildred and Elizabeth).
Helton, James. Will pro. Sept. 1786. Names wife, Lucy; and ch. Jesse, James, Jeremiah, Valentine, Charity, Peggy Kitture, and Betty Scruggs.
Hoard, William. Will pro. Aug. 1781. Names wife, Mary, and ch. unnamed.
Holligain, John. Will pro. Nov. 1772. Names wife, Mary; son Patrick; and bro. William
Hooper, William, dec. Apr. returned Aug,1760.
Holt, John, dec. Apr. of estate. Jan. 1779.
Holt, John. Will pro. Sept. 1790. Names wife, Lucy; and ch. Anna, Martha, Joseph, Lucy, Thomas Barrett, and Mathew Watson.
Huddleston, Abraham. Will pro. Nov. 1785. Names wife, Mary, and son, Joseph.
Hunt, Dr. John, dec. Inv. of estate, June 1778.
Hunter, Alexander. Will pro. Mar. 1768. Names wife, Mary; and ch. Samuel, James, Alexander, Betty Order, and John and Alley Heys.
Irving, Christopher. Will pro. July, 1769. Names wife, Mary; and ch. David, and William; grandaughter Elizabetr (dau. of David).
Irving, William. Will pro. Feb. 1767. Names wife, Elizabeth, and ch. no. or names not given—one unborn.
Jackson, Jervis. Will pro. July 1802. Names wife, Mary; and ch. Ann Milam, Lucy Eubank, Elizabeth Williamson, Sarah Eubank, Jemima Dale, Fllener Sharp, Joseph, John, and Jean Starkv.
Johnson, Benjamin. Will pro. Sept. 1769. Names wife, Mary; and ch. Thomas, John,

—37—

Andrew, William, James, Rachel, Elizabeth, Mildred, and Christopher.

Jones, James, dec. Inv. ret. 1783.

Jones, Michael. Will pro. Jan. 1781. Names wife, Ann; and ch. George, Michael, Publias, Susannah, Lucy, Erasmus, Dudley, Daniel, Christian; and a son-in-law, Samuel Leason.

Jones, William. Will pro. May, 1781. Names wife, Agnes; and five sons, names not given.

Keenums, Alexander, dec. Inv. of estate, Feb. 1779.

Kennedy, John. Will pro. Sept. 1781. To wife, and ch., unnamed, land in Ky.

Kern, George, dec. returned, Oct. 22, 1765.

Kerr, William. Will pro. June, 1792. Names iwfe, Lucy; and dau. Frances.

Krantz, Michael. Will pro. Apr. 1802. Names wife, Mary; and ch. Jacob, and Mary.

Lainhart, Christopher. Will pro. Sept. 1779. Names wife, Susanna; and ch. Isaac, Catherine, Adam; a grandson, Jacob Coffer.

Lambert, Charles. Will pro. Dec. 1798. Names wife Catherine; and ch. Charles, and his wife Nancy.

Lane, Joseph, dec. Apr. ordered, Feb. 1773.

Lawson, Jonas. Will pro. Sept. 1771. Names grandch. David, William, John, James, all sons of David Lawson.

Lee, William. Will pro. Sept. 1803. Names wife. Anne; and ch. Thomas, Andrew, Alexander, Garrett. Rebecca, Ane, William, Richard, and Ann.

Leftwich, Augustine. Will pro. June 1795. Names wife, Elizabeth ch. William, Thomas Augustine, Uriah, John, Littleberry, Joel, Jabez, Fanney, Mary Early, and Nancy Pettross. Grand-dau. Nancy.

Linn, Adam. Will pro. Mar. 1772. Names wife, Izebell; and ch. Joseph, Adam, Martha Craig, Agnes (wife James, Young), and Mary Carson.

Loving, William. Wil pro. Sept. 1767. Names wife, Elizabeth; and ch. John, Henry Catty, and Patty.

Maples, Richard. Non-cup. will. Pro. Feb. 1774. Names Samuel Alley, and his wife, Lucy; Also Elizabeth Asbary.

Martin, John, dec. Apr. of estate ret. Oct. 1774.

Martin, Robert. Will pro. Jan. 1781. Names wife, Mary; and ch. William, James, Mary, Peggy, and Samuel.

Mattock, William, dec. Inv. of estate ret. Sept. 1769.

Mays, James. Will pro. June, 1795. Names wife, Mary; and ch. Samuel, James, Joseph, Sinthey Wright.Frankey. Elizabeth Wright.

Mayberry, Frederick. Will pro. Oct. 1801. Names wife, Barbarah; and ch. Henry Abraham Rachel, George, Frederick, Elizabeth, Jacob, John, and David.

McCormack, William. Will pro. Oct. 1775. Names wife, Agnes; and ch. John, David, William, Lucy, Jesse, and Nancy.

McIlheny, Thomas. Will pro. Jan. ,1777. To Col. Wm. Fleming, of Botetourt Co; to bros., and sisters in Loudon Co. To Rosannah, dau. of Richard and Mary Morgan.

McMurtree, James. Wil pro. Mar. 1772. Names wife, Hannah; and ch. Samuel, William, James, Joseph, and daus. no. or names not given.

McRray, Martha. Will pro. July, 1800. Names ch. Sally (wife John Cobb), and Elizabeth (wife of Jesse Cobb). Grand-dau. Nancy dau. Elizabeth Cobb.

Meador, Hambrus. Will pro. Sept. 1795.Names wife, Franky; and ch. Thomas, William, Dmsiller, Bandy, and Frankey Dowell.

Milam, Benjamin. Will pro. Oct. 1780. Names wife, Elizabeth.

Milam, John, dec. Inv. of estate, Nov. 1780.

Milam, Thomas. Will pro. Mar. 1775. Names wife, Mary; and ch. Solomon, and Rush. (May have been others, but hard to tell from reading of will.)

Miller, John. Will pro. July 1785. Names wife, Ann; and ch. Elizabeth and Jean (and her heirs).

Miller, Joseph, dec. Apr. of estate. Nov. 1764.

Miller, Simon. Will pro Feb. 1785. Names wife, Ann; and ch. Simon, John, William, Susannah Calloway, Ann Dishman, Sally Noel, and Margaret Tate.

Mitchell. Daniel. Will pro. Sept. 1775. Names wife, Mary; and ch. unnamed. Bro. Rob't.

Moody. William. Will pro. Dec. 1794. Names wife, Sarah.

Moon. Jesse. Pro. Oct. 1780. Names Father, Jacob; and bro. William.

Moon, Jacob. Pro. May 1781. Names ch. Christopher, and one unborn. Bros. Wm. and Archelius. Wife, name not given.

Moorman, Pleasant, dec. Valuation of estate, May. 1774.

Moorman. Silas. Pro. Feb. 1777. Names wife, Sally; and ch. Martha, Jacob, Pleasant, Bros. Charles, and Andrew.

Moreman, Thomas. Pro. Nov. 1766. Names wife, Rachel; and ch. Mary Johnson, Pleasant, Charles, Aggathy Johnson, Clerk Terrell, Cilly, Rachel, Zacheriah, and Micajah.

Morgan, Thomas. Pro. May, 1774. Names wife, Esther; and ch. Lewis, Thomas, Ann Kinsey, Elizabeth Vardiman, John. William, Leatice Richardson, Mary, Susanna Samuel, Haner Inmon, Reeace, Pheaby, Racheal, Morgan, Mordiciai, and Abranam.

Morris, Daniel. Pro. Nov. 1767. Names wife ....; and ch. Ezekiel, Rebekah, Joseph, Daniel, Joshua, Elizabeth, Mary, Jane, and Sarah.

Morris, Tibithey. Pro. Aug. 1778. Names ch. Betty Ray, Rebekah Hancock, Ezekiel.

Mosley, Walter. Pro. Oct. 1800. Names wife, Ann; and ch. Nancy, Susanna, William, and James.

Murphy, Thomas. Pro. June, 1778. Names wife, Elinor; and ch. James, Mary, Marget, Thomas. Rosanna, and William.

Neal, Daniel. Pro. March. 1791. Names wife, Mary; and ch. Walter, Jessanah, Betty Steal, Mary Varunm. Margaret Millam.

Nickols, John. Pro. Nov. 1803. Names wife, Martha; and ch. Floyd, John, Archibuto, Elisha, and Jesse.

North, Abraham. Pro. Apr. 1800. Names wife, Susannah; and ch. David, John, Sarah Rucker, Susanna Robertson, Betty Miller, and Polly Jones.

Oglesby, Sarah. Pro. June. 1780. Leaves her part of the estate of Thomas Oglesby, Sr., to her brothers, Richard, and Thomas.

Overstreet, Thomas. Pro. Feb. 1792. Names wife, Agnes; and ch. John, Thomas, William, Ann Hall, Mary Witt, Elizabeth.

Pain, Frayl. Pro. July, 1784. Names wife, Sarah; and ch. Thomas, William, Nancy, and Martha.

Pate, Edward. No. pro. date, will dited Nov. 11, 1767. Names wif,e Martha; and ch. Matthew, Anthony, Thomas, Judith, Jeremiah. Grandson, John, son of dec. son, John, and his wife, Judith.

Pate, John. Pro. Sept. 1767. Names wife, Judith; and an unborn child. Ex. Jeremiah Early.

Parker, Mildred, dec. Apr. returned, March, 1768.

Phelps, John. Pro. Feb. 1772. Names wife, Mary; and ch. Jane, Judith, Sarah, Ann, Mary, Betty, John, James, Jr., also Nathan Turner, relationsh'p unstated.

Phelps, John. Pro. Sept. 1801. Names ch. Mary Hall, Jemima Ferguson, Nancy Ferguson, John, James, Richard, Tmohas, Bathsheba Grayson, Lucy Haynes, Glenn, Ida, Betsy, Randolph, William, Jeanny, Cverton, Robert, and Susanna.

Phillips, Feesil. Pro. May, 1789. Names daus. Mary, and Margaret.

Phillips, Stephen. Pro. Feb. 1788. Names wife, Nancy; and bro., William.

Pickens, John, dec. Adm. account returned, Nov. 1774.

Pollard, Francis. Pro. July, 1771. Names wife, Betty; and ch. Thomas, John, and others, no. or names not given.

Poor, Stanley. Pro. Dec. 1782. Names wife, Ann.

Prather, James. (Late of Prince George county. Md., which is not called Frederick). Will pro. June, 1759. Names father-in-law, Robert Allen; my mother, Joice Allen; sister. Sarah Stone, and "my mother's two daughters, Margaret and Catherine Coleman". Says his father was Thos. Prather.

Prator, Jonathan. Pro. June 1772. Names wife Catherine, and ch. Thomas, Jonathan, Mary, Elizabeth, Rease, Isaac, Ann and Tabitha.

Preston, Philip, dec. Apr. returned, Mar.1775.

Preston, Thomas. Pro. Feb. 1798. Names ch. Stephen, Joel, Susanna, Thomas and John.

Pullem, Moses. Pro. June. 1790. Names wife, Name not given.

Ramsay, Bartholomen. Pro. Feb. 1793. Names ch. Margaret, Simon. Joseph, and James.

Rauton, Richard. Pro. Feb. 1792. Names ch. Elizabeth James, John. and Richard.

Rawlings, Benjamin. Pro. May, 1777. Names mother, Ann Rawlings; a sister, Ann Rawlings, and brother, John—"all the wages that is due me for being a soldier, and my riffle gun."

Ray, Joseph. Pro. May. 1767. Names wife, Martha; and ch. Andrew, Mary, Pricilla.

Read, John. Pro. May, 1773. Names wife:and ch. William, Jonadab, Daniel, Elizabeth Simmons, Thomas (and his ch. Abraham, Marianna, and Isaac.)

Read, William. Pro. Sept. 1798. Names wife, Joanna; and ch. Sanue, John, Thomas, Wyatt, and Edmund.

Rector, Jacob. Pro. Nov. 1779. Names wife, Jane, and daughter, Charlotte.

Rentfro, Joseph. Pro. Mar. 1776. Names wife, Mary; and ch. James, Mary Jones, Joseph, John, Susannah, William, Joshua, Mark. The husband, Moses Rentfro, of a deceased dau., Hannah.

Richardson, Jonathan. Pro. May. 1773.Names wife, Anne; and ch. Jesse, Amos, Joseph, Mary, Nancy, Aimy, and Thomas.

Richardson, Randolph. Pro. Oct. 1782. Names wife, Lucy; and ch. Randolph, John, Berlaman, Clinton, and Richard.

Roberts, Daniel, Inv. of estate, Nov. 1781.

Roberts, Thomas. Pro. Mar. 1781. Names wife Christiana; and ch Richard, James, John, Rhoady, Milly, Maryann, Fanny, Daniel, Thomas, and Elizabeth Prewitt.

Robinson, James. Pro. July, 1778. Names wife, Betty; and ch. Anne, Molly, John, William, Thomas, and Bettsy.

Robinson, Thomas, dec. Apr. of estate, May, 1774.

Rogers, William. Will pro. Mar. 1759. Names wife,........; and ch. William, Clement, and David. Also Barcle Lawson, relationship not stated.

Rosebrough, Robert. Pro. July, 1801. Names wife, Isabell; and ch. Helkiah, Mary, Jean, Margaret, Sally, and John.

Ross, William, dec. Inv. of estate ret. May, 1781.

Row, John, dec. Apr. of estate ret., June, 1775.

Rowland, Henry. Pro. Aug., 1773. Names wife, Penelope, and four ch., unnamed.

Rust, George. Pro. Oct., 1775. Names wife, Anne; and ch. Jeremiah, Elizabeth, Daniel Hammack, Anna Hammack, Samuel, and Sarah Martin.

Salmon, John. Pro. Jan. 1790. Names sons, John, Joel, Robert, Nathan, and James.

Sampson, Benjamin, dec. Apr. returned, Mar. 1774.

Scott, William. Pro. Dec. 1793. Names ch. James, George, Peter, Sarah, John, Joseph, Thomas, William, Charles, Axton, and Evan.

Scruggs Gross. Pro. July 1788. Names wife, Elizabeth; and nephews. William Arthur (son of Benjamin Arthur), and Gross Scruggs, (son of Thomas Scruggs).

Shaw, John. Pro. Sept., 1786. Names wife, Isabella; and ch., unnamed.

Sherwood, Gadde. Pro. Apr., 1802. Names wife Mary; and ch. Joseph, James, Hannah, Ben, Polley, Nancy, Elizabeth, and Martha.

Singleton, Philip, dec. Apr. returned, May, 1775.

Sinn, Adam (See Linn)

Skidmore, Jeremiah, dec. Apr. returned, Dec. 1773.

Smelser, Paulser. Pro. May, 1778. Names wife, Catherine; and ch. John, Abraham, Stephen, Paulser, Jessey, Betty, Rebekah, and Mary.

Smith, Bowker. Pro. Mar., 1768, Names wife, Judith; and ch. John, Elizabeth, Judith, Stephen, Bowker, Guy, William, and Archilles.

Smith, Guy. Pro. Sept, 1781. Names wife, Anne; and ch., Elizabeth Smith, Anne Trigg, Joanna Hall, Bird B., Guy, Lucy, Susanna, Kate Bowker, and Jenny Bird Bowker.

Snow, Henry, dec. Inv. returned, Mar., 1778. Heirs: Wife, Mary, and John, Jane, and Thomas Snow; John Williamson, and William Holligan.

Snow, Thomas. Pro. Aug. 1781. Names wife, Winefred; and ch. John, William, Thomas, Henry-others, unnamed.

Staton. Thos. pro. Mar. 1778. Names wife, Ann, and ch. unnamed.

Stemon, Martin. Pro. May, 1768. Names wife, Mary; and ch. Jacob, Martin, and Henry; a brother, Alexander.

Stevens, Thomas, dec. Inv. of estate, June, 1779.

Steward, James, Pro. Aug. 1784. Names ch. Thomas, Charles Harris, William Snelson, Nathaniel, and one unborn.

Stockton, William. Pro. Oct. 1795. Names father, Dan'l Stockton, his mother, and bros, and sisters, unnamed.

Stone, Stephen, dec. Apr. of estate, Nov. 1778.

Stovall, John. Pro. June, 1778. Names wife, Elizabeth; and ch. Mary Robinson, Bartholomew, Ralph, Barns, Elizabeth, Delilah, Ann, Ezekiah, and John.

Straton, Henry. Pro. Dec. 1799. Names wife, Sarah; and ch. Judith Davis, Mary, William, John, Thomas and Henry.

Stump, John. Pro. July 1782. Names wife; and ch. Thomas and Ellender.

Talbott, Charles. Pro. Aug. 1779. Names wife, Drucilla: and ch. Williston, Charles Nolle, Mary Thurston, Christinah, David Givin, Providence, George, and Zackey.

Talbott, Matthew. Pro. Nov. 1759. Names wife, Jane; and ch. John, (a Dr.), Isham, Charles. Matthew, James and Martha Arther. Godsons, Abr. Chandler, D. Raines.

Tally, James, dec. Apr. returned, Jan 1776.

Tanner, Michael. Pro. May, 1777. Wife, Catrin and dau, Elizabeth Dooly.

Tanner, Nathaniel. Pro. Oct. 1781. Names wife, Mary; and ch. Nathaniel, Joel, Susanna, Elizabeth Danniel, Benjamin, and Mary.

Tate, Charles. Pro. Dec, 1792. Names wife and minor ch. no names given.

Taylor, Henry. Pro. Aug, 1777. Names wife Sarah; and ch. Christopher, Skelton, Tannah, Sarah, and Sherlot.

Taylor, Isaac. Pro. Feb, 1778. Estate to Wm. Read.

Thatcher, Henry. Pro. Dec. 1800. Names ch. Henry, Isiah, Phebe Clerk, Mary Hancock, Edith Burton, Jeremiah, Sarah Hensely, Margaret Terry, and Sary.

Thompson, John. Pro. May 1778. Names wife, Sarah, and ch. Elizabeth, Sarah, and Mary.

Thompson, William. Pro. May, 1763. Names wife, and ch. Samuel, Thomas, William and Mary.

Thornhill, William. Pro. Sept. 1790. Names ch. William, Ezekel, and Rachel.

Thorp, Amos, dec. Inv. of estate, June, 1775.

Trigg, William. Pro. Feb. 1773. Names wife, Mary; and ch. Stephen, William, Dannel, John, Abraham, Nancy, and Lockey.

Trueman, William. Pro. Jan. 1797. Names sons, Ikey, and Moses.

Turner, Richard. Pro. June, 1769. Names wife, Ann; and ch. Mary Leftwich, James

Jesse, Prudence, and Ann.

Wade, Jeremiah. Pro. Sept. 1772. "Divided equally between all my ch",-no names.

Walker. Robert. Pro. Mar, 1767. Names wife, Agatha; and ch. Elijah, Sally, and Judea.

Ward, John. Pro. Dec. 1782. Names wife, Catherine; and ch. Mary Scarborough, Betty, and heirs of dec., son, Zacheriah.

Watkins, Thomas. Pro. July, 1773. Names his mother, Elizabeth; bros. George and Ruben; a sister, Elizabeth; Robert, Benjamin, and Wm. Hall, sons of his wife; and bulk of estate to Judith Pruett, dau. Michael Pruett.

Watson, Johnson. Pro. July, 1801. Names wife, Anne; and ch. William, John, Joseph, Johnson, Elizabeth, Nancy, Sally, Mary, udy (wife James Clagg).

Watts, Edward. Pro. Apr. 1793. Names wife, Elizabeth; and ch. Jaon, Benjamin, William, Elizabeth, Milley Richards, Mary Sinclair (and her son, Edward).

Welch, Nicholas. Pro. July, 1767. Names wife Mary; and ch. Nicholas, Mary Henry, Pawlin. His father, Nicholas Welch, Sr.

Whitehead. Joseph. Pro. Feb. 1778. Names wife, Grizzel; and ch. Molley Perkins, and her ch. Abraham, Betty, and Henry Perkins.

Williamson, John, Apr. 1795. Letter filed written to his father, while he was in army. Estate to bro. Elisha Williamson.

Willson, John. Pro Nov, 1780. Names wife, Hannah; and ch. James, William, and others, unnamed. Mentions his "old and Honored mother, Jennet Morrison".

Wilson, Matthew. Pro. Mar. 1771. Names wife, Mary; and ch. James, Robert, Thomas Matthew, Martha, Elizabeth, John, Mary, Margaret Litford, Jane Meecher, and Sarah Misiber.

Wimmer, John. Pro. Oct. 1780. Names ch. Adam, Jacob (and his sons, Abraham, John and Jacob), Christian Runyon, John, Abraham, and Isaac.

Womack, Jesse, pro. Aug, 1782. Names wife, Sarah, and son, William.

Woods, Thomas, dec. Inv. of estate, Nov. 1764.

Woods, Thomas. Pro. Jan. 1781. Names wife, Elizabeth, and ch. names or no. not given.

Woodward, Richard. Pro Apr. 1796, Names wife Elizabeth; and ch. Lance. Urcilia Hall, Randolph, Isaac, John, William, Richard, Frances Taylor, Warwick.

Worley, Francis. Pro. Nov. 1780. Names wife, Martha; and ch. Flayll, David, & Joanna.

Worley, William. Pro. Oct. 17?7. Names wife, Mary; and ch. Elizabeth Rountree, Raneny Kerr, Easter Sheppard, Matthew, and Zacheriah.

Wright, John, Pro. Sept. 1803. Names ch. Tommy, Sarah. Anthony, Nancy Ashberry, Betsy, Polly, Rhoda, John, Joseph, and Ruth.

Wright, Thomas. Pro. Nov. 1763. Names wife Mary; and ch. Elizabeth, Mary, Abagall, Sarah, Dorcas, Catherine, John, and Joseph.

Yarbough, Jeremiah, dec. (of Amelia City), Apr. of estate Oct. 1765.

Young, James. Pro. May, 1778. Names wife, Agnes, and ch. Margaret, Adam, Isabel, David.

Aikens, Redmon. Pro. Nov., 1781. A non-cupative will. Names ch. William, Jean, Isabell, Hannah, Elizabeth and Ellinor. Wife mentioned, but name not given. Sickened whle on tour of duty in army.

Alderon, Curtis. Pro. Feb., 1804. Names wife, Elizabeth, and ch. Bur, Thomas, Elizabeth Cress, and Hester Woltz Grand-ch., Elizabeth Cloyd, and Curtis Alderson, son of Thomas.

Alderson, James, dec. Apr. of estate returned, March 1775.

Alderson, John, Pro. Nov., 1780. Names wife, Jane, and ch. John, Curtis, Benjamin, Thomas, and Simon. Grand-ch. George, (son of John), and Thomas, (son of Curtis).

Allen, Hugh. Pro. June, 1776. Names wife, Anna; ch. Anne Moore, Jeny Comton, Malcolm, Thomas, William, John, James, Betsy Miller, Metildy, Polly, Robert, Patsy, Rebecca, and Moses.

Allen, Malcolm. Pro. Jan., 1792. Names ch. Hugh, Robert, Moses, Rebecca, Mary, Martha, Elizabeth, Letty, and John.

Allen, Moses. Pro. March, 1812. Names wife, Lydia; ch. Polly Biggs (wife of John Biggs) Rebecca Byrd (wife Wm. Byrd), Jane, Malcolm (wife, Alice), and John, (wife Martha).

Alexander, James. Pro. May, 1775. Names Mary Crawford, Cousin James Tosh, Cousin Sarah Keachy, Thomas Tosh, and others, relationship not given.

Ammen, Durst. Pro. Sept. 1805. Names wife, Eve; ch. Barbara, (wife of Christian Herchbarger), Eve, David, Jacob, and Michael.

Ammen, Eve, dec. Inv. returned, Feb., 1713.

Amiss, Samuel. Pro. Jan., 1819. Names ch. Isaac, Andrew, Peggy Taylor, Elizabeth Preston, Esther Lamb, Susannah. and Ellnor.

Anderson, William. Pro. Feb., 1820. Names wife, Nancy; and children, Sally, Samuel, William, and Alexander.

Armstrong, Ellnor. Pro. Apr., 1791. Names ch. Andrew, David, Robert, Alexander, Thomas, Archibald, Elliner, and Esebell.

Arnold, Andrew. Will pro. Feb. 1821. Names wife, Catherine, and ch. Rebekah; Abraham; David; Joseph; Jacob; Hannah; Susannah; John; Daniel, and Samuel. Grandch. Peter Myers, (son, Rebekah); Mary Ann Black.

Baker, Martin, dec. Apr. of estate returned, July, 1782.

Baldwin, Samuel. Will pro. Sept, 1793. Names wife, Mary; and ch., Elizabeth; Sarah; William; Joseph, Hanna Morris; Thomas Lewis; Alexander; and Mary James. Children by a first marriage, living in Penn, un-named, except a daughter, Charity. A brother-in-law, James Wills.

Bandy, Richard Will pro. Sept. 1795. Names wife, Lucy; and ch. Thomas; Richard; John; George; Mary Lewis. (Wife of Thomas); Eliza, ("Relic of Aquilla Greer"); Sarah, (wife of Benjamin Jordon,); Katy, (an infant,); also names Henry Bandy," son of Ann Bandy, now wife of James Neighbors", presumedly a grandson.

Beale, John, dec. Dower assigned his wife, Mrs. Rhoda Beale'; and slaves assigned following ch., Madison; George; John; Eliza; Robert; Charles; and Mary. March, 1811.

Beale, Madison, dec. Devision of land, naming wife, Charlotte; and heirs; Charles; Mary; George; John; and Eliza B., wife of Thomas Lewis. Note: These were evidently his bros. and sisters. May, 1820.

Beale, Tavenaner. Will pro. June 1810. Names wife, Betty; and ch., Catherine; Jordon; John; Charles; and James Madison Hite; Thomas; and Mary Higgans.

Bear, Gothab. (German). Will pro. Apr. 1814. Names Ciria Nobles-relationship not stated.

Beckner, John. Will por. Sept. 1822. Names "John Beckners' four eldest ch. by his first wife, Elizabeth, viz: David, Mary Catherine, and John. Also bros. and sisters, unnamed.

Beckner, Lawrence. Will pro. Oct. 1802. Names ch. Jonathan; Daniel; Jacob; Elizabeth; Simmons; Susanna Garmon; and John.

Beldin, Hezekiah. Will pro. Oct. 1809. Names brothers, William, and Samuel, of Conn.

Bilbro. Betsy. Will pro. July, 1811. Names niece, Rebecka Carey; brother, John Bilbro.

Bilbro, William. Will pro. Oct. 1807. Names wife, Mary; and ch. Sarah Terril (of Elk River); Rebecca Wallace; Betsy; Rachel; John; James; Benjamin; and Thomas. Grand-ch. Rebecca, Sulla, and William Carey.

Bishop, Jeremiah. Will pro. May, 1820. Non-cupative will. One third estate to wife ,and balance to ch., Abram, and Mary Conner.

Black, Christain. Will pro. Aug. 1812. Names wife, Franche; and ch. un-named, except one, Elizabeth.

Blain, William. dec. Apr. of estate returned, June, 1819.

Blount, Wilson. Will pro Oct. 1819. Names friend, Wm. Sheppard, of Newburn; nephews, Ebenezar Petegrew, Fredrick Beasley, Clement Blount; niece, Sarah Fuller; and grand-niece, Nancy B. Pettegrew, who he states is the daughter of William Sheppard.

Boindrager, Andrew. dec. Estate pro. Aug. 1815.

Boindrager, William. Will.pro. Oct 1798. Names wife Susanna; and ch. Nancy, Martin, Susanna Peffly, and David.

Bowyer. Thomas. Will pro. Aug. 1785. Names Pricilla Madison, nad a nephew, Henry Bowyer.

Boyd, Andrew. Will pro. June, 1820. Names ch. John, Thomas, Sarah Ann Buckanon, Ann Margaret, Pricilla ("my unfortunate dau"), Alexander C. and the heirs of his dec. ch. Jane, and James.

Boyd Andrew. Will pro. Feb. 1821. Names wife, Catherine; and ch. Andrew; Margaret; Mary; and James.

Boyd, James. Will pro. July, 1816. Names wife, Mary; and ch. Andrew; and William Watson.

Breckenridge, Robert. Will pro. Nov. 7, 1773. Names wife, Lettice; and ch. William; John; Alexander; Robert; James; Preston; and Elizabeth.

Brown, Hugh. Will pro. Feb., 1802. Names ch. Mary Moore; Sarah Wilson; Jane Taylor;

—41—

Peggy Brown; Nancy Brown; John; Hugh of whom he state that "his whereabouts are unknown".

Brown, James, dec. Inv. returned, Sept, 1812.

Brown, Thomas. Will pro. Aug. 1823. Names ch. Easther; Rebecca; Massa; Kesia; Mary Thompson, William; and Thomas. His dec. wife was dau. of William Terry.

Brugh, Harmon. Will pro. Oct. 1794. Names wife, Catherine; and ch John (eldest); Jacob; Daniel; Harmon; Cathren (wife Henry Nell); Mary (wife John Stouffer); Signed in German.

Brunk, John, dec. Inv. of estate, ret. May, 1811.

Bryan, William. Will pro. Oct. 1806. Names wife, Elizabeth J.; and ch. William; Catherine Cole; James, and John.
Note: a 1st wife was named Margaret Watson.

Buckhannon, Theodon. Will pro. Oct. 1814. Speaks of wife. two sons, and one daughter-all un-named.

Bumbgardner, Paulser, dec. Sales bill ret. Dec., 1822.

Burwell, Lewis. Will pro Oct. 1804. Names bros., and sisters, but gives names of only two-Nathaniel, and Francis. Speaks of his dec. father, Nathaniel, and a dec. Uncle, Lewis Burwell.

Caldwell, John. Will pro. Apr., 1820. Names wife, Susannah; and ch. William; Rosanah: Sarah; Jane; Archibald; Nancy; John; Joseph; Susannah; and Robert.

Caldwell, Mary. Will pro. Apr. 1814. Names ch. Granvill; John, (and his dau., Sally); Edmison: Samuel. The heirs of a dec. dau., Jane. A grand-dau., Mary M'farran. A brother, Hugh.

Caldwell, Robert, dec. Apr. of estate returned, Feb. 1790.

Campbell, Archibald. Will pro. Apr. 1774. Names his brother, William, and Wms. eldest son. (Says Wm. eldest son of Thomas Campbell The two sons, John and Archibald, of Wm. Simpson; and a sister, Jean, but disinherits her should she marry Peter Evans, designated as "brother to Nathaniel Evans".

Campbell, Arthur, dec. Valuation of est. ret. Mar. 1775.

Campbell, William. Will pro Oct. 1804. Names wife, Susannah; and ch. Thomas. Archibald; William; James; John; Rhoda; and Polly. Leaves sons land "in the western country".

Campbell, William. Will pro. Sept, 1818. Names wife, Magdalene, and nine brothers and sisters, un-named.

Camper, Peter, dec. Inv. returned, Jan., 1789.

Camper, Solomon. Will pro. Jan. 1824. Names wife, Lessaley; and children; Thomas Grimes; Mary Ann Croft; Lydia Falls; Harman; Lilly C.; Lucy Leadlin; Lucy Camper; Bussey; Valentine G.; the heirs of a dec. son, John.

Carlton, William. Will pro. Sept. 1813. Names ch. Henry; William; Joseph; Rebecca Thomas; Mary; Susannah; James; grandch. William and Susanna Pawley.

Carpenter, Leah. Will pro. Sept. 1806. Names ch. Judy Shawver; grandch. Polly Gillaspie and Becky and Leah Shawver.

Carpenter, Joseph. Will pro July 1792. Names wife, Leah: and ch. Abagail Maloney; Mary Viers; Sarah Gillaspie: Judy Shawver; Marthew; Samuel and William.

Carper, Nicholas. Will pro. May, 1813. Names wife, Elizabeth; and ch. Jacob; Benjamin; Elizabeth Harvey; Mary M'ferran; Joseph; Sally Holestine; and Isaac.

Carriagan, Patrick. Will pro. Jan. 1795. Names wife, Mary; and "my beloved relation, Jacob Carriagan, son of Michael, of Pa."

Cartmell, Henry. Will pro. Feb. 13, 1787. Names wife, Mary; and ch. Henry, Jr.; John; and James. Sons-in-law, James Green; William Patterson; James Huston; and Robert Stewart (and Robts son, Henry.)

Carvin, Richard. Will pro. Nov. 1823. Names wife, Lucy.

Carvin, William. Will Pro. Sept, 1804. Names wife ...., and ch. Edward; Elizabeth; Richard; Mary; Nancy Alley (or Tally.)

Chenowth, Thomas. Will pro. June, 1780. Names wife, Ann; and ch. Elizabeth; Mary; James; Francis; John; Thomas; Nicholas. Among his bequests is "my suit of a purple colour."

Christian, Elizabeth. Will pro. Sept. 1789. Names ch. Anne, (wife Wm. Fleming); grandch. Elizabeth Fleming; and Fleming, Stephen, Mary, and Elizabeth Trigg.

Circle, Peter. Will pro. Oct. 1818. Names wife Fanny; and ch. Andrew; Mathias; Emanuel, Lewis; John; Peter; sons-in-law, George Knisley; Jacob Knisely; Isaac France; John Nieconger; and Christley Fisher.

Clear George, dec. Apr. of estate ret. Sept. 1790.

Cleck, Baldas. Will pro. Dec. 1803. Names wife, Sophia; and ch. John; Margaret; Christinah; Jacob; and Elizabeth.

Cloyd, Michael. Will pro. Apr. 1807. Names ch. John; David; Michael; Samuel; Joseph, (land on Cloyds Street, in Amsterdam); Jesse; and Elizabeth Law. (land on Round Oak St., Amsterdam.)

Cochran, Peter, dec. Ap. returned, July, 1771.

Cofmon, Henry, dec. Inv. ret, Mar. 1804.

Coffman, Jacob. Will pro. June, 1807. Names wife Barbra; ch. Benjamin; John; Fanny Hanes; Jacob.

Compton, John, dec. Inv. ret. Sept. 1778.

Coon, Michael. Will pro. ......, 1813. Names wife, Doratha; and ch. John; Eve (wife of John Ship); Catherine, (wife Michael Davis); Sarah, (wife Wm. Ireland); Rosannah, (wife Andrew Zimmerman); Doratha, (wife Amry Teacrist); Elizabeth, (wife John Kelly); and Jacob. The heirs of dec. son, Daniel.

Cooper, James. Will pro. Dec. 1784. Names wife. and ch. no names given.

Cox, Edward, dec. Inv. of estate ret. May, 1784.

Crawford, Andrew. Will pro. Feb. 1791. Names wife, Ufee; and ch. John; James; Eunice; Crawford, John, ("son of John"). Will pro. June, 1795. Names wife, Margaret; and ch. John: William: Andrew: James: Samuel; Margaret: and his brother, William.

—42—

Critts, George. Will pro. June, 1805. Names wife, Mary; and ch. John; Elizabeth; Cunrad; Mary; George; Tunay; Anney; Cattey; Henrey, and Philip.

Cross, William. Will pro. June, 1798. Names wife, Elizabeth; and ch. William, Jr.; Mary Jane; John; and Elizabeth Eath.

Crouse, Daniel. Will pro. Oct. 1818. Names wife, Catherine; and daughter, Anny.

Cunningham, Hugh. Will pro. May, 1772. Names wife, Sarah; and ch. Jesibel; and ten (10) others, names not given. A stepson, James Davis; a son-in-law, John Young.

Darick, John. Will pro. Sept. 1790. Names wife, Mary, and ch. names or number not given, but speaks of "my little son, Jonathan."

Davidson, William, Will pro. Oct. 1812. Names wife, Martha; ch. Ginny M'Cartney Joseph, and three other sons, and three other daus.

Deardroff, Henry, dec. Apr. of estate ret Feb. 1792.

Deaton, Martha, dec. Inv. of estate ret May, 1822.

Dennis, Joseph. Will pro. June, 1794. Names wife, and ch. no. or names not given.

Dennison, John, dec. Apr. returned, May, 1776.

Depew, John. Will pro. Sept. 1811. Names, wife Catherine; and ch. Elijah; Isaac (eldest); Lewerecia Datzell; Abraham; James; John; Jacob: the heirs of dec. son, Samuel and a grand-daughter, Mary, child of his son, James.

Depew, Samuel, dec. Apr. of estate, Jan. 1792.

Detzell, James. Will pro. Sept, 1815. Names wife, Martha; and ch. James; Hugh; Nancy; Sally; and Betsy.

Dill. Henry. Will pro. June, 1818. Names wife, Thrias (this name in will, but in division of land the name is Mary); and ch. Andrew; Esther; Susanna; Anne (wife of Abraham Brubaker); sons-in-law, Daniel Dilman. and Michael Rule.

Dilmon. Daniel, dec. Sale recorded. Dec., 1819.

Dodd, William. Will pro. .. 1822. Names wife Mary; and ch. Thomas; Sally Hipes, William; John. A gran-son, Adney Dodd.

Dollman, Henry. Division of land, June, 1824. Names widow, Sarah; and ch. Sarah Nancy (wife Philip Snider); Barbara (wife George Knode); Mary; Eve; and Catherine.

Douglas, Benjamin. Will pro. June, 1816, Names wife, Charity; and ch. James; John, William; Francis; Elizabeth Saintelair; Behethelon Monson; Benjamin Jileon; and Mary Anderson.

Dryden, Thomas. Will pro. Apr. 1777. Names wife, Agnes; and ch. Nathaniel; David; Thomas, and others, no. or names not given.

Duncan, Robert. Will pro. June, 1787. Names wife, Cattron; and ch. Mary; Eastair; Rachel; Robert; Nancy; Margaret; Elizabeth; Rebecca; Isobel; and Janet.

Egar, Martha. Will pro. Apr. 1789. Names "my beloved child, Jane Logan". Bequeaths to her. 'one horse, one calico gown, one stiff gown, a silk bunnit, a cotton handkerchief. a silk h'd'k'f., and all that she was to get

of Moses Eagers estate.'

Eakins, Nathan. Will pro. 1823. Names wife, Susannah; and ch. Thomas; William; Mary Rice; Nathan; Nancy Walker; Samuel; Stephen; Joseph; John; Rebekah; Susannah; Equilla Broyles, (who is seperated from her husband, Soloman Broyles,); and Preston.

Eakin, Thomas. Will pro. Feb. 1810. Names wife, Agnes; and ch. Joseph; William; and Thomas.

Eakin, William, dec. Inv. of estate, Sept. 1815.

Eason, Frances. Will pro. Aug. 1786. Names ch. Samuel; Joseph; Nancy, and Elizabeth. Says the two daughters are "now in captivity" and provides for them should they be found.

Emack, Matthew, "yeoman". Will pro. Apr. 1779. Names ch. James Matthew; Samuel. A son-in-law, James Smith.

Evans, Peter. Will pro. Jan. 1797. Names wife Mary; and ch. Mark; Thomas; Jonathan; William; John; Betsy, and Catren.

Evans, Thomas. Will pro. Mar. 1785. Names friends, James Gost; David Porter, and James Pergrain.

Ferrel, Gabriel. Pro. Jan. 1803. Names wife, Anna; and ch. Elizabeth; Milly Hanes; Abner; and Stephen.

Francesco, Ludewick. Will pro. Apr. 1799. Names wife, Elizabett; and ch. Jacob; George; Elizabeth; Ester; Christina; Marget; Lodewick; Susanna; Mary, and Sarah.

Frantz, Christian, dec. Order for appraisement, Dec., 1822.

Frantz, Michael. Will pro. May, 1817. Names wife, Elizabeth and ch. Michael (of Kentucky); Elizabeth (wife Adam Shanke of Ky); Catherine, (wife Henry Britz); and Polly, (wife Daniel Stovers.)

Firestone, Nicholas. Will pro. Nov. 1808. Names wife, Eve Catherine; and ch. John; Eve, (wife John Kalfbfleisch); Nicholas; Magdalene, (wife John Wren); Susanna (wife Philip Hyleman); Elizabeth; Catherine, (wife Charles Long); Matthias.

Fleming, William. Will pro. Oct. 1795. Names children, Leonard Isreal Christian; Elizabeth. (wife Cary H. Allen); Dorathera, (land in Ky.); William; John; Annie; Christian; and Pricilla.

Freeman, Derry. Will pro. Sept. 1804. Names wife, Aggy, and son, Isaac.

Fulhart. Henry. Will pro. Feb. 1819. Names, wife, Mary; and ch. John, and Henry.

Galloway. Robert. Will pro. Aug. 1779. Names wife. Elinor; and ch. David; John; Esebell; William; Jean: Mary; and Robert.

Garmon. John. Will pro. Sept. 1799. Names wife. Susanna; and ch. Adam; and Mary Elizabeth.

Garst, Nicholas. Will pro. Oct. 1803. Names wife, Mary; and ch. number or names not given. except one son. John Nicholas.

Garwood, Joseph. Will pro. June, 1823. Names wife. Samuel (land in Kv.); Sarah: Elizabeth: Peggy; and John.

Gatty, John. Will pro. April, 1801. Names brothers, Dennis; Jerry; Jeremiah; a sister. Bridget: and two other sisters in Ireland, names not given.

Gaunt, James, dec. Inventory ret. Sept, 1778.

Gentry, John. Will pro. May 1779. Names

wife, Mary; and ch. no. or names not given.
Gerard, John, dec. Apr. of est. Wife, Rachel. Dec. 1807.
Getty, Dennis, dec. Apr. of estate ret. Aug. Aug. 1779.
Gilleland, James. Will pro. Apr. 1811. Names wife, Susannah; and ch. Sally Shepherd; Joseph; James; Betsy; Mary; John; William; Samuel; Tency; Nancy, and Susannah.
Gillespy, Hugh, dec. Inv. ret. Mar. 1777.
Gillespy, Robert. Will pro. Apr. 1798. Names ch. William; Isabel; Mary; Robert; John; James; Alexander; and Jean: grand-son, John Gillaspy.
Gillespy, Simon, dec. Apr. ret. Wife, Nancy. Nov. 1821.
Gish, Christian. Will pro. June, 1796. Names wife, Sophia; and ch. Christian; Elizabeth; Caty; George; Abraham; Jacob, and others, names or no. not given.
Givens, Daniel. Will pro. March, 1823. Names ch. Anna Webb; Susanna, (wife John Walker); Oalinda Peck; William; Lsiah; Elisha; Joseph, and Daniel. Grandchildren Daniel (Wms. son); and Patsy Peck (dau. Jacob Peck).
Glenn, Jean, dec. Apr. of estate ret. Aug. 1803.
Gortner, Catherine, dec. Apr. of estate Sept. 1819.
Gortner, Philip, dec. Settlement of estate, naming heirs: Mrs. Catherine Gortner (widow); Charlotte (wife Michael Mallow) Mary Gortner; Jacob (wife, Catherine); Elizabeth Gortner; John and Mary, (wife Joseph Key).
Goulding, Thomas. Will pro. May, 1778. (Of Rockbridge). Names Thomas Goulding of Long Bav, N. C.
Graham, William. Will pro. Sept, 1786. Names wife, ..; and ch. Elizabeth, (wife Joseph Robinson); Francis; Catherine (Wife Edward Springer); Nancy (wife Walter Giver); and George.
Green, George, dec. Devision of estate, Oct. 1784. Naming heirs: Thomas M'Clanahan* John Reburn; John Green; and Janet Green.
Greenwood, William. Will Pro. Oct. 1812. Names wife, Jane; and ch. Robert; Margaret; Jane, and Mary.
Gregor, Christine. Will pro Jan. 1809. Names grand-ch. Rebeccah and John Gregor. (See Grogan).
Greybill, John. Will pro Sept. 1818. Names wife, Hannah; and ch. John; Daniel; Solomon; Elizabeth, (wife John Fisher); Shem: sons-in-law, Daniel Arnold, and Jacob Garman.
Grist, John, dec. Inv. returned, Oct., 1791.
Grogan, John. Will pro. Dec. 1803. Names wife Christine. (See Gregor)
Gross, Jacob, dec. Inv. returned, Dec. 1804.
Gross, Martin. dec. Dower assigned widow, Margaret, Feb. 1798.
Gulliford, Allen. Will pro. Oct. 1815. Names wife, Anna; and ch. Henry; Anderson; Pricilla; Elizabeth Wilson; James; and Allen.
Gurney, Henry, (of Pa.). Will pro. June, 1792. Names Elizabeth Doughty," brought up by him"; sister, Elizabeth Brookfield; nep-

hew, Rev. Stephen Tucker; and nieces, Catherine and ....
Hall, William. Will pro. Feb. 1773. Names wife, Jean; and ch. Andrew; Agnes Berry; John; Jsabel Buchanan; William; Nathaniel; and James. Grand-ch. William, and James, sons of Andrew.
Hamilton, Andrew. Will pro. Nov. 1823. Names wife,.., and ch. James Alexander: Wilson Cary; and daughters, no. or names not given.
Hamilton, Godfrey. Will pro. July, 1795. Names Catherine and William Koger, ch. of Peter Koger.
Hamilton, John. Will pro. May, 1811. Names ch. James; John (land in Ky); and others, names or no. not given.
Hamilton, John. Will pro. May, 1823. Names ch. John; William. Samuel; Mary Croft; Susannah. and Margaret.
Hammon, Peter, dec. Adm. appointed-wife, Barbara. Mar. 1822.
Handley, Alexander. Will pro. Sept, 1781. Names wife, Mary; and ch. "little dau. Marthew Breaker", and one other, name not given- A bro-in-law, William Ewing.
Hannah, Alexander. Will pro. Sept. 1820. Names wife, Mary, and ch. James; Joseph; Peggy Gibson; and Anna Taylor.
Hanson, David. Will pro Jan. 1800. Names wife, ...; and ch. Samuel; Daniel; Mary Bags (?); Martha grandch. Elizabeth; Sally, and Annie Caldwell (dau. John Caldwell). Disinherits son, Samuel if he marries Rachel Gulliver, "who he is now courting, or any of her family."
Harbison, William. Will pro. Mar. 1775. Names wife, Mary; and ch. David; Hannah; William; George; Agnes; Mary; Jean; Grizzle; Rebecca; Elizabeth. Son-in-law, Nathaniel Evans.
Harmon, Jacob. Will pro. Apr. 1792. Names wife, Margareta; and ch. John; Lewis; Jacob; Margareta; Elizabeth; Catherine Mase.
Harmon, John, dec. Apr. of estate, Mar. 1778.
Harmontrout, George. Will pro. Oct. 1798. Names wife, Barbary; and son, Fredwick; and heirs of a dec. dau. Catherine Russell: viz- George, Mary and Catherine.
Harrison, John, dec. Inv. ret. Aug. 1786.
Harshbarger, Mary. Will pro. Dec. 1802. Names ch. Christley; Jacob; and Samuel.
Harvey, Matthew. Will pro. Nov. 1823. Names wife, Magdalen; and ch. Lucy Magdalen. Frances; Jane: Elizabeth; Virginia: Polly (wife Robert Kyle); Maria H., (wife Wm. A. McDowell); John.
Hawk, James. Will pro. Jan. 1824. Names fiends, Emund Richeson, and Peter Keyfogger.
Hawkins, Benjamin. Will pro. Mar. 1779. Names wife, Martha, and ch. William, James John, Burden, Magdelin, and Sarah.
Haynes, John. Will pro. June, 1797. Names wife, Jannett, and ch. Jennet Harriot Haynes, Granville Haynes (a dau.), William Henry, Ann Gulleland, Elizabeth Holeday, and Agnes Kitchen. A brother, Wm. Haynes.
Haynes, Nicholas. Will pro. June, 1797. Names wife, Elizabeth; and ch. Isaac, John, Mar-

garet, Miffert, Catherine Luder, Chirstopher, and Jacob.

Hays, John. Will pro. Nov. 1822. Names ch. John, Thomas, Jonathan, Ruth Measlls(?), and Lewis. Grandch., James, son of Thomas, Harrison, son of Jonathan, and Henry, son of Lewis.

Hazelwood, Joshua, dec. Apr. returned, Feb. 1812.

Heavins, John. Will pro. Aug. 1784. Names wife, Sarah; and ch. James, Mary, (wife of Thomas Finley, of N. C.), Howard, and John.

Henry, William, dec. Inv. of esetate ret. June 1816.

Hewett, John, dec. Inv. returned, Sept. 1812.

Hill, Edward, dec. Venue bill ret. Apr. 1811.

Himes, John. Will pro. Jan. 1808. Names ch. Abraham, John, Isaac, David, Elizabeth, Barbary, and Daniel—the youngest.

Hindmon, John, dec. Settlement of est. Feb. 1798.

Hiner, John. Will pro. Dec. 1801. Names wife, Mary; and ch. Henry (eldest son), Gertrude, (eldest dau. and wife of Solomon Lets), Catty, Polly, (wife Samuel Nofsinger), Elizabeth, Susannah, Abraham, John, Peter, and Anthony.

Hiner, Peter, dec. Heirs named—"L. Latshaw's wife, P. Deards' wife, J. Boyds' wife, John Moor's wife", and Anthony, John and Peter Hiner.

Hiner, Peter, dec. Dower assigned Catherine Fellers, former wife Peter. Dec. 1823.

Hipes, Nicholas. Will pro. Apr. 1802. Names wife, Apolonia, and ch. John, Peter, Henry, Maria, Elizabeth Able, Barbary, ("late Hammon"), Magdaline Gross, and Margaret.

Hively, Jacob, dec. Adm. of estate, Aug. 1819.

Hof, Lewis. Will pro. Aug. 1823. Names wife, Rachel; and ch. Abraham, Daniel, David, Peter, Catherina, John, Maryan, and Samuel.

Hoffes(?), Nicholas, dec. Apr. of estate, Sept. 1802.

Hontz, Jacob, dec. Adm. appointed—his wife, Polly. ....1818.

Howard, Edward. Will pro. May, 1785. Names wife, Elizabeth, and son Ezekiel.

Howell, Abner. Will pro. Sept 1812. Names wife, Hanah; and ch. James, Samuel, Thomas, Jesse, David, Jamimah, Rader, Mary Gist, Virth Gist.

Howery, Jacob, dec. Apr. returned. Dec. 1809.

Huddle, George. Will pro. Sept. 1794. Namés wife. Margaret; and ch. George, Elizabeth, and Christian—all minors.

Hugart, William, dec. Inv. of estate ret. May, 1775.

Hutchinson. William. Will pro. Apr. 1778. Names "kinsman. James Hutchinson, Sr."

Inglebird, George. dec. Est. settles. May, 1778.

Ingram, Alexander. Will pro. May, 1782. Names wife. Mary; and ch. Ann, ("and her husband"), John, William, James, Mary, and Alexander, Jr.

Janhoward, Samuel. Will pro. Dec. 1824. Names wife. Ann: and ch. John, Thomas Jefferson. Timothy Newel. Cynthia Magdalen (wife Henry W. Kelly), Jacob, Betsy Cahoon, Susan Camper, Samuel, and Barbera.

Jenkins, Jeremiah. Will pro. Feb. 1821. Names Eliner Falts, and her sons, Peter and Benjamin, and Amelia Williams—no relationship stated.

John, Jacob. Will pro. Oct. 1806. Names wife, Cathren; and ch. Henry, and Jacob, son-in-law, Daniel Bare. Leaves one dollar "to each of my children by my first wife"—un-named.

Johnston, Eve. Will pro. Nov. 1809. Names ch. Henry Persinger, Jacob Johnston, William Johnston, Sarah Porter, Rachel Linkhorn, and Margaret Smith. Granddaughter, Rebecca Smith.

Johnston, Ezekiel. Will pro. Aug. 1781. Names wife, Eve; and ch. Andrew, Sarah, Rachel, John, Jacob, William, and Margaret.

Johnston, Peter, dec. Apr. returned, Dec. 1794.

Jones, Ambrois. Will pro. May, 1822. Names wife, Elizabeth; and ch. Polly Jones, Allen, Ambroise, Catherine Moyer, Milly Watkins, Mary Watkins, (her heirs), Nancy Watkins, (her heirs), and Sally Russell.

Jones, John. Will pro. July, 1773. Names wife Elizabeth; and ch. Nathaniel, John, Margaret M'Coy, Elizabeth, John, Marthew, Sarah, Jean, Hannah, (wife Thomas Harrison).

Jones, John Grabriel. Will pro. Nov. 1779. Names brothers, Samuel, (a surgeon), Gabriel, Thomas, A brother-in-law, Thomas Griffith, a friend, Patrick Lockhare, his mother—name not given; sisters, Elizabeth, Ann Margaret Jones, and Charlotte Griffith? (Property in England). Says his father was John Jones of England, and his grandfather Samuel Slade, also of England.

Keefauver, Katherine. Will pro. Jan. 1820. Names ch. Mary and Elizabeth.

Kent, Jacob. Will pro. Feb. 1777. Names wife, Mary; and ch. John, Joseph, Robert, Jacob, Jane , and Nancy.

Keslar, Jacob. Will pro Sept. 1824. Names wife, Elizabeth; and ch. George, John, Jacob, Henry, Catherine, Daniel, Andrew, Benjamin, David, Samuel, and Elizabeth.

Kilmer, George. Will pro. Mar. 1823. Names wife, Catherine; and ch. Elizabeth Hanmel, Susanna Eve Cup(?), Barbary, Magdalene Johnson, Esther, Margaret, William, Nancy, Sarah, and George.

Kimberling, Paulzer. Will pro. Oct. 1808. Names wife, Sarah; and ch. James, Martha Matthews, Agnes Pitzer. Rebecca Pitzer, John and Jacob.

Kinny, John. Will pro. Nov. 1813. Names wife, Elizabeth; and ch. William, James, Joseph, David, Sampson, John, Sally Betsy, Susanna.

Kinny, William. Will pro. Nov. 1774. Names wife, Elizabeth, Marrey. Jean, Elizabeth, Marrey.

Kitchen, Henry, dec. Apr. of estate, Jan. 1792.

Kyle, Archibald. Will pro. Mar. 1784. Names wife, Mary; and ch. Sally, Rhoda, Fanny, and Marvin.

Kyle, Jane. Will pro. Nov. 1820. Names ch. Christopher, Jane Pitzer, Robert, and Dinguid.

Kyle, Joseph. Will pro. 1808. Names wife, Jane and ch. Robert, Duiguid, William, Christopher, Anne, and married daus. no. or names not given.

—45—

Kyle, Mrs Mary, dec. Adm. return, Sept. 1784.
Kyle, Nancq, dec. Apr. returned, Oct. 1811.
Kyle, William. Will pro. Dec. 1809. Names bros. Christopher, Robert, Dinguid; sister, Ann Kyle, Martha Jane Kyle, (relationship not stated). Mentions his dec. father, Joseph.
Kyle, Wiliam. Will pro. Feb. 1821. Names wife Sarah; and ch. Jane Womack, Barclay, Sally Rowland, and James. Sons-in-law, John Dickerson, and Charles Beale. Grandsons, James Pitzer, ("Born Oct. 1805"); and Robert Pitzer, (" Born 3rd. Dec. 1807"), both sons of eGorge Pitzer.
Lackey, James. Will pro. Oct. 1823. Names wife, Mary; and ch. Thomas, Nathan, Martha McKnight, Agness McKnight, Mary Lakey, and Samuel.
Lange, Christian Charles. Will pro. Aug. 1817. Names wife, Elizabeth; and wifes sister, Christina Schlengliss.
Lantz, Peter. dec. Inv. returned, Nov. 1822.
Lawyers, Sampson. Will pro. Apr. 1819. Names wife, Mary; and ch Andrew, Mathew, Rebeccah, Alexander, and Archer.
Larkins, Henry. Will pro. Feb. 1773. Names wife, Jain: and ch. James, Henry, Mary, David, Thomas, Elizabeth, Sarah, Jain, Margaret, Nancy, Marthew.
Lawrence, James, Jr. Will pro. Nov. 1773. Names wife, Frances; daughter, Elizabeth; and brothers, Henry Hunter, William, Samuel, David, John, Solomon, Isaac, Joseph, and Robert.
Leforce, Rene. dec. Apr. returned, Oct. 1781.
Lemmon, George, Sr. Will pro. Apr. 1807. Names wife, Elizabeth; and his third son, Jacob; other heirs, no. or names not given.
Lester, Nancy. Will pro. Sept. 1823. Names ch. Polly, John, and others, nomes or numbers not given.
Lewis, Andrew. Will pro. Feb. 1782. Names wife ....; and ch. John, Sauuel, Thomas, Andrew, William, Anne. Grandsons, Andrew, Sam'l, and Charles (sons of John). His bros. Thomas and William, sister, Margaret.
Lewis, Andrew. dec. Dev. of land, 1821. Names John, Wm. Patsy, Sam'l, Emel..........., Eliza, and Jane Ann Lewis: Sally Woods, (wife James L. Wood).
Lewis, John. Will pro. Aug. 1783. Names wife Marthew, and ch. Andrew, Samuel, Charles, Elizabeth, and one unborn.
Likins, Andrew, dec. Inv. returned, Nov. 1780.
Likins, Marcus, dec. Inv. ret. Nov. 1781
Lindsay, Margaret. Will pro. Apr. 1804. Names sons, Samuel, Matthew, and Walter; grand ch., Samuel (son Nathan), Samuel, (son Walter L.), Margaret, (dau. Walter), and Margaret and Samuel Cantley. A niece, Agnes Smithey.
Lindsay, Robert, dec. Apr. returned, Feb. 1776.
Lindsay, Samuel. Will pro. Apr. 1784. Names wife. Margaret; and ch. Matthew, Erling Cantley. Samuel, and Walter.
Linkenhonker, Elias, dec. Adm. return, Dec. 1821.
Linkenhonker, Elizabeth, dec. Inv. returned, Dec. 1822.
Little, David. Will pro. Dec. 1813. Names ch.

John, Robert, William, James, David, Sarah, and Rebeccah.
Little, John. Will pro. July, 1793. Names wife, Elizabeth; and ch. David, John, William, Mary, Fannah,an d Sarah. "Moneys to be devided equally amongst my children: the males shall have 20 shillings each, and the females 15 shillings."
Little, William, dec. Apr. of estate, Sept. 1819.
Loggan, John, dec. Apr. returned, Mar. 1773.
Long, Elizabeth. Will pro. Jan. 1824. Names friend, Peter Bush.
Looney, Absolum. Will pro. June. 1796. Names ch. Michael, Elizabeth Potts, Peter, Mary Swanson, Margaret Caldwell, Jonathan, Absolum, Ruth, Ann Harberson, Catherine, Pricilla Caldwell, and Benjamin.
Looney, John, dec. Devision of land, Dec. 1823. Naming heirs: widow, Elizabeth; and Sarah, Joseph, John, and William Looney. (Note: widow, Elizabeth. at this time wife of .... Reynolds.)
Looney, Robert. Will pro. Nov. 1770. Names wife, Elizabeth; and ch. Joseph, an others no. and names not given.
Loop, Philip. Will pro. Oct. 1824. Names wife, Catherine; and ch. Sarah Menga, Simon. Christian, Catherine. John, Jacob, Rebecca, Barbara, Philip, Elizabeth, and Susanna.
Love, Philip, dec. Inv. returned, Jan. 1793.
Lyth, John. Will pro. Dec. 1781. Names Mrs. Betsy Brekenridge. Made on leaving home to enter army.
Madison, John. Will pro. Mar. 1784. Names wife, Agatha; and ch. Rowland, George, Thomas; daughter-in-law, Elizabeth Madison (widow of dec. son, William), and her ch. Elizabeth Smith Madison. and Agatha Strother Madison: A daughter-in-law, Susanna Madison; son-in-law, Andrew Lewis.
Madison, Thomas. Will pro. Sept. 1798. Names wife ....; and ch. Agatha, (wife Col. Bowyer), John H., Thomas, Patrick, Peggy Sale, Annie, and Jennie.
Mann, William. Will pro. Nov. 1778. Names wife, Jeane; and ch. Moses, Thomas, William, John, Catie, Jenny, Sarah, and one, unborn.
Mann, William, dec. Inv. ret. Feb. 1795.
Markey, Nicholas. Will pro. Feb. 1824. Names wife, Barbara; and ch. George, and others, unnamed, or no. not given. Bro. David Markey, of Pa.
Martin, Johnson. Will pro. June. 1818. Names wife, ..., and ch. Nancy Bartel, Judy, Sarah, and Feby.
Martin, Josiah. dec. Dower assigned wife, Polly, Nov. 1820.
Matthews, William. Will pro. Nov. 1772. Names wife, Frances; and ch. Ann, Flizabeth, John, Joseph, James. Brothers, Samson, and George.
Mason, James. Will pro. ....1808. Names William Crawford, Samuel Crawford, Mason Crawford, Jane Pate, Elinor Jennings, Margaret Crawford, Sarah Crawford, all ch. of Samuel and Janet Crawford of Ky. (Says Janet his sister and best friend). Heirs of dec. bro. William Mason: Heirs of dec. sister, Mary (wife James E. Edgar, of Bedford Co.): heirs sister, Margaret (wife Joseph Snodgrass, of Tenn); A

brother, Joseph Mason, of Beckenridge Co., Ky.

Mason, Jonathan, dec. Apr. returned, Mar. 1822.

Mason, Martin, dec. Apr. returned, Dec. 1794.

Maura, Conrad. Will pro. Feb. 1824. Names son, Conrad, of Somerset Co. Pa., and son-in law, Henry Painter.

Mays, Mary. Will pro. May, 1822. Names ch. Susannah Tate, Mary Cross, and James.

Maze, William, Sr. Will pro. Mar. 1783. Names wife, Margaret; and ch. William, Richard, Sarah McMurray, and Mary Scott.

McCarty, Nancy. Will pro. Nov. 1823. Names sister, Elizabeth Kidd (and her dau. Elizabeth) of King and Queen Co.; brothers, John and Luray Campbell; niece, Susan, dau. of brother John.

McClananghan, Robert, dec. Inv. returned, 1774.

McClanahan, Washington. dec. Settlement of estate, Sept. 1819.

McClanahan, William. Will pro. Nov. 1819. Names wife, Sarah; sons, Elijah, James, and Green. The widow, Lucy, and ch. William and Charles, of a dec. son, John. Heirs of a dec. son, Washington. Wife Elizabeth, and ch. Washington, and John, of his son, Green. Grandchildren, William McClanahan, William Lewis Cook, William Lewis, Jr., William McClanahan, Jr. William Markle.

McClung, John. Will pro. May 1779. Names bro. James, and sister, Agnes Gray.

McClure, John. Will pro. Feb. 1778. Names wife, ...; and ch. Samuel, Alexander, Mary, Agnes, Jannet, Malcolm, Hannah, Rebeccah, John. Holbert, Moses, and Nathaniel.

McClure, Malcom. Will pro. June, 1791. Names wife, Elizabeth; and ch. John. and Mary. A brother, Samuel, and nephew, Samuel, Jr.

McConnell, James. Will pro. June, 1813. Names wife, Nancy; and ch. James: Peter, Jesy, and the heirs of dec. son, John.

McConnell, James. Will pro. May, 1821. Leaves estate to friends.

McConnell, Nancy. Will pro. Sept. 1818. Names ch. Peter and James.

McCown, Patrick, dec. Apr. of estate, Dec. 1772.

McCrery, John, dec. Apr. ret. Oct. 1802.

McDonnald, Bryan. Will pro. Feb. 1777.Names wife, Susannah; ch. James, William, Thomas, Edward, George, Mary, Susannah, and Jane.

McDonnald, James. Will pro. Mar. 1778. Names mother, Susannah; and sisters and brothers, Edward, William, George, Mary, Susannah, and Jean.

McFerran, Archibald. Will pro. Aug. 1777. Names brother, Isaac McFerran, "can he be found"; an dan Uncle. John McFerran, living in county Derby. Ireland.

McFerran, James. Pro.. Sept. 1806. Names his mother, Anne McFerrand.

McFerrand. John. Will pro. May, 1776. Names wife, Margaret; ch. Samuel, Martin, Agnes, Martha, Mary Watkins (and her son, Robert). Jane, James, Thomas; a grandson, John MsFerran.

MeFerran, Martin. Pro. Feb. 1816. Names

Hetty and Martin McFerran, the ch. of Samuel McFerran, of Tenn.

McFerrow, Samuel. Will pro. Feb. 1820. Names wife........; ch. Ann, Martin; mother, unnamed; niece, Hetty McFerrow.

McKeechy, James. Will pro. Sept. 1605. Names wife, Rebecca, and son Andrew.

McKnight, George. Will pro. Aug. 1815. Names ch. James, Jane, Sarah, William, Elizabeth, Nancy, George, John, and Thomas.

McMath, William. Will pro. Oct. 1782. Names wife, Margaret; a brother, James, and James' son, William.

McMullin, Edward. Will pro. June, 1788. Names wife, Sarah; and ch. John (eldest), Elizabeth, Margaret, and Agnes (these four by a first wife); James, Edward, Joseph, Samuel, Sampson, Lovia, Jean, Ester, Sarah, Lettice, and Mary.

McMurray, William, dec. Adm. settlement, 1798.

McNeal, Daniel. Will pro. Aug 1.818. Names wife, Sarah; ch. Jane, (wife Robert Filson) Polly, (wife George Bright). Grandson, Thos. Jefferson Bright.

McNeal Hugh. Will pro. Feb. 1796. Names wife, Martha; and ch. Mary McGlaughin, Lida Gordon, Martha Murphy, John, Sarah Duke, Margaret, and Elizabeth.

McNeal, James. Will pro. Nov. 1778. Names wife, Mary; and ch. Joseph, and Mary. A brother,, Jonathan.

McNeal, John. Will pro. Feb. 1773. Names wife, Mary; and ch. Rebecca, Nancy, Mary, Sarah, and one unborn.

McNeel, John, dec. Apr. returned, Dec. 1789.

Merrett, Samuel, dec. Apr. returned, Sept. 1821.

Mifford, Jacob, Will pro. June, 1798. Names wife, Peggy; and ch. Elizabeth Nugent, Polly, John, Jacob, Catherine, Peggy, and Pricilla.

Miller, David, dec. Wife Hannah, made administrator. Sept. 1811.

Mills, Hugh. Will pro. May, 1785. Names brothers, Blaney and John, and John's son Hugh.

Mills, John, dec. Apr. estate, Feb. 1782.

Mitchell, Joseph, dec. Settlement by executor, Mary Mitchell, Feb. 1810.

Moore, Henry. Will pro. Dec. 1822. Names wife, Elizabeth; ch. John, William, Elizabeth.

Moore, James. Will pro. Aug. 1780. Names ch. James, John, Martha Ralston, Jean, (wife Samuel McClanahan).

Montgomery. Samuel, dec. Valuation of estate ret. Mar. 1777.

Mosley, Bennett. Will pro. Nov. 1811. Names wife, Elizabeth; and ch. Henry, Mary, and George. A brother, John Mosley.

Mound. John James, dec. Dower assigned wife, Harriet, Aug. 1815.

Mover, Jacob, dec. Apr. returned. July,1795.

Mull, James. Will pro. May, 1782. Names Thomas Tatum, a friend.

Murphey, Dennis. Will pro. Sept. 1808. Names friends, James, Joseph, Anna, and Peggy Hannah. Land in Ky.

Murray, John. Will pro. Jan. 1775. Names wife, Elizabeth; and ch. Richard, Martha, Charles. (In inventory he is "Capt. John

Murray").

Muson, James, dec. Inv. returned. Nov. 1782.

Myars, Henry, dec. Inv. returned. Aug. 1821.

Nealley, John. Will pro. Aug. 1778. Names wife, Elizabeth; and ch. Robert, Andrew, John, and Elizabeth Cloyd. Grand-ch. Betsy and Sam'l Nealley.

Neeley, John. Will pro. Jan. 1802. Names wife, Sarah; executor, Major Robt. Neely.

Neeley, Robert. Will pro. Sept. 1780. Names wife, Ann; and ch. John; James; Andrew; William, and Robert.

Nicholas, George. Will pro. Aug. 1812. Names wife, Ann, and ch. names not given, or number-all minors.

Nicholas, John, Gent. Will pro Oct. 1803. Names, Wife, Mary.

Nofsinger, Joseph. Will pro. Sept. 1815. Names wife, Betsy, and ch. unnamed.

Norville, Thomas. Will pro. Sept. 1812. Names ch. Rebeccah; Elizabeth; Nancy; Young; Samuel; John; Hugh; Thomas, and William.

Ocheltree, Michael. Will pro. June, 1799. Names wife, Elizabeth, and bros. and sisters no. or names not given.

Olds, Edward. Will pro. June, 1819. Names wife, Elizabeth; and ch. Nancy Head; Elizabeth; Charles; Anderson; Luellow, and Henry. Grand-ch. Elizabeth Epps, dau. Patterson Olds.

Oldshoe, Jacob, dec. Apr. returned July, 1795.

Owen, Thomas, dec. Apr. returned, Jan. 1775.

Palmer, William, dec. Apr. of estate, Nov. 1772.

Parrish, Julius, dec. Apr. of estate-wife, Betsy–Sept. 1803.

Pate, Jeremiah. Will pro. June, 1797. Names ch. Rhoda; Amelia; Minor; Polly Compton Matthew; Jeremiah; Judith; John, and Edward.

Patrick, Jamie, dec. Apr. returned Dec. 1804.

Patterson, George. Will pro. Apr. 1789. Names wife, Margaret; and ch. George, and Jean-the two youngest. Others, but no. or names not given.

Paul, Andley. Will pro. Apr. 1810. Names ch. Anna Taylor; Andley, Jr.; Margaret Walker; John; Rebecca Taylor; James; Jane Harris; Elizabeth Defreese. The following relationship not stated: John Walker; Cawfield Taylor; and James Harris.

Peck, Jacob. Will pro. Oct. 1801. Names ch. Benjamin; Jacob; John; Adam; Joseph; Mary; Ester, and Hannah. Wife was Lydia Borden. A son-in-law, Jacob Carper.

Peck, John. Will pro. Sept. 1820. Names wife, Mary; and ch. Susannah, (wife Allen Jones); Margaret, (wife John Sites); Ann, (wife William Camell); Jane Peck; George Joseph; William; Martin, and Jacob C. A daughter-in-law, Mary W. widow of a dec. son, Lewis, and her son, George.

Parsinger, Christopher, dec. Inv. returned Jan. 1802.

Persinger, Jacob, dec. Apr. returned Dec. 1789.

Peters, Abraham, dec. Inv. returned Mar. 1818.

Phillips, Samuel. Will pro. June, 1812. Names wife, Elizabeth; and ch. Samuel; Richard Nancy, Sarah, and Elizabeth. A brother,

John, and Mary Anderson, relationship not stated.

Phipps, Joseph. Will pro. Feb. 11, 1772. Names ch. Joshua; Aaron; Caleb; Mary, (wife Isaac Lewis, of Chester Co., Pa.); Rachel, (wife Owen Astin of Chester Co., Pa.); Hannah, (wife George Astin of Botetourt Co.); Easter Crosby (and her son, Benjamin); Joseph, (and his ch. Jonathan and Anne). Were Quakers.

Poage, George. Will pro. Dec. 1786. Names ch. Elizabeth Shirky; Rachel; Margaret; Experience; Mary; George, and John, (six yrs. old).

Poage, John. Will pro. Apr. 1789. Names wife, Marthew; and ch. names or no. not given.

Poage, Robert. Pro. Sept. 1788. Names sons, William, Robert, and John. Also, Thomas Goodson, and Nathan Scott-relationship not given.

Pollston, Benjamin. Will pro. Aug. 1770. Names wife, Mary; a daughter, Margaret (under age); and a brother, Swain Pollston.

Porter, William, dec. Apr. returned July 1790.

Potts, Amos. Will pro. Aug. 1780. Names wife Hannah, and ch. John; Nathan, and others, number or names not given.

Potts, John, dec. Inv. retuned Jan. 1793.

Preston, Jane. Will pro. July, 1813. Names ch. Polly and Thomas.

Preston, Thomas. Will. pro. Apr. 1802. Names wife, Jane; and ch. Thomas; Anne; Mary; Jane Snodgrass, and the heirs of a dec. son, John.

Price, Thomas. Will pro. 1823. Names wife, Margaret; and ch. Sophia, (wife Jacob Price); Madoriah; Agnes; Rebecca (wife John Hank); Polly Scott; Sarah Littlepage; Margaret Bennett, and Thompson. Four others by last marriage, un-named: grand-ch. Alfred Holston; Sophia Price: a brother-in-law, Thomas Beard.

Pryor, Luke. Will pro. Oct. 1783. Names wife, Susan, and an unborn child. Brothers John, Joseph, and Luke: heirs of dec. bro. Samuel.

Reed, Rev. Joseph, dec. Inv. returned, Oct. 1813.

Reed, Samuel. Will pro. Jan. 1793. Names ch. Samuel; William; Michael; Nancy; Rachel; Elizabeth Telford; Sarah Richardson; Jane Charter; Margaret Gritton, and John.

Reed, William. Will pro. Dec. 1801. Names wife, Ruthe; and ch. William; John; Sarah McMullen; Ruth New; Anne Knox; Margaret Persinger; Rebekah Nysonger; Thomas; Mary Kimberling, and Archibald.

Reiley, Francis. Will pro. Feb. 1778. Names James Reiley, and Catherine Patterson, "both of the Kingdom of Ireland, Co. Cavin".

Rentfro, William. Will pro. June, 1789. Names Patrick Lemon, and John Targert.

Revnolds, Magdalan. Will pro. Nov. 1820. Names ch. James; Thomas; John; Ann Givens; Fanny Taylor, and William, (and his dau. Ann.)

Reynolds, Thomas. Will pro. Dec. 1804. Names wife, Ann; and ch. John (eldest); Harry Byne; Sarah Loyd; Pattie King; and Betty McGee. Grandch. John Givin (son Joseph and Ann Givin) and Nancy Ann Taylor. (Note; Wife, Ann, is evidently the Magdalan above.)

Reynolds, William, dec. Apr. returned Feb. 1796.

Richards, Richard, dec. Inv. returned Apr. 1803.

Richardson, Samuel. Will pro. Oct. 1821 Names son, John, and other ch. names or number not given.

Richey, John. Will pro. Aug. 1780. Names wife, Sarah; and ch. James; Stephen; John Mary and Aunice (?).

Rinehart, Francis. Will pro. Jan., 1814. Names wife, Rebekah; and ch. John, and others, names or no. not given.

Ripp, Frederic, dec. Apr. returned, Feb. 1790.

Robinet, Samuel, dec. Inv. returned, Apr. 1772.

Robinson, David. Will pro. June, 1787, Names wife, Catron; and ch. William; George; James; Pricilla; Jane; Catherine; Mary; Elizabeth; Ann; Annable; Phebe, and Prudence. Son-in-law, Wm. McDonald.

Robinson, Elizabeth, dec. Inv. returned Aug. 1772.

Rowland, James. Will pro. June, 1805. Names wife, Margaret; and ch. Mary; Elizabeth; Jane; Margaret; Agness; Prudence; Robert; George; James, and William.

Rowland, James. Will pro. Apr. 1819. Names wife. Sarah, and ch. Charlotte and James.

Rowland, Robert. Will pro. Feb. 1782. Names ch. James; Thomas; George: and heirs of dec. son, William, (only one by name-Robert).

Rowland, Thomas. Will pro. Aug. 1814. Names wife, Mary; and ch. Jesse; Silas; Joel; George (land in Jessimine Co. Ky.); Milly Gilmore; William, and David (also land in Ky).

Rowland, William. Will pro. Mar. 1777. (Noncup. will) Equal devision between all his ch. no. or names not given.

Ruddell, Cornelius. Will pro. Apr. 1798. Names wife, Ingebo; and ch. Andrew; John; Stephen; Chear Reader; Deborough Rutledge; Catherine Sangler, and Elizabeth Alcorn. Brother George Ruddells' daughter, Ingobo.

Rute, George. Will pro. Sept. 1823. Names Cathreine Rute, "alias Shute", Rosanna Rute, "alias French", Christinah Rute, "alias Dasher", Jacob Rute, John Rute,Michael Rute; a grand-daughter, Sally French.

Savour, Elizabeth. Will pro. June, 1890. Names Julies Webb, Sr.

Scott, James. Will pro. Sept. 1783. Names wife, Esther; and ch. William, Samuel, and four daughters unnamed.

Scott, Nathan. Will pro. Oct. 1819. Names ch. Robert, William. Jane, (wife David Short), Sarah, wife Philby Whitmore) Isabella Scott, Peggy, (wife Andrew Mellon. (States that these four daughters have "removed to the western country"): Mary, Rebecca, Nathan, John, James, and Joseph.

Seacat, Elizabeth. Will pro. June 1824. Leaves estate for upkeep and fencing of her, and her dec. husband, George, graves.

Seachrist, John. Will pro. June 1815. Names wife ....; and ch. Daniel, and others, un-named.

Sever, Casper. Will pro.Feb. 1782. Names wife ....; and ch. Henry, Casper, and John.

Shamblin, Aaron. Will pro. Feb. 1789. Names ch. William, Aaron, George, Jesse, and Mary. Mary's ch. George and Cittle.

Shanklin, Richard. Will pro. Oct. 1800. Names wife, Agnes; and ch. John, William, Robert, Andrew, Cathernie, and Elizabeth. (and her son Absolum.

Shanklin, Robert. dec. Apr. of estate, Feb. 1802.

Shanks, David. Will pro. Aug. 1821. Names wife, Temain; and ch. William, David, Thomas, James, Lewis, Carey, Cassey, Geo-rge Washington, also a sister, Sarah.

Sharkey, Patrick. Will pro. Mar. 1786. Names wife, Anne, and ch. James, John, and Patrick.

Sharp, Edward. Will pro. June, 1770. Names wife, (names not given); ch. John, Anthony, and one other—names not given. Father-in-law, John McCiellon; bro.-inlaw, Wm. McClellon. Note: in 1786 an account gives wifes name as Jane, and ch. Anthony, John and Annis.

Shaver, Andrew. Will pro. Mar. 1816. Names wife, Wisula; and ch. Andrew, Betsy, Saly, Lucy, and others, unnamed. A bro. Adam.

Shaver, Peter. Will pro. Apr. 1798. Names father, Andrew, and a brother, Andrew.

Shewsbury, Dabney(dec. Apr. returned, Feb. 1803.

Short, Jacob, dec. Inv. returned, June, 1805.

Shrido, John, dec. Apr. returned, Sept. 1772.

Sigle, Nancy, dec. Sales bill, Oct. 1811.

Simmons, Jacob, dec. Inv. returned, Feb. 1789.

Simms, Ignatius, Jr., of Charlotte Co., Md. Will pro. Nov. 1786. Names mother, Sarah Simms; brother, James Simms; sisters, Mattingley; Sarah, and Ann Fowler; nephew, John Simms, and niece, Maddox Simms.

Skidmore, James. Willpro. Dec. 1807. Names wife ....; and ch. Ann, Joseph, John, Randolph, James, and Sarah.

Skillern, Elizabeth. Will pro. Oct. 1808. Names dau. Nancy.

Skillern, George. Will pro. Apr. 1804. Names wife, Elizabeth; and ch. William Preston, Elizabeth Beals, Peggy Beals, and Nancy Skillern.

Skillern, William. Will pro. Feb. 1817. Names wife ...., and son George.

Sloan, Archibald. Will pro. Oct. 1804. Wife, Nally; and ch. Mattie Elizabeth, George, Sarah Kirk, Rosannah McClendish, Nelly Skidmore, Polly Ferguson, David, and James.

Smiley, Walter. Will pro. June, 1807. Names ch. Alexander, George, Daniel, James and Nancy. Says Nancy has six ch.

Smith, David, dec. Apr. returned, July 1782.

Smith, James, dec. Apr. returned, Mar. 1780.

Smith, John. Will pro. Mar. 1783. Wife living, names not given. Son James. Mentions an officers claim warrant.

Smith, John. Wil lpro Apr. 1806. Names wife, Mary; and son, Samuel.

Smith, William, dec. Apr. returned, Nov. 1786.

Smyth, Rev. Ad. Will pro. July, 1786. Names ch. Nancy V. Moxley, Alexander, and others, unnamed Father, and step-mother, names not given.

Smythe, James,("of the Kingdom of Ireland, son of Benjamin Allen Smythe, dec.") Will pro. June, 1790. Names brother, Alexander Smythe.

Smythe, Jane, dec. Apr. returned, Feb. 1820.

Snider, Jacob. Will pro. Sept. 1821. Name ch. by first wife: Elizabeth Kely; Mary, Molly Felty, John, George, Christian, Barberry, and Eve. Bequest to his housekeeper, Miss Huddle. Names Jacob, Flany, Nickls, and Lilly, relationship not stated, but possibly ch. by last marriage.

Snider, Philip. Will pro. Sept. 1803. Names brother, Henry, and sister, unnamed.

Snodgrass, Elizabeth, dec. Inv. returned Feb. 1783.

Snodgrass, Jane. Will pro. Nov. 1823. Names sister, Maranda; brother, Tighlmanand his wife, Mary, and their ch. Robert L. Henry W., and William N. Says her dec father was Robert Snodgrass.

Snodgrass, Joseph. Will pro. Oct. 1782. Names wife, Hannah; and ch. Robert, Joseph, Lidia Cammeron, Margaret McClanahan, Hannah, Rebecca, (wife John Potts), Phebe Baker, Isaac. A grandson, Joseph Potts.

Snodgrass, Joseph. Will pro. Sept. 1809. Names wife, Mary; and ch. Robert, John, Joseph, Caroline, William, Elizabeth St-Clair, George, Bartley, Henry and Polly. "Ex bro.-in-law, John Walker."

Snodgrass, Robert. Will pro. Nov. 1806. Names ch. Tilgman, William Adams, Sabra, Elizabeth, Jenny, and Miranda. Brothers, Joseph and Tilgman West.

Snodgrass, William. Will pro. June, 1791. Names wife, Isabella· and ch. Joseph, James, William, John, Shusan Tweedy, Jain Fisher, Margaret Seel, Isabella McClenalhan, and Elnor George.

Spechard, Philip, dec. Inv. returned, Jan. 1793.

Spillar, Jacob. Will pro. Mar. 1820. Names wife, Fanny, and ch. Michael, Barbara Cram(?), Daniel, Elizabeth Peters, Jacob, Hannah My........, and Magdeline.

Star, Henry, dec. Apr. returned, June, 1810.

Statler, Abraham. Will pro. May, 1813. Names ch. Abraham, John, and Elizabeth Write. Sons-in-lew, John Write, and John Good.

Stuart, James, dec. Inv. returned, Dec. 1803.

Stuart, Robert, dec. Inv. returned, Dec. 1819.

Switzer, Henry Will pro. June, 1798. Wife, Chloe; and ch. William, Nathan, Thomas, John, Mary, and Joseph.

Switzer, William. Will pro. Feb. 1812. Names wife, Nancy; and ch. William, Sarah, Cloe. Bros. John and Joseph Switzer.

Sympson, Solomon. Will pro. Oct. 1785. Names wife, Margaret; and ch. Solomon, and Elizabeth.

Tapscott, James, dec. Devision of slaves: ¾ to widow, rest to ch. Robert, and Allen.

Tate, Nathaniel, dec. Apr. returned, Mar. 1810.

Taylor, John. Will pro. June 1812. Names wife, Mary; and ch. Andrew, Elizabeth, (wife Tom Price), John Isaac, Thomas, James. The heirs of the dec. daughter, Mary—her husband, Moses Bonont, also dec.

Teel, Thomas. Will pro. Jan. 1824. Names wife, Martna· and ch. Henry, Betsy Johnson, Peter, John, and Jacob.

Thomas, Lodaneck. Will pro. Sept. 1778. Names ch. Magdalin Runnills, Margaret Christian, Elizabeth, Abraham, Mary, and Catherine.

Thomas, Richard. Will pro. Oct. 1782. Names mother, Mildred Thomas; sister, Sarah, and brothers, James, and George.

Thompson, John. Will pro. June, 1822. Names wife, Judith; ch. Bartlett, John W., Creed T., Anderson, Elizabeth Eubank (wife, Elias M.). and Mary Shirky.

Tosh, Jonathan. Will pro. Feb. 1782. Names wife, Dina; ch. Nancy and one unporn. Bro. James; a cousin, Jonathan Tosh.

Tosh, Thomas. Will pro. Feb. 1778. Names wife, Mary; and ch. Mary, Jonathan, a son-in-law, James Crawford.

Tosh, William. Will pro. Feb. 1773. Names bros. Jonathan, James, and sister, Jean.

Trimble, James. Will pro. Apr. 1776. Names wife Sarah, and ch. John, Isaac, Moses, Alexander, William, Agnes, Sarah, Rachel, Jean McClure. A brother, Moses Trimble.

Triplar, Henry, dec. Devision of land, Jan. 1820. Names heirs: Sally, George, Moses, William. Jacob, Henry, Peter, Nancy, Michael. Barbara,(wife Wm. Persinger), Mary (wife Adam Quickle), Catherine, (wife George Mallow), and Elizabeth, (wite Jacob Pence).

Trisslar (see above).

Trout, John. Will pro. Dec. 1816. Names wife, Elizabeth; and ch. John, Philip, Elizabeth Michel, Emanuel, Jacob, and Rosannah.

Turman, Benjamin. Will pro. Oct. 1784. Names wife, Frances, and ch. Charles, George, John, Elizabeth, James, Ignasus, Benjamin, William, Mary, Ann and Frances.

Turner, James. Will pro. Apr. 1823. Names wife, Sally, and children, no. or names not given.

Vanbibber, Isaac, dec. Inv. returned, Apr. 1776.

Vineyard, Christian. Will pro. June, 1798. Names wife, Christinah; and ch. Christian, John, and others unnamed. ("Trans. from German").

Vineyard, Christian. dec. Devision of land, May, 1819. (Same as above?). Names heirs: Nicholas, Taylor, John, Peter, Nancy, William, Christian, Abraham, Elizabeth (wife James Bryant), Catherine (wife Wm. Stuart), and Tabler.

Vineyard, Christinah, dec. Inv. returned, Feb. 1805. (wife of above).

Waddle, James. Will pro. June, 1809. Names Anny McCleur.

Wadle, Martin. Will pro. Mar. 1783. Names wife, Kathrean; and ch. Benjamin, and Barbara (wife John Philsthimer).

Waggoner, James, dec. Adm. of estate—wife, Mary. Sept. 1819.

Walker, Alexander. Will pro. Aug. 1771. (Non-cupitive will.) Names sister, Martha Mineely; brother, John Walker, and to two nieces and a nephew 'in Carolina'. Witness states that he "died Saturday about ten o'clock in the morning, July 6, Anno Domini, 1771".

Walker, Henry. Will pro. ...... 1803. Names wife ....; and ch. Andrew, William, Robert, Henry, Archibald, Mary, Joseph, and George.

Walker, James, dec. Inv. returned, Oct. 1822.

Walker, William. Will pro. Sept. 1810. Names ch. John, Esther, George, James, William, ("and my dau.-in-law, Martha Walker, equally"); Son-in-law, Thomas Harmon; Grand-sons, William (son of John); and William, (son of William).

Watkins, John. Will pro. Oct. 1784. Names wife, Elinor; ch. Joel, Jonathan, Agnes, and Mary.

Wax, Henry. Will pro. 1797. Names wife, Catherine; and "children, grand-children, and son-in-law will doesn't distinguish between these): Peter, John, Henry, Jacob, Mary, Christanne, Mandilson, Hannah, Hetty, and Susanna Wax. Mary Boyer, George Etter, Henry Price, and Margaret Hatsimpillar.

Wax, Peter, dec. Inv. returned, July, 1804.

Weaver, Leonard. Will pro. July, 1800. Names ch. Conrad (eldest), Catherine, Barbara, and Leonard.

Welch, Thomas. Will pro. Oct. 1802. Names wife Jene, and sons of his son Thos.

Wernor, Daniel. Will pro. June, 1802 Names ch. George (and his son, Daniel), Mary Lake, (and her ch. Frances and Daniel); Anne Bowyar, Willia, Sarah, Philip, and Aaron.

White, Peter, dec. Apr. returned, Oct. 1810. in June, 1812, dower was assigned Mary Campbell "from the estate of her first husband, Peter White."

Whitley, Paul. Will pro. May, 1772. Names wife, Jane; and ch. Michael, Sarah, Moses, Thomas, Anne, Samuel, and Paul—all minors. Sister Ann.

Willis, John, dec. Inv. returned, July 1773.

Wilson, Elizabeth. Will pro. Nov. 1824. Names daughter, Sarah.

Wilson, John. Will pro. May 1823. Names wife, Elizabeth; and ch. Ann, Thomas, Pricilla, Sarah, James, and John.

Wilson, Matthew. Will pro. Dec. 1795. Names wife, Mary; and ch. Thomas, John (of Ky.) Steel, Samuel, Matthew, (of Ky.), Jennet, Betsy, Polly, Sally, and Nancy.

Wilson, Patrick. Will pro. Apr. 1774. Names ch. William, Alexander, Moses, Andrew, John, and Thomas.

Wilson, Richard. Will pro. Mar. 1779. Names wife, Mary; and ch. William, and Thomas.

Wilson, Thomas, dec. Inv. returned, June, 1801.

Wilson, William. Will pro. May, 1823. Names wife, Rebecca; and ch. John L., David J., and others, no or names not given.

Witturs, John. Will pro. Oct. 1805. Names wife, Elizabeth; and ch. names or number not given.

Woods, Andrew. Will pro. Aug. 1781. Names ch. James. Andrew, Archibald, Robert, Martha, Mary, Elizabeth Cloyd, and Rebekah Kelly. Wife, Martha.

Woods, Arthur, dec. Apr. returned, Sept. 1773.

Woods, Jane. Will pro. June, 1816. (Noncupative will). Died Apr. 3, 1816. Names dau. Margaret; son, William, and granddau. Demarius Flint.

Woods, Jonathan. Will pro. Feb. 1804. Names bro. James, of Montgomery Co. Nephew John Woods, so of bro. Jeremiah.

Woods, Joseph. Will pro. Apr. 1816 Names ch. Carlos, Edward, Thomas, Joseph, James

Anna, Elizabeth, Mary Stull, Martha, and Sally.

Woods, Michael. Will pro. March, 1777. Names wife, Anne, and ch. Jane Buster, Susannah Cowan, Samuel, Elizabeth Shepherd, William, Magdaline Campbell, David, Martha, and Sarah.

Wright, Peter. Will pro. Dec. 1793. Names wife, Jane; and ch. Peter, Elizabeth, Sprowl, Mary Smyth, Rebecca Kirkhead, Thomas (and his ch. Jane and James), Agnes Clark, Jane Estill, and Rachel Proctor.

Wrightman, John. Will pro. Sept. 1810. Names ch. John, Samuel, Michael, Daniel, Solomon, Mary, Christina, Lohre.

Young, Isaac. (of Augusta Co.) Will pro. June, 1818. Names bros. John White, Hugh, Thomas, David, and others, un-named.

Zeglar, Paul. Will pro. Jan. 1812. Names ch. Elizabeth, and others, un-named.

CARROLL COUNTY

Ailsworth, George, (of White Co. Tenn). Will pro......... 1843. Names wife, Susanna, and grandson, Alvis A. Swift.

Baskerville, John. Will pro. July, 1848. Names sisters, Alice G. Pringle and Polly Guthrie of Halifax Co., Va; Elizabeth Baskerville, of Sumner Co., Tenn.; Patsy Steele, of Graves Co., Ky.; heirs of sister, Fanny (wife Henry Seal, of Graves Co., Ky.; and John B. and George W. Baskerville, of Pulaski Co., Va.

Beamer, Peter, dec. Adm. settlement closed, Jan. 1843. Begun, 1835.

Bobbitt, James. Will pro. Mar. 1849. Names wife, Rosanna; and ch. William, Lacy, Ann Moore, Acenah Wheeler, Jane Moore, Patsy Williams, and Celesta Goad.

Bryant, Thomas. Will pro. Nov. 1843. Names wife, and ch. No names given.

Carico, Simms, dec. Dower assigned wife, Margaret, Dec. 1944.

Cock, James, dec. Apr. returned, May 1845.

Cooley, Benjamin. Will pro. May, 1847. Names wife, Jane; and ch. Amanda, Elizabeth, Juliann Martin, William D. James D. Polly Smith, (dec. her heirs), Nancy Smith, and Rebecca Worrell.

DeHaven, James. Will pro. Jan. 1847. Names sisters, Drucilla Shockley, Patsey McClure, Nancy DeHaven. A niece, Drucilla DeHaven dau. of Bro. Abraham. Bulk of estate to Ruth ,wife of Granville Burnett.

Durnel, John. Will pro. July, 1843. Names ch. Eli, James, Andrew J., Febe Philips, Sarah Dalton, Alley Goad, Mary Stillwell, and Hetty Dalton.

Edwards, Annuel. Will pro. Mar. 1846. Names wife, Mary; and ch. Isaac, Jeremiah, Sally and others. no. or names not given.

Farmer, James. Will pro. Oct. 1850. Names sisters, Elizabeth and Rebecca Newman; brothers, Michael and Isaac. His father was James dec.

Franklin, John B. Will pro. Oct. 1850. Names ch. Henry, Joel, Mary, John, and Robert.

Gardner, James. Will pro. May, 1849. Names wife, Tabbitha; and ch. Matthew, Andrew Washington, Sarah, Mary Jane, Elizabeth, James, William, Alexander, John, and Nancy.

Gray, William. Will pro. Dec. 1846. Names wife, Mary; and ch. R. T., and others, no. or names not given.

Jackson, William. Wil lpro. Nov. 1849. Names wife, Jemima; and ch. Patsy Spence (wife Eli), Margaret Silvan, (wife Wm.), Matson, Branson, William, Elizabeth Haley, (wife John), Sarah Ann Bowman, (wife Elisha), Mary, John, and Carroll.

Jennings, Thomas. Will pro. Jan. 1850. Names wife, Sarah; and ch. Jonathan, Andrew, William, Clifton, James, Peter, Nancy Durnell, Sally Huff~ and Mary Jane.

Johnson, Levi. Will ~ro. Mar. 1846. Names wife, Elizabeth, and ch. Charles A. Warner, Edaline, Fontlyroy, Jane, and Joseph.

Kenny, William. Will pro. Jan. 1852. Names ch. Robert, and William, and three daughters, names not given.

Lindsey, Henry. Will pro. Dec. 1845. Names wife, Elizabeth; and ch. Sally, Henry, and Elizabeth.

Lineberry, Jacob. Will pro. Feb. 1852. Names ch. Jeremiah, George, Francis, Martha Farmer, Catherine Coulson, Elizaoeth Coulson, Polly Edwards, Lorana Wilkinson, Euphreny Robinson, Joseph, and Jacob.

Mabry, Joshua. Will pro. Apr. 1849. Names ch. Lemina, Mary Francis, Jesse, and Joshua P. C.

Mallory, George. Will pro. Mar. 1846. Names wife, Elizabeth, and ch. Nicholas, Joel, Benjamin, Henry, Stephen, George, Mary Stone, and Hannah Kenny.

Moore, George. Will pro. Aug. 1843. Names wife, Nancy, and ch. Goodson M., Judidiah. Edawrd, George, Anderson, William, and others, no. or names not given.

Nester, William, dec. Estates apr. ordered Feb. 1843.

Phillips, Tobias, dec. Settlement of estate Jan. 1843. (begun in 1841).

Pratt, Elisha. dec. Inv. of estate, May, 1844.

Puckett, Woodson, dec. Apr. of estate ordered. Apr. 1844.

Quesenberry. Moses. Will pro. ...., 1843 Names wife, ... and ch. George, James, Rhoda Davis. Mila Hogan, Patsa Durnell, Sarah Phillips, Ginia Gallimore, Nancy Henson, Frederick, and Amos. Heirs of Polly Largin, (Patsa, Theopolis, Caroline and Nancy Quesenberry); sons-in-lew, John Bullard, and Aaron Largin.

Smith, Polly, dec. Apr. of estate, June, 1843.

Spence, Burwell. Will oro. May, 1844. Names wife, Nancy; and ch. Isham, Drury, Uriah, Joseph, John, James, Elizabeth, Mary, and Lewis.

Standiff, Oliver, dec. Inv. ordered, May, 1843.

Starr, Jeremiah, dec. Inventory ret. Aug. 1846.

Stephens, Peter. Will oro. May, 1849. Names John Early; his brother, James Stephens, and the widow of his dec. brother, Joseph.

Stilwell, Elias. Will pro. Apr. 1844. Names wife, Susannah, and ch. Iven, Amos, Polly, William, Vincent, and Lewis.

Wilson, Jeremiah. Will pro. Dec. 1844. Names heirs of dec. son, John (living in Selby Co. Ohio); heirs of dec. dau. Nancy Osburn, and his ch. Jeremiah, Jesse (of Ill.), Ann Hodson (of Hendricks Co. Ind.), Katherine Sickfrit, (of Guilford Co., N. C.), Mary

Hodson (of Hendricks Co. Ind.), Elizabeth Ward, and Ruth Williams, (both of Jackson Co., Tenn.).

FLOYD COUNTY

Altizer, John, dec. Apr. of estate ret. Feb., 1851.

Beckett, John. Pro. Nov. 1835. Names wife, Anna; and ch. Elizabeth Terry, Ann Walters, John, Samuel, and William.

Bird, John, dec. Apr. ordered, Aug. 1843

Booth, Abner. Pro. Sept. 1836. Names ch. Phroniah, Alfred, George, John, Catherine, Diannah, Abner, and Angelina.

Booth, Isaac. Pro. Sept. 1837. (Of Lawrence Co. Ark.) Names wife, Mary; and ch. Permelia. George, Daniel. Isaac, Freelove Powers, Anna Alexander, Zilla Sanfson, Adah Henry, Stephen, Wright, Ferguson, and Robert. The heirs of a dec. son, Abner.

Bowers, Christopher, dec. Inv. returned, Mar. 1841. (Wife married adm. of estate, Walter Richards).

Bowles, Reuben. Pro. Jan. 1844. Leaves estate to his housekeeper, Elizabeth Sowell, and her ch., Rody, George, Robert, and Lucy.

Burnett, Josiah, dec. Inv. returned, May, 1850.

Carrell, Elizabeth (of Montgomery Co.), Pro. Feb. 1832. Names ch. Ann Bright (wife of George), Elizabeth Beemer. and Fanny Baber; grandch. Emily Beemer, and Elizabeth and John Baber.

Castle, Edwards R. Pro. Aug., 1849. Names wife, Malinda; and ch. names not given

Clower, Jacob, Pro. June, 1847. Names wife, Elizabeth; and ch. Nancy, Sally, Elizabeth, Daniel, John, Jacob. and Lewis.

Cole, Joseph, dec. Inv. returned, Feb. 1832.

Conner, Andrew. Pro. May, 1845. Names wife and ch. John, William, Aaron, Nancy, Bethany, Daniel, and Nancy Ann Hoback.

Maston, Aris F., Dicey Bishop. Lucy Burks, Sarah; and ch. Luke, Ambrosa, Braxton,

Maston, Aris F., Dicey Bishop, Lucy Burks, Sarah Quesenberry, Mary Phillips, Elizabeth Wade, Eunice Wilson, and Nancy Lester.

Duncan, Blanch, dec. Apr. returned, Jan., 1831.

Duncan John, dec. Account ret. Aug. 1814.

Duncan, Thomas, dec. Apr. of estate Sept. 1847.

Earl, Timothy, Pro. Feb. 1846. Names daus, Rebecca, and Susannah.

Edwards, Benjamin, dec. Inv. returned, Aug. 1844.

Epperley, Christian, dec. Inv. returned, Mar. 1845.

Epperley, Jacob. Pro. June, 1849. Names ch. Betsy, John, Catherine, Philip, Sally, Polly, Peggy, George, and Daniel: heirs of dec. son Jacob.

Ferrow, John, dec. Apr. returned, Sept. 1832.

Gardner, James, dec. Inv. of estate ordered, Aug. 1832.

Gilham, William, dec. Inv. returned, Dec. 1831.

Goodson, Mary, dec. Sales bill, Dec. 1844.

Goodson, Robert, dec. Inv. ordered July 1834.

Goodson, Thomas, Pro. Sept. 1837. Names wife, Elizabeth; and ch. John, Elizabeth, Mary, William, George, Thomas, Charlotte Reader, Jane Kilgore, Grandch. Jane Elizabeth, and Ruth Shelor (ch. of Daniel Shelor), Samuel K. Vest (son Philip Vest), and Robert Goodson.

Goodson, Thomas, Pro. Oct. 1838. Names wife, Mary; and ch. James, George, Samuel William, and America.

Graham, Robert. Pro. July, 1834. Names wife Rachel; and ch. Luke, John, Samuel, Nancy Thompson, Mariam Howerton, Sara Reed, and Elizabeth Akers.

Gunson, William, dec. Inv. returned, Aug. 1840.

Hancock, William. Pro. Nov. 1841. Names wife, Nancy; and nine ch. only one, Elizabeth Hill, being named. Grandch. William Hill and Jenny Terry.

Harmon, Solomon, Pro. Sept. 1842. Names wife, Elizabeth; and ch. Mary Ann Phlegar Benjamin, Jacob, John, Paeter, Margate Fingar, and David.

Helms, Jacob, dec. Adm. act. returned, Aug. 1835. Names wife, Eliza; and ch. Madison S., Malinda C., Henry Dillon, and John W. Heeden.

Hewett, William. Pro. May, 1837. Names wife Elizabeth, and ch. John, Mary Jefreys, William, Sally Prater, and Elizabeth Nester. Heirs dec. dau., Aley Goad.

Holt, Spratley. Apr. returned Sept 1849.

Howard, Sarah. Pro. Dec. 1846. Names ch. Nancy Moor, Elizabeth Banks, Joseph (eldest), Major, and Ira Grandch. Richard Wells (son dec. dau. Sarah), and Sarah Banks.

Howell, David. Pro. Mar. 1851. Names wife, Jane; and ch. Rhoda; Neomi, Stephen, Charity Speklehimer, Dorcas James (of Indiana), Elizabeth Hewett, Jenny Hungate, Daniel; and the heirs of dec. sons, Dariel, and James.

Howell, Mark, dec. Apr. returned, June 1851.

Hundley, Hiram. Pro. May, 1844. Leaves wife, Martha his entire estate.

Hungate, William. Pro. Jan. 1833. Names ch. John, Richard, Clark, Nancy Sumners; also a Nancy Hungate, and her son-relationship not stated.

Hylton, George. dec. Settlement ordered, Sept. 1841.

Hylton, George. Pro. Mar. 1845. Names ch. Elijah, Archillius, John, James, Nathaniel, Elizabeth, George, Simeon, Nancy Quesenberry, and Sally. The heirs of dec. daus. Lucy Hylton, (husband was named John, and her ch. were: Betsy Ann, Tabitha, and George) and Susannah Howell.

Jones, Henry. Pro. Nov, 1831. Names wife, Cassander; and ch. Abraham J., Henry, Hannah Wade, William, Joshua, Neomy Stanley and Robert.

Kersey, Isaac. Pro. Auᵍ 1849. Names wife, Nancy; bros. John, and Thomas; a sister, Sara Billups.

King, John. Pro. Mar. 1843. Names ch. Henry Catherine, Catey, Mahala (wife Isaac Wimmer), Rosanna, Elizabeth Shilling, Nancy Burnet, and Masey Wimmer.

Kitterman, George, dec. Apr. returned Aug. 1847.

Kitterman, John. Adm. settlᵉment, Oct. 1835. Names heirs: wife. Juliann: George, David, Daniel, Henry, Philip, and Solomon Kitterman: George P. Roup, Isaac Phlegar, and John Morricle.

Lee, William, Pro. May, 1851. Names wife, Polly; and ch. John, Samuel, Alexander, William, Abel, Jonathan, Nancy, Emela, Sarah Elizabeth-all by a first wife. Polly has minor ch. but no or names or not given.

Lester, Jacob, dec. Apr. made, Mar. 1844.

Lester, John, Pro. Oct., 1851. Names wife (or Masy); and ch. Malinda Booth, Katherine Booth, Noah L. Hewline, John, Amos, Bird, and William. Grandch. George Washington, and Emmeline Lester (ch of dec. son, Jacob): two daus of a dec. son, Hewline, by his first wife, Margaret: and Juliann Weddle (dau. of Matilda Weddle.)

Peterman, George, dec. Apr. of estate, Dec. 1834.

Philips, John, dec. Apr. of estate, Jan. 1836.

Philips, Tobias, dec. Inv. returned Sept. 1832. Wife, Lucy, and minor children.

Phlegar, George, dec. Settlement of est. names heirs: Joseph, David, Rhoda, Lydia, and Elizabeth Phlegar.

Reed, George. Pro. Dec. 1837. Names wife, Elizabeth, and ch. Elijah, Mark, and others unnamed.

Richards, William, dec. Apr. returned Apr. 1843.

Sandifur, Matthew. Pro. Sept. 1844. Names wife, Mary (2nd wife); and their ch. Elizabeth, and Jane. Names only one ch. by first mar. America H. Goodson—"only child unapposed to my 2nd marriage".

Scott, John, dec. Apr. ordered, July, 1836.

Shelor, George W., dec. Inv. ordered Aug. 1841.

Shelor, William, Pro. Apr. 1847. Names wife, Margaret, and ch. Rhoda Epperley, Elizabeth Wells, Thomas G.; sons-in-law, John Goodson, and Major Howard: dau.-in-law, Elizabeth Shelor; grandcʰ., Cyrus and Matilda Goodson, Sarah A. Howard, and Rufus Shelor.

Simmons, William. Will pro. Jan. 1852. Names wife, Rhoda; and ch. James, ᶜlorina L., Harry, Erasmus M., William C., Ady Sowers. Rhoda Booth, Molly, Polly Graham; and heirs of dec. daughter, Sally Graham.

Slaughter, Martin, dec. Inv. returned, Sept. 1847.

Slaughter, William, dec. Inv. returned Sept. 1847.

Slusher, Christopher, dec. Inv. ordered Jan. 1846.

Slusher, David, dec. Inv. ordered Feb. 1840.

Slusher, John B., Inv. returned, 1849.

Sowers, John, dec. Apr. ordered, Apr. 1836.

Smith, Catherine, Pro. July, 1845. Names ch. Mary Magdelene, and others, names not given. Grandch., Catherine, Frederick, and Elijah Hylton.

Smith, Humphrey. Pro. June, 1847. Names ch. Sarah (wife James Light), Eliza Kennerly (widow), and two sons, unnamed.

Smith, Jazeb, dec. Apr. of estate ret, July, 1844. Wife now Elizabeth Iddings.

Smith, John W., and his wife, Mary, dec. Inv. ret, Jan. 1835.

Smith, Mary. Pro. Oct. 1847. Names bros. Christopher, and Henry.

Smith, Peter. Pro. Nov, 1837. Names ch. Margaret, Elizabeth, Jacob, Alexander, Peter, William, and James. The heirs of dec. son, John.

Stanley, Samuel (of Guilford Co., N. C.) Pro.

Feb, 1835. Names wife, Sarah, and ch. Richard, Joshua Isaac, Samuel, Jesse, William, Nathan, Elizabeth Pitts (wife Cadwalleder Pitts), Dorcas (wife George Hunt) Mary (W. James Meredith), and Sarah Newly.

Terry, Patience. Pro. Feb. 1847. Names Isaac (son Miles Terry); Elizabeth, Mary, and James Cole; James Craig; and Patience (wife Lewis Day).

Thompson, Elisha. Pro. May, 1848. Names wife, Nancy; and ch. Elizabeth, Nancy, Sarah, Clabourne, Willson, and Levi.

Thompson, John W. Inv. ret. Aug. 1839.

Tice, Manassas, dec. Inv. returned, Aug. 1849.

Turman, Charles. Pro. Mar. 1849. Names wife and ch. Matthew (wife, Sarah), Elizabeth (W. John Sumpter), Susan (W. John Stype. Emancipates all slaves.

Turman, George, dec. Apr. estate Aug 1839.

Turner, Peter, dec. Apr. of estate, Nov. 1847. wife, Perina.

Underwood, Eleanor, dec. Sale bill, Nov. 1846.

Underwood, Jesse. Pro. May. 1850. Names ch. Jesse, William, Sarah, Joseph B., Alexander Miseniah, Richard, Samuel, Charles, Burwell: heirs of dec. son, Isham. Wife was Eleanor.

Wade, John, Pro. Apr. 1849. Names ch. Henry Nathan, John, Olven, Anna Cox, Frances Legleman, Elizabeth Epperly, Mary Weddle, Nancy Slusher, Ally (W. Wm. Slusher), Ruth (W. James Magatha), and Isaac. Grand dau., Hannah Magatha.

Walters, Martin. Pro. Nov. 1843. Names wife, and ch. Rebecca Blackwell (W. Moses), Catherine Richardson, and five others, unnamed. Grandch, Andrew Cross. Heirs of dec. ch. Abraham. and Elizabeth Cross.

Weaver, John, dec. Sale bill, Mar. 1851.

Weddle, Andrew. Apr. ordered, Aug. 1847. His father was Benjamin, and wife, Elizabeth.

Weddle, Barbary, dec. Adm of estate, Jan., 1846: heirs, Samuel, Permelia, Ascue, Dennis and Moses.

Weddle, Jonas. Pro. Jan. 1846. Names wife, Polly; and niece, Sopia Weddle, dau. Peggy Huff.

Wells, Jane. Pro. Sept. 1836. Names Ira Howard, and Asa Howard, "trusty friends".

Wells, Richard. Pro. Sept. 1832. Names wife, Jane; nephew, Jobe Wells (and his sons, Richard and Major H.), bro, Abner (and his ch. Richard, Eli, John, Anna, Abner. and Deborah); bro. John (his ch. Isiah, Elizabeth, and Susannah). Heirs of dec. bro. Benjamin.

West, Esther, Dec. nv. returned Feb, 1840.

Williams, Philip. Pro. May, 1834. Names wife, Jane, and ch. Elizabeth, Joseph, John, James Ryley, Isabella and Sarah.

Winthers, Paulus. Pro. Dec. 1839. Names wife Sarah, and ch. Barbary, Susannah, Mary, Nancy, David, and George. Heirs of dec. daughter, Elizabeth.

Zentmeyer, John. Pro. Sept. 1844. Names wife, Barbary; and ch. Elizabeth. Daniel. John N., Catherine Priddy, Rebecca Mary Ronald, and David.

GRAYSON COUNTY

Alderman, Jacob, dec. Inv. returned May, 1824, Rosannah.

Allen, William. Estate Inv. July, 1823.

Anderson, John. Pro Aug 1830. Names wife, Mary; ch. George, William, Jonathan, Isaac, Joseph, Nancy, Milley, and Elizabeth.

Baldwin, Thomas. Pro. March, 1826. Names son, Thomas; heirs of dec. dau. Rebecca Jackson; other ch. names or numbers not given. A son-in-law, Thomas Ward; grandson Thos. Baldwin: granddau. Hannah Gallimore.

Ballard, Amos. Pro. Feb. 1850. Names wife, Jane; ch. Amos, William K; Bryon, and Ellener.

Ballard, Bryon. Pro. Aug. 1817. Names wife, Elizabeth; ch. Philip, Moses, Ruth, William, Amos, Mary Chadwallader, and Judith Cunningham.

Barber, Allen. Pro. Dec. 1849. Names wife, Jane; ch. Jeremiah, Thomas, Susannah Stone, Stephen, Margaret Houghery, Elizabeth Jackson, Joseph, Violet Hatch, Mariah Sally, Nelly Byrd, Nancy, and Malinda.

Beamer, Henry, dec. Apr. returned, Feb, 1841.

Beamer, Phillip. Pro. Nov. 1832. Names wife, Roady; ch, Frances, Teney, Ireney, Manoak (youngest son), Peter, Henry, Isaac, Richard; grand-son, Philip Edwards.

Bedwell, Robert. Pro. Oct. 1804. Names ch. Mary, Micha, Reuben, Elisha, Robert, John and Thomas.

Beeson, William, dec. Inv. returned, Feb. 1828.

Blair, Thomas. Pro. Jan. 1806. Names wife, Mary; ch. Rebeccah M'Kenzie, Nancy Bobbitt, and John.

Blevins, Jefferson, dec. Inv. returned Oct. 1834.

Bobbitt, Lacy. (A non-cup. will) Pro. Aug. 1816. Names Vincent and Matilda Bobbitt.

Bourn, Stephen. Pro. May, 1849. Names ch. William, Martin, Elizabeth Dickey Cynthia Pugh; heirs of dec. daughter, Nancy, and her husband, Spencer James.

Bourn, William, Pro. June 1836. Names ch. William, Stephen, Polly Dickenson, Milley M'Kinney, Celea Johnston, Patience Thomas, Charity Blair, Elizabeth Hail, and Frances Hail.

Bourn, William, dec. Inv. returned July 1841.

Boyer, William H. Pro. .., 1821. Names wife, Elizabeth; ch. Samuel, John, Jacob, Daniel, Margaret, Susan, Hannah, and Elizabeth.

Bremer, Lewis. Pro. Apr. 1839. Names ch. Martin, Rufus, Sally Parks, William, Sinnur, and Samuel.

Brown, John. Pro. Apr. 1815. Names ch. Mary, Nancy, Martha and John.

Bryant, John. dec. Anr. returned Feb. 1795.

Byrd, Samuel. Pro. Oct. 1820. Names wife, Mourning Bird; ch Sally. Mourning, Nancy Mollary, Betsy Swinney, John, Garnet, Polly Bourn, and Samuel.

Cannoy, Barny. Pro. May, 1817. Names wife, Catherine; ch. Polly, Betsy Ann, Sally, Jacob, John, Phebe, Caty, and Molly.

Cannoy, Jacob, dec. Apr. returned Nov. 1831.

Carlan, Daniel, dec. Apr. ret. Aug, 1822.

Clark, Stephen. Pro. Jan. 1838. Names wife, Sally (says she is his "Present wife") and ch. John H. (eldest son), Jeffry, Andrew, and Silvester.

Coleman, Peter. Pro. Sept. 1808. Names wife, Abagail; ch. Abraham, Peter, Richard, Daniel, Mary Williams, Rachel Burcham, Jerusha Wells, Charity, and Stephen.

Coltrane, David. Pro. July 1834. Names wife, Hannah; and ch. Nancy, Rachel, Hannah White, Purnia Elder, Martha Elder, Mary Roblin, Emily, and Alexander; the heirs of his dec. son, William: the sons of his dau. Nancy-viz. inv. Morgain and Clark Coltrane

Combs, Zedikiah, dec. Est. inv. Aug. 1821.

Cooley, Daniel. Pro. May 1812 Names wife Elizabeth, and ch. Tucker, and Sally.

Cooley, Peter. Pro. May 1832. Names wife, Mary; ch. Andrew, Harden, Jeffry, Benjamin, Matilda, Ruth, Elizabeth, Rachel, and Justen (a dau.).

Cornelius, Francis. Pro. June, 1840. Names sister, Rachel.

Cornutt, Archelous. Pro. June 1847. Names wife ...., and ch. Stephen B., other ch. names or number not given.

Cornutt, David. Pro. Sept. 1847. Names ch. William, James, John, Reuben, Sally Hooten, Roda Graham, Diada Sutherlin, Pheroby Anderson; sons-in-law, Thomas Sutherlin and John Anderson.

Cornutt, James. Pro. Aug. 1524. Names wife ...., and ch. Archelius, John, Jesse, Reuben: grandchildren, Polly James, Rhoda, and Aughtive—all children of his dau. Milly.

Coulson, Isaac, dec. Apr. returned, Feb. 1795.

Coulson, Jacob, Pro. May, 1811. Names wife, Elizabeth, and ch. Jeremiah, Isaac, Rachel Hill, Sarah, Jane Carlan, Pricilla Newman, and John.

Cox, David. Pro Apr. 1819. Names ch. Samuel, Ann, Catherine, Blevins, Mary Philips, Margaret Douglas, Joshua, Andrew, Alexander, and Richard.

Cox, David. Pro. returned, Feb. 1840.

Cox, Enoch, Sr. Pro. Apr. 1840. Names wife, Sally; ch. Ruth Warren, Nathan, Solomon, Onoch, Polly Love (Lady), Jesse, Jeremiah, (all these by a first wife): Joshua, Elizabeth, Nancy, and John by present wife.

Currin, George, dec. Inv. ret. Jan. 1825.

Daniel, Nathaniel. Pro. Aug. 1821. Names wife Anny; ch. Clara Morris, Nancy Allin, Tempy Allen, Polly, Sally W. Willion, Robert, Fanny Hains, Drucilla, and Nehemiah.

Davis, Daniel. Pro. Jan. 1848. Names wife, Jane; and sons, Hugh, and Elias.

Dell, Peter, Pro. Apr. 1849. Names Gaines Wright, and Peggy Delp.

Delp, Jane, dec. Inv. of estate, Oct. 1803.

Dickerson, John. Pro. May, 1838. Names wife, Mary, and sons and daus. no. or names not given.

Dickenson, Martin, dec. Dower as. wife, Poley, Mar. 1835. Following heirs named in division of land: Samuel McCamant; Hugh Gwyn; William Dickenson; James Mrrk, Jane Gwyn, Caroline Dickenson, John Dickenson, and Stephen Hall.

Dickey, Matthew, dec. Apr. ret. Jan. 1828.

Dickson, William. Pro. Jan. 1837. (Of Ruthford Co., Tenn). Names bros. James, of Madison Co., Ala: Enoch, of Rutheford Co. Tenn: John, of Virginia: two nieces, Luretia and Margaret Martin, of Va.

Dillard, Edward, dec. Inv. ret. Feb. 1827.

East, Drury, dec. Apr. ret. Feb. 1825.

East, William. Pro. Aug. 1803. Names wife, Fanny; ch. William, Mary, Rebecca, Franke Isom, Sarah Fitzpatrick, Usly Venerable, Elizabeth Biles, and Martha Jones.

Edwards, Catherine, dec. Inv. ret. Mar. 1835.

Edwards, Isaac. Pro. Aug. 1825. Names wife, Katherine; ch. John, Isaac, others names or number not given: grand-daughter, Polly Bedsalt.

Edwards, John. Pro. Aug. 1810. Names ch. Elijah, William, Thomas, Nancy Shockley, Caty Sexton, Jeny, Burk, and Easther.

Farmer, Barnet. Pro. Jan. 1818. Names wife, Elizabeth, and ch. Names or number.

Farmer, James. Pro. Aug. 1838. Names wife, Susannah; ch. Elizabeth, James, Isaac, Michael ("in the west") and Rebeccy Newman.

Fielder, Dennis. Pro. May 1834. Names wife, Delia: ch. Charles, Sarah Cox, Elizabeth, Byrd, Randel, Enos, Martha Cane, Mourning Wright, Thomas, Dennis, Delia Clark, Jane, Lucy, Samuel, States that Delia is his second wife.

Fielder, Delia. Pro. June, 1845. Names ch. Thomas J., Dennis, Delia, Jane , Lucy, Charlotte, Randolph, and Samuel K.

Fisher, Jacob. Pro. Nov. 1846 Names wife, Elizabeth: ch. Joshua, Joseph, Elijah, James, Catherine Hutzell (wife Joseph Hutzell), Hester Ann, Andrew, Ruben, and Rebecca; and the ch. of his dau. Catherine —Rebecca and Lucinda Hutzell.

Frost, John. Pro. May. 1837. Names wife, Mary ch. Ezekiel, James, Jonas, Simeon, Sally Rebecca, John, Stephen, and Betsy Farmer.

Fulton, David. Pro. May, 1822. Names wife.. ...., and ch. Ann Whitehead, Isabella, Jane Johnson, James, Peggy, and David.

Goad, Robert. Pro. March, 1836. Names wife, Jsbell; ch. Sarah Webb (wife of James A.), Aaron. Mary Nester (wife of William).

Greer, Isaac. Pro. Nov. 1813. Names ch. John, Alice, Reuben, Abigail Chew, Lydia Hunt, and Susanna Hunt.

Greer, William. Pro. Oct. 1802. Names wife, Sarah; ch. Shadrack, Aquilla, Elizabeth, Sarah, Rachel, and Hannah.

Hacklin, Peter, dec. Apr. returned, Apr. 1840.

Hail, Dudley. Pro. Feb. 1815. Names wife, Nancy; ch. Preston, Burris, Lewis, Polly, Franklin, Sally, Jesten, Olive, and Elizabeth.

Hall, John, dec. Assignment of dower to wife, Rosemond, Jan. 1850. Heirs named: Thomas, James D., Warner, John, William, Stephen, Loranza D., Johnson, and Sidney Hall.

Hail, Lewis, dec. Apr. returned April, 1802.

Hail, William. Pro. May, 1847. Names wife, Lucy; ch. Peyton, Susannah Bryant, Rosemond Dickerson, Elizabeth Whitman, Stephen, Charles, Samuel M.; sons-in-law, Morgan Bryant, John Dickerson, and David Whitman. The children of his sons Lewis and John Hall, and the ch. of his daughters, Nancy Gose, Susannah Bryant, Elizabeth Whitman, and Rosemond Dickerson.

Hall, Thomas. Pro. Sept. 1827. Names wife, Anne; ch. Eliza, Anne, Martha, Polly, Frances, Lankford, Thomas, John, and Richard.

Hampton. Wade, dec. Dower assigned wife, Elizabeth, April, 1831.

Hanks, Thomas, dec. returned, Aug. 1840.
Harden, William, dec. inv. of estate ret. May, 1803.
Harmon, Joseph, dec. Inv. of est. returned, Feb. 1826.
Harmon, Sally, dec. Inv. returned, Sept. 1818.
Harrison, William. Pro. Aug. 1844. Names wife, Rhoda; ch. William Jr. Rhoda, Bethany, Ann, Elizabeth, Arlakes (?), and Fielding.
Hays, Jacob, dec. Devision of property, June, 1837. Heirs; wife, Elizabeth; William Hays, Randolph Collins, Bailey Hayes, William Ballard, Sam'l Low, Elizabeth Hays, John Collins, John Ramey, and Andrew Ramey.
Helton, Elias. Pro. Jan. 1825. Names wife, Sarah; ch. Joshua, Jesse, Elisha, Newman, Pleasant, Alexander, Mary Beady, Sarah, Nancy, and Charity.
Hiatt, Amos, dec. Inv. ret. Jan. 1816.
Hiatt, Asher, dec. Valuation of est. Nov. 1804.
Hiatt, Joseph. Pro. March, 1826. Names wife, Keziah; ch. Sarah Montgomery, (w. Wm.) Zacheriah, Martha Montgomery, (wife of Robert); grandson, Robert, son of Wm. Montgomery.
Higgins, Vincent, dec. Apr. returned, Dec. 1849.
Hill, John, dec. Apr. ret. Feb. 1824.
Holland, George. Pro. July, 1802. Names wife, Mary; ch. Agothy .... obliterated, (begins with a B or R), Wm., Fanny Hatfield, Sarah Sope, Judith Vaughn, and Elizabeth Basham.
Isom, John. Pro. Feb. 1830. Names wife, Rebecca; ch. Spencer, and others, names or number not given; son-in-law, Jacob Toliver.
Isom, John, Jr. Pro. .... 1831. Names wife, Charity; ch. Spencer, Hugh and four daughters, names not given.
Isom, Spencer. Pro. Oct. 1849. Names wife. Susannah: ch. John. James, Isom. Cyntha Williams, Nancy, Polly, Patsy, and Rebecca; grandson, John R. Isom.
Jackson, Joseph, dec. Apr. of estate, June, 1809.
Johnson, Jaber. May, 1840. Names wife, Polly; ch. Greenberg, John, Alexander, Lewis, Elizabeth, Frances, Keziah, William, Martin, Newell.
Johnson, Jacob, (non-cuo. will). Pro. Dec. 1820. Leaves estate to ch., Martin, Holland, and John.
Johnson, Joseph, dec. Apr. returned March, 1826.
Jones, William, dec. Sept. 1825. Dower assigned wife. Sarah; ch. David, William, George, Polly Mash, Rebeckah, and Batsy.
Judson, Joseph. Pro. Dec. 1815. Names ch. Hannah Powell, Mary Morgan, Deborah Jessop, Jane, Rebeccah Cock, and Ruth.
Keith, George. Pro. Nov. 1804. Names wife, Nancy: ch. George, Daniel. Polly Porter. Susanna Porter. Prudence Porter; grandson, Robert Keith.
Kenny, John. Pro. Nov. 1820. Names wife, Eleanor; ch. William, Elizabeth, Margaret, Jane Miller, and Eleanor Dick.
Kester, Eli, dec. Apr. of estate. June, 1841.
Larrew, Richard Pro. July, 1831. Names wife, Hannah: ch. Anna, Mary, Joel. and Jesse.
Leonard, William, dec. Inv. of est. ret. Oct. 1826.

Linton, William. Pro. April, 1827. Names wife, Mary Ann; (" his money coming from the United States"), children, Mary, Margaret, Hayns, Ann, and John.
Long, William. Pro. Feb. 1822. Names wife, Caty; ch. Margaret, William, George, Caty, Henry, Samuel, Polly, Betsy, Benjamin, Lewis, and John.
Lundy, John. Pro. May, 1831. Names wife, Rebecca; ch. Rachel, Amos, Ruth, Aaron, Joanna, Anna Darlin, Achasa Wells, Edith Woods.
Lundy, Richard. Pro. May, 1822. Names wife, Mary; and ch. Azariah, Daniel, Isaac, Richard, Rhoda Beamer, Mary Harrold, Elizabeth Davis, Samuel, and Sally Davis.
Mabry, Charles, dec. Apr. of estate, June, 1840.
Mallory, Thomas, dec. Dower assigned wife, Nancy, June, 1824.
Martin, Joshua. Pro. April, 1845. Names wife, Patsy; and ch. George W. Eliza A., Matilda G.
Martin, William. Pro. May, 1848. Names wife, Jane; and ch. John, Clasy Moore, James, Martha, Elizabeth, William, and Henry.
McCleur, James. Pro. Oct. 1821. Names wife, Martha; and ch. Samuel, Mary, Tabbatha, Martha Hill, and William.
Morris, Isaac, dec. Inv. of est. returned Mar. 1826.
Murphy, John. Pro. July, 1848. Names wife, Rebecca; ch. Lewis, Polly Moore, Greenbury, Timothy, Anna......... Todd, and Lorenza. Note: Settlement of estate shows the following additional children—Tamsay, James, Peggy, Manala—sons-in-law Aaron Simcock, and Armstead Todd.
Newman, Conrad, dec. Inv. returned Aug, 1806.
Ogle, Thomas Pro. March, 1803. wife, Elizabeth, and ch. John, Thomas, William, James, Sarah Sargen, Elizabeth Jennings, and Hannah Rioheson.
Oglesby, William. Pro. March, 1839. Names wife, Nancy, and ch. unnamed; a brother, Macajah Oglesby.
Ott, Silvester. Pro. June, 1803. Names ch Frederick, Margaret, Lovice, Mary, and Catherine.
Parks, James. Pro. Feb. 1806. Names wife, Hannah, and ch. Elizabeth, James, John, and Andrew.
Parsons, Robert. Pro. May, 1846. Names wife, Anna; ch. James, Robert, Solomon, E....
........, William Isaac, John W.. Polly (wife of Stephen Jones), Nancy (wife of Benjamin Lawrence), Sarah (wife of John Davis), Anna (wife of Sam'l Baker), Isabella Austin.
Patton, Thomas, dec. Dower assigned his wife, Isabella. Feo. 1823.
Perkins, Aria. Pro. Jan. 1828. Names wife, Polly; ch. David, Christopher L., William, M., Matilda, Linnia M. Daniel, and Morrison.
Perkins, Stephen. Pro. Aug. 1844. Names ch. Samuel, Isaac, Timothy, John B., Amy, Lucy, Rebecca, Linton, and Stephen; grandchildren, John Wesley, Mary Ann, Amy, Joshua, Lucy, Kinsey, (ch. of son Timothy); Stephen C. Russell, Philip Francis Russell, and James Fleming Russell; son-in-law, James Thomas.

Phillips, Tobias. Pro. March, 1809. Names wife, Peggy; ch. Hannah Henson, Franky, Nancy, Rachel, John, Joseph, Molly Quesenberry, Jany Cock, Wm. Thomas, Robert, Richard, John, a..d Joseph

Phillips, Tobias, dec. Inv. returned, Feb. 1840.

Philips, James. Pro. Aug. 1814. Names wife, Peggy; ch. Polly, John, James, Thomas, and Luchresy.

Phipps, Benjamin, dec. Inv. returned, June, 1841.

Phipps, James, dec. Apr. returned, Oct. 1840.

Phipps, Joseph. Pro. Sept. 1848. Names wife, Nancy; ch. Ireny Young, Larkin, Gincey Cox, Alexander, Emily Thomas, Peggy Pugh John McCleman, Maryann, Jane, Drucilla, Joseph, and Nancy; grandson, Jackson Phipps.

Pool, William. Pro. Jan. 1808. Names wife, Mary; ch. Edward, Isaac, John, William, Sary Cole, Mary Bedwell, Elizabeth Hanks, Rebekah Thomas, and Nancy Pool.

Pool, William. Pro. Aug. 1837. Names ch. Piety, Mourning, and Rebecca.

Porter, James, dec. Inv. returned April, 1830.

Prichard, James. Pro. April, 1796. Names wife, Jane; ch. Sarah, Rebeckah, James, Rhoda, Jessse, Thomas, Joseph, and William.

Pugh, David, dec. Inv. returned Oct. 1807.

Pugh, David, dec. Dower assigned wife, Sarah, June, 1823.

Pugh, William, dec. Dower assigned wife, Lucy, Jan. 1839.

Rector, Jacob. Pro. July, 1811. Names wife, Mary; ch. Peter, James, Jesse, Bennet, Elizabeth Hays.

Reeves. George, dec. Valuation of property ret. May, 1811.

Reppard, Milkion. Pro. April, 1827. Names brothers, John. Stephen. Peter and Jacob; sisters, Elizabeth, Mary Murrilstvorin, Roosy Beck, and Elizabeth. Bulk of property to Jacob Hines—relationship not stated.

Ring, Hester, dec. Inv. returned, Dec. 1840.

Ring, Martin, dec. Inv. returned. Oct. 1839.

Ring, Martin, Pro. July,1811. Names wife, Caty and ch. Molly Shuler, Elizabeth, and others, no. or names not given.

Roak, Charles. Pro. Nov. 1849. Names wife, Isabel; and child, Polly Malena.

Roberts, William, dec. Apr. of estate, April, 1841.

Roberts, William. Pro. May. 1838. Names wife, Lydia; and ch. John, William, James Johanthan, Isiah, Fielden B. Zachariabus, Febe D., Jestianna Pool, Sally Porter, Elizabeth Hackler, Phebe D., and Eliza Ann (youngest child).

Robinson, John, dec. Apr. returned, Oct, 1832.

Rowark, Timothy, Pro. June, 1811. Names wife Rachel; ch. Moses, Tomothy, Charles, Rebecca, William, Mary Raimey, and Sarah Miller.

Rudy, Jacob. Pro. Jan. 1818. Names wife, Julvanna: and ch. Jacob, George, Stephen, David, Polly, Barbary (dec.), and Betsy Howell.

Rudy, Julia. dec. Inv. returned, Oct. 1825.

Russell, Charles. Pro. Oct. 1807. Names ch. Charles, Channey, Channel, Barnet, Erwin, and Clerky (a girl).

Sage, James. Pro. March, 1820. Names wife..:, and ch. Samuel, James, Mary, Loves, Margaret, Sampson, Esther, Ann, Charles, Elizabeth, and William.

Schooley, Samuel. Pro. May, 1832. Names ch. Margaret, John. Benjamin, Nathan, Elizabeth, and Samuel.

Scudders, John. Pro. July, 1833. Names wife, Noncy; ch. Polly, Phebe, Sythe Jones, and Nancy Carter.

Stanfield, George. Pro. Aug. 1827. Names Jane and William Combs and their son, Zedekiah; a nephew, William Harvey; brother, William Stanfield, and sisters, Lydia Hiett, and Mary Harvey.

Starr, John. Pro. Feb. 1834. Names ch. Lewis, Jeremiah, and Sally Hylton.

Stone, Jeremiah. Pro. Aug. 1827. Names ch. William, Stephen, John, Betsy Hail, Micajah Nancy Hambleton, Richard, and Jeremiah.

Stone, Micajer. Pro. Sept. 1842. Names wife, Nancy; and ch. no. or names not given.

Stone, William, sr. Pro. April, 1843. Names wife, Elizabeth; ch. John, Jeremiah, William, Anna Atkins, Susanna Davis, and Menoah.

Southerland, Alexander. Pro. Nov. 1843. Names wife, Peggy; ch. Thomas, John, Joseph. Jane, Fillis, Peggy, Polly, Barbary, and Phebe.

Southerland, John, dec. Apr. of estate, April 1844.

Southerland, Polly. Pro. Sept. 1845. Names mother, Isabella; brothers, Jonson, Samuel, John. Leonard, Francis Morgan; sisters, Elizabeth, and Isabella

Taylor, Simpson. Pro. April, 1824. Names wife, Batty; ch. William, John, James, Benjamin, Nathan, Mary, Becky, and Fenley (dau).

Thomas, Owen. Pro. Dec. 1814. Names wife, Mary Ann; and bro. Stephen.

Thompson, Catherine. Pro. Mar. 1820. Names ch. Robert Hammock("by my first husband William Mammock"), Margaret Thompson. Jane Simmons, Mitchel, David, Nelson. and John Thompson. States that her husband Robert Thompson, is dead.

Wadsworth, Jeremiah. Non-cup. will. Pro. Jan. 1824. Names bros. Abner, and William

Ward, Nathan. Pro. March, 1803. Names wife ...., and ch. Wiliam, Wells, Nathan, and Enoch.

Watson, Michael. Pro. July, 1841. Names ch. Terry, Davis. Margaret King, Sally McCoung, and Nancy Spence.

Welch, John, dec. Apr. returned. Feb. 1827.

Wells, Barney, dec. Apr. June 1822.

Wells, John, dec. Inv. returned. Feb. 1803.

Wells. John. Pro. July, 1846. Names wife. Rhoda: ch. Allen, Melinda Perkins. Sarah F. Ross, Synthia Johnson, Ceroline Ellrod, Margaret. Hazy M., and Fidella.

Williams, William. Pro. Aug. 1828. Names wife, Nancy; ch. Jonathan, and others names or no. not given.

Worrell, Esau. Dec. 1838. Names wife, Nancy: ch. Esau, Jesse, Sally, Nancy, and others. not named; James W. M'Clure, relationship not given. (Note: other ch. were: William. Amos, John, Peter.)

Worrell, James. Pro. Jan. 1802. Wife, Barbary;

ch. Esau, and six others, names not given; a step-son, John Pennick. (Note: James Worrell's first wife was Elizabeth........, their ch. were: Esau, James, Sarah, Amos, Catron, and two others.)

Wright, Richard. Pro. March, 1820. Names wife, Seney; and ch. Susannah, John, Sally, and Hiram, (all these by present wife): William, Richard, Abraham, Jacob, Neomy Surginor, Polly Harper, Sally Kirk, Betsy Anderson, Rachell Cornutt, James, Susanna, and John—by first wife.

Young, Ezekiel. Pro. June, 1800. Names wife, Ruth: ch. Robert, Joseph, Ezekiel, William, and Thomas. (A non-cup. will.)

Young, Timothy, dec. Apraisment ret., Sept. 1841.

Young, William. Pro. Apr. 1809. Na. wife, Caty and ch. Mildray and Joseph.

PULASKI COUNTY

Addair, James. Appr. of estate returned Apr. 25, 1845.

Allison, Charles. Will pro. May 5, 1846. Names brothers, Robert. John, and Francis; sister, Martha Childress, and nephews. Charles (son of Robert), Robert (son of John), and James Cole (son of Stephen Cole).

Anderson, Christinah. Will pro. Sept. 10, 1846. Names ch. Elizabeth Woolwine, Peggy Gray Eve Songer, Polly S. Barger, Jacob, John, and William; the heirs of her deceased ch. George, Nancy Shepherd, and Susan Hues.

Anderson, Jacob. Will pro. Apr. 7, 1842. Names wife, Christinah, and ch. Elizabeth Woolwine, Peggy King, Polly S. Barger, Eve Songer, Susannah Hughes, Jacob. John, William, Nancy Shepherd, and Malinda.

Baskerville, GeorgeW. Will pro. Oct. 1849. Names wife, Nancy B., and ch. Cynthia M., Martha A.. John B,. and Spencer.

Bell, John. Guardian Appt. for his ch. viz: John. Hannah, Elizabeth, Peyton, Nancy. and Sarah.

Bish. Peter. Will pro. Apr.7. 1842. Names wife, Phebe. and ch. Isaac. Abraham. Samuel, Emmanuel. David. Catherine Cain, Susan Gordon. and Sally Bish.

Black, John. Will pro. Aug. 8. 1850. Names ch. Polly Jones. Martha Warden. James John, William, Hugh; and the heirs of his dec. son. Robert.

Caddall, Nancy. Apr. returned, Aug. 24. 1841.

Calfee, William. Bill of sale returned, Oct. 1851.

Carnahan. John. Will pro. May 6, 1858. Names ch. Mary Ann, Isabella E.. Thomas S. William B.. Samuel W., and John N.

Carper, John. Will pro. July. 1845. Names ch. Frederick, Henry: leaving to each of them "One draw of my pension money."

Cloyd, David. Will pro. Apr. 6, 1848. Names ch. Joseph, Gordon, James M. Son-in-law. David McGavock, (and HIS ch. David and Sarah). Grandson, David Kent.

Cloyd, Thomas. Will pro. Oct. 1849. Names wife, Polly; and ch. David and Lucinda—wife of Gordon Kent. (Thos. Cloyd owned Dunkards Bottom.)

Cook, Henry. Will pro. June, 1849. Names

wife, Polly; and ch. Alexander, Henry and George.

Crockett, James. Apr. returned, July, 1842.

Davis, Sarah, (Of Reed Island) Will pro. Feb. 1855. Names ch. Joseph, William, Hugh, Joannah Sloan, and the heirs of a dec. son, James. Speaks of her mother, Joannah Stephens, dec. Names grandchildren, Sarah, William, Rhoda, and Joannah, all ch. of her son Joseph. Mentions land inherited thru her dec. brothers, Peter and James Stephens. Also grandson, James, son of Hugh.

Draper, Margaret. Will pro. Feb. 1859. Names ch. Margaret P., Jane C. Tate, John S., and Susan S.

Eaton, Crozier. Will pro. Dec. 18, 1857. Names wife, Keziah; bros. Joseph, David, Edward, sister, Elizabeth Williams; the ch. o this dec. sister. Nancy Scott, and of his dec. brother, Richard.

Farmer, Martha. Sale bill returned, May, 1850.

Fulkner, Elizabeth. Inventory returned, Feb. 1841.

Galbreath, Catherine. Will pro. July, 1857. Names ch. Mary A. Rayel (wife of John), William, Bartram, Sarah Mitchell, and the widow, Catherine, of her dec. son, Thomas.

Glendy, John. Will pro. Jan. 1858. Names wife, Polly, and ch. William I., Margaret Darst, Mary A., Elizabeth D., Robert, and Gilly A.

Gordon, Giles. Apr. returned, Sept. 1841.

Guthrie, Richard. Will pro. June 6. 1850. Names wife, Elizabeth; and ch. Elizabeth Stone, Cassandra Graham, Eliza Munsey Hetty Munsey, Cynthia Wygal, John, William, and the heirs of his dec. son, James G. (viz. Harry, Hugh, Elizabeth, Lieza. Margaret, Jane, Almina. and Stephen R.)

Guthrie, Elizabeth. Inv. returned, Aug. 7, 1851.

Hoge, Elizabeth. Will pro. July, 1851. Names ch. John Matthew, Matilda Loyd, Rebecca McIntyre, Nancy R., Margaret Hickman George D., Moses H., Eliza Long, Jane Peterman; grandch. Edward Thomas, Mary Elizabeth, Margaret Virginia(ch. of Moses) and Thomas and Rachel (ch. and a daughter, unnamed).

Hoge, John. Will pro. Aug. 1847. Names wife, Elizabeth; and ch. Moses H., Eliza A. Long, Jane Peterman, Matilda Loyd, Nancy. Margaret R. Hickman, John, Rebecca McIntire. Grandch. John M. Thomas, and Rachel Peck (ch. of a dau. unnamed); Margaret Jane, John Montgomery, James Thomas, and Ann Eliza (ch. of daughter unnamed).

Howard, Alexander. Account ret. Aug. 1854.

Hurst, John. Will pro. Aug. 1855. Names ch. Delila Nunn, Elizabeth Herrill, William, Mark, John, Matida (wife of Hillary Ashworth); the heirs of his deceased ch. Jesse, Catherine Holly, and Thomas.

Hurst, William. Inv. returned, Dec. 1839.

Ingram, Aaron. Apr. returned. Oct. 1839.

Jordon, Michael. Apr. returned, Feb. 6,1857.

Lesley, William. Apr. of estate returned Dec. 9, 1852.

Martin, Robert. Will pro. May 5, 1859. Names

wife, Elizabeth; and ch. David, William, Robert, and John.

Medidith, Jeremiah. Will pro. Oct. 1855. Names wife, Sarah Ann: and ch. Belllveidra, Florence Jane, Salome Snow, Cephus Shelburn, and Jeremiah.

Miller, James. Will pro. May 20, 1855. Names ch. William, Andrew, Alsey Raines, Joseph, Eliza, Polly, John, and Samuel.

Miller, Margaret. Will pro. Feb. 8, 1849. Names ch. William, Elizabeth Vermillion, Witnesses: Daniel, Elizabeth, and John K. Miller.

Miller, Daniel. Apr. of estate returned, July 25, 1840.

Monnahan, Martha. Will pro. Dec. 7, 1854. Names ch. John Bell, William Hellums, David Heavener, Catherine Scott, and Ann. Also Ann's ch. Martha, George, David, and Elizabeth.

Morris, Robert. (of the City of Philadelphia) Will pro. May 21, 1804. Names wife, Mary; ch. Thomas, Henry, Hetty Marshall, Maria Minor(?).

Morris, Mary, (Of Philadelphia) Will pro. there Feb. 1, 1827. Names ch. Thomas, and Henry.

Meurhead, Andrew. Will pro. May 7, 1857. Names wife, Jane; and ch. George W. F., John C., Benjamin F., James W., Crozier E. Ralph, Edwin W., Sarah, Joseph M., Samuel C., Andrew, Nancy Vernillion. and Martha.

Patton, Henry. Will pro. June 7, 1849. Names wife, Eleanor; and ch. William. Stephen. Peggy Ingram, Nancy Neal, Thompson. Austin, Maria Cummings, and the heirs of his deceased ch. Calvin, Eliza Thorn, and Lucinda McDonnald. (These ch. were by a first wife, named Martha).

Peck, Jacob. Will pro. Feb. 9, 1854. Names ch. Louisa Robinson, Catherine Weeks, Christopher, Nancy Burton, Fadela Burton, Mary Brookman, and William.

Pierce, James A. Will pro. Aug. 10, 1854. Names ch. David S., and others, names or number not given. Wife living, but unnamed. Brother William. Ch. all minors.

Pryor, John (Of City of Richmond) Will pro. there, March, 1823. Names wife, Elizabeth Graves; nieces, Dorcas Bryan, Elizabeth Taylor, Rebecca Taylor, Charlotte Morrson (of W'msburg, Va.), Elizabeth Hazelwood: nephews, Thomas Pryor, and Archer, William, Romert, John, and Pryor Hankins. Friend, Lewis Burwell. First wife was named Ann.

Raines, Meridith, Apr. returned, Jan. 1841.

Rankin, James. Will pro. June 7, 1849. Names wife, Mary. At her death all his slaves were to be freed, and his entire estate sold " and proceeds to be used to remove said slaves to some free state, and to fix them comfortably."

Shepherd, Will pro. Dec. 1840. Names wife, Elizabeth.

Sifford, Harmon. Apr. of estate? Dec. 9, 1852.

Steel, James. Sale bill, Dec. 5, 1852.

Swope, John. Will pro. Apr. 10, 1856. Names sisters, Elizabeth Sheets, Catherine Powell, Rosanne Smith, and his brother Henry's sons, Peter and George.

Tipton, William. Will pro. Mar. 6, 1856. Names wife, Patsey, and ch. number or names not given. Witnesses James S. Tipton, and others.

Trollinger, John. Will pro. Nov. 5, 1840. Names wife, Elizabeth; and ch. Henry, John, Sally Trinkle, Polly Elliot, Elizabeth Jordon (wife Michael), Phebe Shifflebarger. Also a half sister, Elizabeth Lincos. (Han another dau. Not named in will— Eliza Durham).

Turner, Francis, dec. Apr. of estate, July, 1847.

Vermillion, Rizen. Will pro. June 6, 1854. Names wife, Amelia;, and ch. Edwin H. John H., Uriah, Thomas B., James H., Mary A. and Sarah E.

Wygal, James. Will pro. May 4, 1854. Names wife, Mary, and ch. James G. Rhoda, Mary Trollinger, Thomas C., and Nancy Yost.

Wygal, John. Will pro. Dec. 5, 1844. Names wife, Catherine, and ch. Birdine (a son), James, Sebastain, Jefferson, Abraham, Jackson, Ann, Sarah, Keziah, and Mary E.

Wysor, Henry. Will pro. Feb. 1844. Names ch. James, Henry, Polly Dills, Elizabeth Grayson, and Caty Blackwell.

ROANOKE COUNTY

Abbott, Andrew. Will pro. Apr.17, 1848. Names wife, Mary; and ch. Thomas, Harriet Lord, Hannah Jones, Cassandra Niday, Mahalay Hufman. Witnesses: John Abbot, Richard Abbott, and James Abbott.

Abbott, Richard. Will pro. Aug. 1848. Names bro. James, and nephews, Ormandine W. Abbott, Linkilan C. Abbott, son of bro. James.

Blain, George Washington. Will pro. Mar. 29, 1843. Names wife, Catherine; son, James Calloway; and brother, James Blain.

Branch, Ann M. Will pro. Dec. 1854. Names Dr. A. L. Reed, and Laura, his wife.

Brubaker, Henry. Will pro. Nov. 1848. Names wife, Sarah; ch. Christian, Jacob, Jonathan, Joel, John, Joseph, Abraham, Isaac, Benjamin, Henry, Catherine Barnhart, Elizabeth Beekner (wife of John), Nancy Worts, Madgalene, Elias and Moses (Two last, youngest).

Burnett, Joshua. Will pro. Sept. 1852. Names wife, Sarah; and ch. Joshua, Jonathan, Obediah, Mahala Robertson, Jane Smelser, and Elisha.

Burnett, Sarah. Will pro. Dec. 1854. Names her brother, Absolum Smith, and his wife, Martha.

Bush, Peter. Will pro. Aug 1841. Names wife, Alice, and children, Thomas J., Elizabeth Stewart (wife of James Stewart), William, Robert, Criffin, and Sarah Gish, wife of Wm. Gish).

Burns, Samuel. Will pro. Nov. 1838. Names wife, Sophia: and ch. Elizabeth, John, Mary, and Geo ge.

Carney, Charles. Will pro. Aug 1853. Names wife, Susannah; and ch. Ann Womack, William, David, Robert E. Jones ("my lawful son"), and Eliza Pace.

Chapman, John S. Will pro. Dec. 1854. Names wife, Nancy; and ch. Nathan, and others, unnamed.

Cirkle, John. No probate date; will made Nov. 25, 1839. Names wife, Elinor; and ch. ch. Lewis, Margaret Roof(?), Eleanor Gordon, Elizabeth Dulaney, Phebe Windle, Rutha Hagy, and John.

Coffman, David. Will pro. Jan. 1855. Names wife, Ann Elizabeth; and ch. Susan Owens, Mary M. Parnnel, Lenna F. Butt, Margaret Pannel, Lydia L. Bear, Palomy W. Butt, Frances N., Moses, Rhoda I. Coffman, Esther A. Coffman, Clarissa R. Coffman, David M., and John.

Craig, Robert. Will pro. Dec. 1852. Names wife, Malinda.

Deaton, Frances. Will pro. Feb| 1849. Names husband, John; sister, Sophia Hubbard, and Francis A. Deaton, Hardyman Deaton, Polly Goodwin, Hester Day, Eliza Horn, and Sally Temple; the last six, relationship not given.

Denton, Phebe .Wil pro. Apr. 1853. Names John Neff; relationship not stated.

Dillard, ... Will pro. Mar. 1853. Names wife, Elizabeth.

Dillard, Louisa. Pro. Aug. 1850. Names friends only.

Dingledine, Balser. Pro. Apr. 1850. Names wife, Susan; ch. Elizabeth Saver (of Indiana. Land to her children by her first husband, John Moore; has no children, this date by Saver); Susannah W. McCauley her son, William): and a step-son, Dan'l Hiteman, of Rockbridge.

Farley, William. Pro. June, 1846. Names wife, Fanny W. and their children, Seth. George, Ann Hazletine, Sarah Mildred. The following children by his first wife: James H., Joseph, Catherine Read (wife Wm.), Nancy Baldwin (wife Wm), Eliza Kenzie (wife Christian), and Emeline Angel (wife Jacob).

Francesco, Lewis. Pro. Sept. 1850. Names ch. George, John, Lewis, Garner, Jacob, Cnristopher, Sarah Hypes, Mary Hughs, and Elizabeth, and Margaret Francesco. Says he is " Old, and well striken in vears."

Frantz, Peter. Will pro. Aug. 1854. Names wife, Sarah; ch. Catherine Grill, Mary Fullhart, Nicholas, Ann Fullhart. Magdaline Christ, Elizabeth Trout, Sallv Garst, and Barbary Howard.

Gaines, Kemp. Will pro. June, 1851. Names wife, Mary: sons, Thomas and James; grandson, William, the son of James.

Garman. Adam. Will pro. June 1854. Names wife, Catherine: and ch. Sarah, Joseph, Flizabeth Eanoch, Nancy Everly, John, and Magdalene Bean.

Garst, Frederick. Will pro. Sept. 1842. Names wife, Magdalene; and ch. Frederick, Anna Gordon (wife of Richard). Magdalene Echols (wife, Joseph). Elizabeth. Jacob, John. Peter George, William, (whose wife left him in 1822.)

Garst, Jacob. Will pro. March, 1854. Names wife, Magdalene: and ch. Jacob F., Philip, Flizabeth, Hannah, Abraham. Catherine Hartman, Christina Akers, Anna Clarke, Rosena Hinkle. Nicholas Christian, Eve Shewly, Mary Lockett, and Lydia Mason.

Gish, David, Sr. Will pro. Mar. 1849. Names wife, Polly; and ch. David, John, George.

Greaso, Jacob. Will pro. Feb. 1844. Names

wife, Sarah; and ch. James, Elizabeth, Katherine Mateson, George Hawkins, John Sarah, Rebecca, and William.

Green, John W. Will pro. Mar. 1846. Names Mrs. Nancy Preston, Mrs. Washington Smith (the dau. of Capt. Phillips), Nancy Kyle, wife of Col. James Kyle; and his brothers,. Thomas, Timothy and Samuel Green.

Grounds, George. Will pro. Jan. 1842. Names ch. George, Peggy Lowry (wife, James), Catherine Britt; grandson, George Moyers (son of David Moyers), son-in-law, William Fizer, and Lewis Circle.

Hall, William. Will pro. Nov. 1849. Names wife, Nancy; and ch. James, David, William, John, Lewis, Archibald, Allen, and others, no. or names not given.

Hannan, Esom. Pro. Mar. 1843. Names wife, Mary; ch. Mary Ann Cooper, Thomas, William, John, Esom, Edward; and the ch. of his dec. ch. Elizabeth Hutcheson (3ch.); Jane Baker (3 ch.); and Abraham.

Hannah, Patterson. Pro. June, 1853. Names wife, Edney, and ch. Martha Jane Harvey (wife, Matthew—has ch. Irvin Patterson Harvey); Julia Ann Rorer (wife, Ferdinand, and ch. Patterson Hannah Rorer).

Hartman, John. Pro. Nov. 1846. Names ch. John Abraham, George Lewis, Catherine Snider, Elizabeth Kittinger, Susanna Kittinger, Sarah Brooks; also, Mary, the wife of his dec. son, Michael.

Hartman, Luke. pro. Aug. 24, 1839. Names brother, George.

Henry, William. Pro. Jan. 18, 1841. Names wife, Bethsheba; ch. John, William, Mary Owens, Anna Johnson, Sarah Wartz, Sophia Neighbors, Rachel Owens, Margaret Leffler, Catherine Henry, Helen Hartman, Stephen, and Magdalene Henry.

Howbert, George. Pro. Jan. 24, 1839. Names wife, Elizabeth M. and ch. Samuel Esther, Jacob, Michael, John, Moses. George Elizabeth, Catherine, Esther, Mary, Barbary, and Ann.

Howell, James. Pro. Sept. 1852. Names Jesse, Abner, and Ann Howell, Sally Armintrout, Elizabeth Baker, Jemima Gaultney, Mary Gaultney, (all ch. of Jesse Howell dec.) Relationship unstated. The ch. of his dec. sister, Mary Gish—Elizabeth Love, Sarah Holleman, Hannah Williams. The ch. of his dec. Sister, Ruth Gish—William, David and Mary Mangus.

Johnson, John. Pro. July, 1845. Names wife, Elizabeth; and ch. Susan, William, John, Joseph, George, and Elizabeth.

Keagy, Henry. Pro. Aug. 1944. Names ch. Henry, Christopher, Jacob (wife, Mary), Anne Frantz (husband, Henry M. dec.

Ledgerwood, Rebecca. Pro. Aug. 1849. Names Nephew, Wm. Hall, and his wife, Nancy. Sisters, Margaret, and Mary Ledgerwood, brother, William, and Wm's. daughter, Nancy.

Ledgerwood, William. Will pro. Mar. 1852. Names wife, Sally; and ch. William, David, Joseph, and Nancy.

Leffler, Joseph. Will pro. April, 1853. Names ch. John, Aaron, George, Richard, Susannah Butler, Patsy, Nancy, and Joanna (and HER son, John.)

Lewis, Jane. Will pro. Mar. 1846. Names ch. John, Samuel (wife Frances), Sarah Woods (husband James S.), Emeline Ingles, Rlizabeth Pitzer (husband, Madison), and the heirs of her dec. son, William, unnamed

Longhorne, James C. Pro. in orphans court of Marengo County, Ala., Aug. 3, 1841. Names mother and father—Catherine and Wm. Langhorne, and their heirs—no. or names not given.

McClanahan, Lucy. Sept. 1854. Names cn. of her son, Charles (says their maternal grandfather named White). Other ch. mentioned, but not named.

Miller, Martin. Pro. Dec. 1852. Names wife, Catherine (was widow of Dan'l Brillhart). Catherine 2nd wife—married June 4, 1846, both having ch. by first marrige. His ch. Magdalen e,Betsy, Esther, Jacob, Susan. (All married). Also gives names of Dan'l Brillhart's ch. (by Catherine) Sam'l, Dan'l, John, and Joseph Brillhart.

Moomaw, Philip. Nov. 1844. Names wife, Catherine, and ch. Mark B., Jacob, Harriet, Catherine, Susannah, John B. Philip R., and David R.

Murray, James. Pro. Sept. 1840. Names wife ....; and ch. William, James, Susan, Samuel, Elizabeth Carper, Elijah.

Muse, John. Pro. not given. Dated Mar. 5, 1845. Names wife, and ch. names not given.

Muse. Sarah. Pro. Aug. 1849. Names stepgrandson, Thomas R. Muse. Mentions a sister, Elizabeth Revere, dec.

Neal, Owney. Pro. Mar. 1854. Names bro. Armstead Neal.

Nighdy, George. Pro. Aug. 1847. Names wife, Eve; and ch. of his dec. son, John. States he has 4 living children.

Oliver, Charles. Pro. July, 1851. Names his son, Yelverton, and son's wife Catherine.

Oliver, Matilda M. Pro. August 1866. Names great nephew and nieces—Chas. Wesley Corter, Mrs. Rebecca T. Bruce, and Kate M. Carter. Also a sister. Mrs. Eliza Walton, wife of Thos. Walton.

Pace, Valentine. Pro. Dec. 1851. Names ch. James E., and others, unnamed.

Pefely, Henry. Pro. June 1842. Names wife, Susannah; and ch. Henry, Solomon, Jonathan, Catherine, Jacob, Elizabeth Smith, Susannah, Solome, and Daniel.

Pettit, William. Pro. Feb. 1854. Names wife, Catherine; and their daughter, Sarah Frantz, wife of Thornton Frantz. Names following children by a first marriage: Catherine, James, Elizabeth F. Stoutmire (W. Berry Stoutmire).

Pouge, John. Pro. Feb. 1840. Names wife, Margaret; and ch. John, Elijah, George, Joseph, and Jane.

Renn, John, Pro. Sept. 1854. Names ch. Isaac, Catherine, Lydia, Elizabeth Shanks (widow of Michael Shanks).

Riffey, Thomas. Pro. Sept. 1854. Names ch. Flizabeth and George.

Robinson, Thomas. Pro. Jan. 1849. Names wife, Sara; and ch. John, Zaceriah, Zirkle, Polly, Tempy, Allen, Lesner, Ruth, Joseph, and Perry.

Richardson, William. Pro. Aug. 1850. Names wife, Nancy; and ch. Lucinda Duckwilder (W. Joseph), Greenbury, Elizabeth Mays,

John S., Phoeby, Joel, Nancy, and Sarah.

Sarver, George H. Pro. Nov. 1845. Names wife, Susan; his mother, Catherine and father, James; and three children - David Callahan Sarver, Demascus Lafayette Sarver, and Harriet Ann Catherine Sarver.

Sarver, James Pro. March, 1840. Names wife, Catherine, and ch. George, Rebecca, and Linny Shawver.

Shepherd, Michael. Will Pro. Jan. 1849. Names wife, Barbara; and ch. Catherine Hickler (land in Tenn.), Elizabeth Evans, John Spesard, Susan Brown (land in Mo.), and Mary Thomas (Wife of Elias).

Smith, Jacob. Will Pro. Sept, 1847. Names ch. Adeline Caldwell, Eliza, Alexander, Margaret, Jacob, John W., Mary Carper, Susan Eggleston, Agnes, Sarah Jane, Abbot, Elizabeth Ann, Lydia Carper, dec; and Floyd.

Smith, John. Will pro. Dec. 1854. Names ch. Washington, John, Polly Humphreys, Milly Gordon, Sarah Riddle, Ned, Nancy Thompson, Philip, Rhoda (and HER son Dick), Absolum (wife, America S.), John, and Melly McGeorge.

Snyder, Christain. Pro. Feb. 1845. Names wife, Margaret, and boy, Jonathan Mason.

Snyder. Henry. Pro. May, 1843. Names wife, Catherine; and ch. Henry, John, Charles, William. James ,Jacob, Polly Anderson, and Peggy Mitchell (wife of Thos.).

Statler, Jacob.Will pro. Dec. 1843. Names wife, Margaret, and ch. Abraham, and a son-in-law, David Roan.

Stover, Mary. Will pro. July, 1848. Names ch. Nancy, Jacob, and others, names or number not given.

Thrasher, Fredrick. Will pro. July, 1852. Names wife, Nancy, and ch. James Foster, Gibson Gaines, John, Paul, Robert, and others,no. or names not given.

Thrasher, Paul. Will pro. Jan. 1849. Names wife, Sally, and bros. and sisters - Susan DeLong (wife of Geo.), Fredrick (and his son Pau)l John (and his son Paul), and Polly Short.

Trout, George. Pro. July, 1850. Names wife ...., and ch. John, Ann (w. Michael Airheart), and others, no. or names not given.

Trout, Michael. Pro. Oct. 1853. Names ch. Alexander, Thompson, Margaret Grady. To follownig ch. of his dec. son, John: Noah, Harvey, David, Alexander, Eliza Sloan, (W-Chas), Lucinda.

Walton, William, Sr. Pro. Feb. 1845. Names ch. Wm. Leftwich, Elizabeth Sherman, Polly Otey, Salley Leftwich, Lucy McClanahan, Lucinda Bane, Maria Lewis, and Malinda Craig.

Webster, Henry. Pro. June, 1854. Names ch. John Jane, Elizabeth, Sarah, David, Robert E. Jones("my lawful son") and Eliza Pace.

Winger, Joseph. Will pro. Aug. 1840. Names ch. Martin, Michael. Others, but no. or names not given.

Woods, Joseph (ofCataba) Will pro. July, 1848. Names wife, Prissela, and her ch. by a first marriage (James, Samuel, Alen, and John McConley); also sons, William, James, of his brother, John. (Note: Pricilla was widow of Geo. McConkley.).

—61—

Woods, Joseph (of Burlington) Will pro. June 18th, 1849.
Woods, Sarah, his wife. This is a joint will.
Names John Ballard (a grandson); Martha Arseman, and their heirs; Elizabeth Wooril, and her heirs, Jane Campbell, and her heirs; Polly Ballard; Sarah Brosius; Susan Brown).

REVOLUTIONARY PETITIONS.

The requirements of the 1818 pension law was very rigid, and comparitively few soldiers applied under this law, but that of 1832 was easier, and by 1840 the last restrictions were removed, and practically all who served could secure compensation.
The petitions, from which briefs below were taken, were most interesting historical documents, and but for the prohibitive cost of printing, I would have included the entire petition in these records.

BEDFORD COUNTY

Boyer, Henry. Makes oath that he was a leut. and adjutant in the first regiment of light Dragoons. Filed May,1818.
Dason, Jonathan, agde 57. Enlisted in 1779 in a regiment called the Deleware Blues; was in battle of Brandywin,e and served until reg. was disbanded in 1783. Filed May, 1818.
Dole, David, aged 64. A private under Capt. Thos. Henson, commanded by Col. Ewing, from Baltimore, Enlisted July 4, 1776.
Lafoy, John, aged 55. Enlisted 1777 under Capt. Jones in Surry County, N. C., in the fifth Reg. of N. C. Served three years and discharged in Charleston, S. C. Filed Sept. 1818.
Lockhart, Philip, aged 65. Enlisted 1781, under Capt. Scott; continued in service 18 months, as waggoner. Filed May 1818.
Melson, Charles. Enlisted Feb, 1776 under Capt. Scruggs in Bedford county; discnarged Feb. 1778, at Valley Forge. Filed May, 1818.
Merrit, Majer, aged 57. Enlisted as private in 1st regiment if light dragoons, in the year 1781: served until disbanded in 1783.
Rose, Thomas. (See Thomas Rose Wharton).
Smith, George, aged 78. Enlisted in 5th under Capt. Scruggs; served later in Morgans' riflemen. Served three yrs. Filed 1818.
Tyler, Daniel, aged 61. Enlisted 1776 under Sam'l Cabell in sixth Va. reg. Delivered his discharge to Col. David Saunders. Filed 1818.
Whorton, Thomas Rose, aged 70. Enlisted under Capt. Booker 2nd Va. reg. Was taken prisoner at Charleston (Written "Thos Rose", and the 'Wharton' written above in another writing). Filed Aug. 1818.

All petitions filed in the order books of Bedford of 1832-34, are all worded as follows: "John Mitchell, an applicant for a pension under the act of Congres of June 7th,, last, this day appeared in court and filed his declaration in the following words, and figures,- viz- "State of Virginia etc..........".
And the court do hereby declare that after the investigation of the matter, and after putting the interrogotories prescribed by the war department, their opinion is that the above named applicant was a Revolutionary soldier and served as he states."

FILED 1832 and 33

Adams, Henry
Andrews, Thomas
Arthur, William.
Austen, Richard.

Baily, Phillip.
Brown, Henry.
Brown, Thomas.

Campbell, Anthony.
Cundiff, Isaac.

Davenport, William.

Franklin, Samuel.

Graham, Michael.
Grooms, Jonathan.

Hackworth, Thomas
Hambleton, James.
Hancock, Samuel.
Handcock, Samuel.
Holley, John.
Hudnall, John.
Hunter, Francis.

Jones, Stephen.

Lambert, Charles.
Lambert, George
Lowry, John.

Markham, John.
McConnahan, ...
Meadows, Benjiman.
Mitchell, James.
Mitchell, John.
Moore, Robert.

Nelms, Charles.

Oliver, William.
Otey, Jacob.
Overstreet, Thomas.

Powell, Aaron.
Pullin, Thomas.

Reynold, Lewis B.
Robertson, Benjamin.

Saunders, David.
Shepherd, Jacob.
Stiff, James.
Swain, George.

Tracy, William.

Wild, Jesse.
Wilks, Samuel.
Williams. Rogers.
Woods, Francis.

BOTETOURT COUNTY

Alverman, John. Filed Sept. 1832. Born Culpeper Co., Va. 1757. Vol. in Capt. Henry Hills co. Discharged because if illness, 1781.
Britt, Jacob. Filed Feb. 1832. Aged 78. Enlisted inCapt. Thomas Boyers' Co. under Col. Archibald Cambell, in1779. In battle of Guilfcrd Courthouse N. C. Discharged at Cambden, S. C. after 18 mo. service.
Camper, John. Filed Aug. 1832. Aged 82.Enlisted at Stovertown, Shanadoah Co. Va., under Capt. Nevill, and Col. Richard Campbell,Lived there until close of war, when removed to Botetourt.
Harrison, James, Filed Dec. 1832. Aged 76. Enlisted 1776 in Augusta Co. Va., under Capt. John Thornton, and Hugh Mercer. Was discharged at Valley Forge, N. J.
Lemmon, Jacob. Filed Aug. 1832; Aged 70. Enlisted in Augusta Co. Va. in Capt John Tate's Co. Was marched to N. C. in Col. Howard of Md. company. In battle of James Town, and acted as sergeant. Service against Indians in 1782.
Sizer, John. Filed Jan. 1833. Born Baltimore Co. 1759. Served under Capt Ewell, and in service for three years.
Tate, John. Filed Sept. 1832. Born Aug. 6, 1761. Served under Capt. Patrick Buchanan, and Thomas Smith; was at Yorktown.

The following petitions were not entered in order books in full, but were all worded as follows:

"Peter Brickey exhibited a declaration in open court, it being a court of record for Botetourt county, in order to obtain a pension under the provision of the late law; and having made oath according to the law, it is ordered copied and transmitted to the War Dept. with the certificate of the court required by law, the provisions of the law having been complied with by the applicant."

Brickey, Peter, filed Dec. 1832.
Crist, Philip. Filed Aug. 1833
Henry, William. Filed Jan. 1832
Hewett, John. Filed Feb. 1833.
Lee, Zacheriah. Filed Aug. 1833.
Miller, Valentine, Filed Mar. 1833.
Ridley, George. Filed Dec. 1832.
Spangler, Charles. Filed May, 1833.
Treanor, James. Filed Nov. 1833.
Wisong, Fiatt. Filed May, 1833.

FLOYD COUNTY

Edwards, Benjamin. Filed Sept 1832. aged 75 on March 15, 1833. Served in 1st Va. reg. under Col. Chas. Dabney. Entered in 1778, and served for duration of war. Saw surrender of Cornwallis. Lived in Goochland Co., Va.

Howell, Daniel. Filed Sept. 1832; aged 75. Served under Capt. Walter Crockett, and lived in Botetourt County, Va.

GRAYSON COUNTY

Auburn, Stephen. Filed 1832. Aged 71. Enlisted as substitute for his father, Jacob Auburn, in 1776 in Winchester township, Pa., Co., Pa., Was under Capt. Stephen Bloom. Moved to Guilford Co., N. C., and to Grayson Co., in 1797.

Austin, Isiah. Filed 1832. Aged 73. Enlisted under Capt. James Shepherd; Leut. Edmund Kirby, and Ensign James Williams. Served as an Indian spy, and lived in Surry Co., N. C. Was born Feb. 18, 1759.

Beasley, Benjamin. Filed 1832. Aged 70. Was resident of King and Queen Co., Va. Entered just before surrender of Cornwallis.

Bryant, Thomas. Filed 1819. Entered at Portsmouth, Va., in 1777, under Capt. Edward Moody in the artillery. Was from Randolph Co., N. C., Had wife and four children.

Byrd, William. Filed 1819. Aged 67. Enlisted in Capt. Morton's Co., fourth Va. Regiment in Prince Edward Co., Va., in 1777.

Clark, Stephen. Filed 1832. Aged 70. Resided in Goochland Co., Va., when enlisted under Capt. Edward Cuid. Was born there in 1762, leaving in 1805.

Cloud, William. Filed 1832. Aged 82. Vol. as private in 1776 under Capt. James Lynn, being in Patrick county, Va.

Comer. John. Filed 1832. Aged 79. Enlisted in Amelia County, Va., as minute man under Capt. Lewis Jones. Born Caroline Co., Va., July, 1753.

Cox, James Filed 1832. Aged 69 yrs, and 9

mo. Born Fort Chiswell, Wythe Co., Va., and enlisted under his father, Capt. John Cox. Was engaged in building a Fort on Peach Bottom Creek; also served as Indian spy.

Fielder, Dennis. Filed 1832. Aged 76. Enlisted under Capt. John Clard in 1776. A resident of Prince Edward Co., Va.

Fielder, John. Filed 1832. Aged 80. Enlisted under Capt. John Clark in 1775 or 6. Born in Goochland Co., Va., in 1752. and resided there until 1791.

Frost, John. Filed 1832. Aged 76. Enlisted in N. J., under Capt. Mitchell. Total service was 5 yrs. Was one of Washington's guards at Valley Forge. Born in Morris Co., N. J., in 1756.

Gardner, James. Filed 1835. Aged 77. Enlisted under Capt. Benj. Hopkins, June 1777, in Sussex Co., N. J. Born Apr. 20, 1758. Moved to Sanadoah Co., Va., at close of Rev., then to Franklin, Montgomery, and Grayson.

Jones, John. Aged 86 on 3 of Apr., 1832. Entered under enlisting master, Andrew Armstrong, in 1776. Born Morris Co., N. J. Was in Henry Co., Va., when enlisting.

Mortimer, James. Filed 1832. Aged 76. Enlisted in 1776 with Leut. Woodstock in N. Y. Artillery. Was in battle of White Plains, Monmouth, and at surrender of Cornwallis.

Phipps, Benjamin. Filed 1832. Aged 70. Was born Guilford Co., N C., in 1761. Captured by British. Enlisted under Capt. Anderson Thomas in N. C.

Rose, James. Filed 1819. Aged 66 or 67. Enlisted with Capt. Mazard. in 2nd Reg., of Va. Artillery for 3 yrs. Has wife and 3 ch.

Shinault. Benjamin. Filed 1824. Aged 64. Enlisted in Bedford Co., Va., under Capt. Samuel Terrill. Family consists of wife. aged 65, and two grown daughters.

Spence. Burrell. Filed 1832. Aged 69. Entered under Capt. Alex Gordon, and Col. Malbry, in year 1781. Born Bedford Co., Va., and resided in Surry Co., N. C., when entering service.

Spencer, Timothy. Filed 1832. Aged 74. Entered service in 1776, under Capt. Smith, of Salem, N. C. Marched against Cherokees. and helped rescue a Mrs. Bean. States "the reunion between Mrs. Bean and her sons, Wm. and Robert was most touching."

Thomas, Jonathan. Filed 1832. Aged 69. Entered in 1782 under Cp. Wm. Douglass in Orange Co., N. C. where he was born. and resided until 1789. Moved to Montgomery Co., after discharge. Born Nov. 19, 1762.

Vaughan, William. Filed 1832. Aged 71. Born Hanover Co., Va. Entered just before battle of Guilford Courthouse. Entered as substitute for William Vaughan, sr. under. Capt. Philip Webber.

MONTGOMERY COUNTY

Anderson, Jacob. Filed Sept. 3, 1832. Was 74 years of age July 5, 1832. Enlisted under Capt. Chas. Thurston in Frederick Co., Va.

Bane, Edward. Testified Oct. 1832. for Dan'l Howe, saying that he, Edward Bane, served about 1880 or 82 on a tour of one month under Dan'l Howe, on an expedition against the Indian on Blue Stone.

Bell, Robert, Sr. Filed Aug. 5, 1833. Was 74 yrs. on Dec. 25, 1833. Enlisted in Montgomery County, Va., where he has lived since age of three yrs. Served under Capt. Aaron Skaggs, and Col. Preston.

Berry, James. Filed Sept. 1833. Age 82. Enlisted in Pa., in 1777, under Capt. Robt. Sample.

Bott, Frederick. Filed Nov. 7 1832. Was 75 yrs., last October. Enlisted in Dinwiddie Co., Va. in 1779, under Col John Bannister.

Caddall, Samuel. Filed Aug. 7, 1832. Aged 73. Served with Capt. Paxton in 2nd. Va. Reg. in Rockbridge Co. Knew Washington well.

Carmikel, Thomas. Filed Oct. 1832. Aged 70. Enlisted Feb. 1778, in Lancaster Co., Pa. under Capt. Peter Shoffner—also under Capt. John McLenon.

Charlton, Francis. Filed Feb. 4, 1833. Aged 74 on the 3rd. day of same month. Enlisted in Montgomery Co., Va., under Capt. Joseph Cloyd, at the time Fort Donnelly, on Greenbrier River was attacked.

Cline, Peter. Filed Sept. 3rd., 1832. Aged 76 yrs. Enlisted 1774 with Capt. Henry Miller, in 12th. regiment of Pa., line. Served until 1776. Resided in Redingtown Barracks, Pa. Now in Pike Co., Ky.

Cooper, John. Filed June, 1818. Enlisted as a drummer in Chester Co., Pa., in Co., commanded by Capt. Marshall. Age not stated.

Fergus, Francis. Filed Oct. 1834. Aged 81. Enlisted in Bucks Co., Pa., Aug. 3rd., 1776, under Capt. John Jamison.

Ferguson, Robert. Filed ...., 1818. Aged 67 yrs. Enlisted October, 1777 in Woodstock, Shanadoah Co., Va., under Capt. Bell. Served three years.

Hall, Asa. Filed Apr. 1833. Aged 74 in June, 1832. Enlisted in Duchess Co., N. Y., March 2. 1776. Was at the taking of Burgoyne, by Gen. Gates. Served under Capt. Nathan Price, also Capt. John Salisbury.

Hall, Jesse. Filed Jan. 1833. Aged 72, on last March. Enlisted Feb. 1776, under Capt. Nathan, Pierce. in Duchess Co., N. Y. Was in Battle of White Plains.

Henderliter, Michael. Filed June, 1818. Enlisted under Capt. Henry Crest, in 2nd., Pa., Regimental line.

Hollv, Peter. Filed Oct., 1832. Aged 79. Enlisted in Fredrick Co., Va., under Capt. William Fields.

Howe, Daniel. Filed June 3. 1833. Aged 75. Was a leut. under Capt. John Lucas, and Col. William Preston. Entered in 1776, served until 1781. Re-inlisted, and was at surrender of Cornwallis.

Kelsey. Thomas. Filed Sept. 1832. Enlisted in Ulster Co., N. Y., May 1776; was under Capt. Sam'l Clark; also under Capt. Peleg Ranson. Aged 78 yrs.

King, William. Filed Jan., 1833. Aged 77, or 78. Enlisted in Bedford Co., Va., under Col. Charles Lynch, in Capt. Robert Adams company. Speaks of his father, Avra King, who was drafted, also in Bedford, by Capt. Charles Watkins. Names following officers: Leut. Wm. Revnolds; Capt. Isaac Webb; Capt. James Calloway; Ensign Wm. Triplett; and Col. Benj. Logan.

Lawrence, Thomas. Filed June, 1833. Aged 69 yrs. Enlisted in N. Y. under Capt. Joshua Champlain, and Col. James Vanderburg. Served two yrs. Removed to Montgomery Co., Va. about 1783.

Lewis, Andrew. Aged 74. Enlisted in Botetourt Co., Va., Feb. 1, 1777, under Capt. Joseph Crockett. Speaks of his father, Gen. Andrew Lewis.

Lucas, John. Filed Aug. 1832. Aged 83 yrs. on July 15, 1832. Engaged in service as Capt. of Malitia in the regiment commanded by Col. Wm. Preston. Resigned at the conclusion of the war.

Meacham, Elijah. Filed, 1818. Aged about 60 yrs. Enlisted in Hartford Co., Conn., Jan., 1778, under Capt. John Harmon.

Heacham, Ichabod. Filed, 1818. Aged 63. Enlisted in Hartford Co., Conn., Dec. 1775. Served until 1781.

Miller, Daniel, Sr. Filed Sept. 1832. Aged 85, next December. Enlisted in Augusta Co., Va., in 1775, or 76, under Capt. Michael Bowyer: Leut. Robert Brammel, in Col. James Woods, regiment, and served two years.

Mitchell, John. Filed Sept. 1832. Aged 72. Enlisted in Amelia Co., Va., in 1776; was fife major, under Capt. Roland Ward.

Peterson, Eli. Oct. 1832. He testified for Daniel Howe, saying that he served with him —Daniel Howe—one month in guarding the frontiers of Virginia in the Revolutionary war, on East River Island Creek

Ratliff, Nathan. Filed July, 1833 Aged 71. Entered May, 1778, under Capt. Joshua Wilson. Henry Bishop of Floyd Co., Va., certified that he served with him

Simpkins, James. Filed Aug. 1832. Aged 74 yrs. on last November. Enlisted in Botetourt Co., Va., in 1777, under Alexander Breckenridge and Leut. Sam'l Lapsley.

Teaney, Daniel. Filed Sept. 1832. Aged 75. Enlisted in New Providence, Philadelphia Co., Pa., in 1776, served until 1777. Subs. for his brother, Henry Teaney. Names of officers, Capts. John Edwards; Arnold Francis; Wm. Davis; James Tate; John Dickey. Cols. Faniel Heister; John Bull; last two tours were in Augusta Co., Va.

Thomas, Giles. Filed, Aug. 1832. Aged 68. Served in Maryland State Regiment, enlisting July 24, 1780.

Walters, John. Testified that he served in same regiment and company with Francis Charlton. (See Charlton, Francis).

Waracott, Richard. Filed June, 1833. Aged 81 years. Entered in 1777; served four years under Col. Henry Skipwith, in Pa.

Wheatfield, George. Filed Sept. 1832. Aged 107 years old. Served in Virginia State Line, with Capt. McGuire, and Leut. Col. Bell. Lived in Frederick Co., Va.

Wysor, Henry, Sr. Filed Mar. 1833. Drafted 1781; served in General Morgans' Rifle Regiment, under Capt. Berry, in Frederick Co., Va.

ROANOKE COUNTY

Applications for pensions by the widows of Revolutionary soldiers.

Henry, William. "On motion of Basheba Henry it is ordered to be certified by the clerk of the court of Roanoke county that she is the widow of William Henry, dec. who was a pensioner of the United States, and who departed this life Sept. 21, 1840 (States below above that Henry drew pension of $28.22 yearly).

Querry, Elisha." On motion of Sarah Querry at is ordered etc....... that she is the widow of Elisha Querry who was a pensioner of the U. S. and who departed this life June 20, 1834.

Riffey, George. 'On motion of Catherine Riffey it is ordered etc. that...... she is the widow of George Riffey who was a pensioner of the U. S. and who departed this life Sept. 12, 1840.'

Williamson, John. 'On motion of Martha Williamson, it is ordered etc—— that she is the widow of John Williamson, who was a pensioner of the U. S. and who departed this life Feb. 15, 1828.

From Order Book 1840-41.

OLD TOMBSTONE RECORDS.

BEDFORD COUNTY

From private cemetery.

Buford, Harry. Born Sept. 19, 1751. died Dec. 31, 1814.

Buford, Mildred Blackburn (wife above). Born Feb. 22, 1753; died Apr. 19, 1802.

Buford, Pascall G. Born Feb. 14, 1791; died July 23, 1875.

Buford, Frances. (Wife above). Dau. Elizabeth Matthew and Isaac Otey. Born Mar. 17, 1798; died Feb. 5, 1882.

Cobb, Margaret Buford. Born Feb. 17, 1835; died Feb. 24, 1920.

Williams private cemetery

Slicer, E. J. Born Jan. 11, 1813; died May 7, 1887.

Williams, Albert G. Died 1850; aged 49.

St. Stephen's Church

Alexander, Bettie, wife Col. Gerard Alexander. Died 1870, aged 81.

Alexander, Gerard. Colonel in War of 1812. Died 1853, aged 81.

Beale, Ann R., wife Charles T. Beale. Born, May 6, 1816; died July 30, 1841.

Bullock, John. Born, July 1, 1779; died Apr. 30, 1858.

Bullock, Mrs. Lucy, wife John Bullock, esq. Born Feb. 27, 1787, married July 19, 1810; died, Jan, 29, 1865.

Bullock, William Galt, died Jan. 21, 1896, aged 81.

Burton, Damares; wife Jesse A. Burton. Died May 28, 1853, aged 44.

Cobbs, Marion; died May 30, 1877, aged 76.

Cofer, Rev. James. Born July 1, 1811; died May 20, 1897.

Cofer, Mary E. (wife above). Died Apr. 10, 1879, aged 60 years.

Gardner, B. G. Died June, 1851, aged 87.

Griffin, Margaret; born Mar. 27, 1817, died Aug. 31, 1896.

Hutter, Edward S. Born Sept. 9, 1812; died Nov. 7, 1875.

Hutter, Emma W. Born Oct. 25, 1822; died July 9, 1870.

Moore, William F. Died May 25, 1887, aged 56.

Moseley, Ann W. Wife of Gen. William Moseley, treas. of Va. Died Feb. 18, 1845, aged 81.

Radford, Elizabeth. Wife ,William Radford. Born Nov. 13, 1785; died Feb. 9, 1858.

Radford, Octavia DuVal; wife Col. R. C. W. and dau. E. W. and Ellen J. DuVal. Born Dardenalles, Ark., Jan. 31, 1829. Married at Fort Smith, Ark., Aug. 8, 1848; died Bedford, Dec. 8, 1877.

Radford, Rebecca, wife William Radford, Sr., of Richmond. Died 1820, aged 59.

Radford, Col. R. C. W. Died Nov. 2, 1886, aged 64.

Radford, William. Born Jan. 27, 1787 in Goochland Co., Va., married Elizabeth Moseley. Apr. 3, 1803 in Powatan Co., Va. Died Jan. 5, 1861 at Woodbourne.

Note: There are also several Radford ch. buried here.

Schenk, John. Born May 10, 1799; died Dec. 17, 1844.

Scott, Elizabeth R. wife Jos. W. Born Dec. 27, 1794; died Oct. 9, 1857.

Scott, Joseph W. Born Dec. 19, 1781, died Nov. 26, 1845.

Slaughter, James C. Died May 30, 1889, aged 77.

Smith, John, Jr., Died in Miss. May 25, 1852. aged 62.

Smith, Martha Ann (wife above). Died Apr. 16, 1840. Born June 7, 1811.

Whitten, William B. Born Nov. 23, 1792; died March 31, 1840.

BOTETOURT COUNTY

The following records have been taken from stones in that old cemetery surrounding what is supposed to be the oldest Presbyterian Church to be found west of Augusta Co., Virginia. This Church lies within the limits of Fincastle.

Ammen, Benjamin. Born Dec. 10, 1800; died June 15, 1869.

Ammen, Naomi (wife of above) Born Mar. 29, 1810; died Nov. 1, 1886.

Anderson, William Col. Born June 2, 1764; died Sept. 13, O. D., 1839.

Anderson, Annie, (wife of above) Born Frederick Co. M., Dec. 29, 1770. Died July 23, 1848.

Anderson, Robert. father of Col. William Anderson, Died July 22, 1825, aged 86 years of age.

Anderson, Margaret. Mother of Col. William Anderson. Born 1738; died July 26, 1810.

Anderson, Chas. William. Born 25th day of March, 1815; dept. this life, July 1840

Anderson, John Thomas. Born Sept. 21, 1343; died Sept. 23, 1846.

Anderson, Mary (dau. of Wm. T. and C. M. Anderson) Born Feb. 23, 1840; died Jan. 1841.

Anderson, Joseph W. Maj. Born Dec. 19, 1836; killed in Battle of Bakers' Creek, May 17, 1863.

Anderson, John T. Born April 5, 1804; died Aug. 27, 1879.

Anderson, Cassandra M. (wife of above) Born Jan. 2, 1807; died Jan. 1, 1837.

Baker, Caleb. "Dept this life 27 May, 1855, in the 57 year of his life".

Bell, James Capt. "Died Dec. 6, 1826 in the 78 year of his age."

Bell, John C. Born Aug. 6, 1827; died July 13, 1858.

Brugh, Lewis. Born July 11, 1818; died Oct. 9, 1856.

Brugh, Elizabeth (1st wife of Lewis) and daughter of Capt. Benjamin Carper died Nov. 7, 1845, aged 27 years.

Brugh, Ann G. (2nd wife of Lewis). Died Dec. 30, 1905.

Carper, George, son of C. W. and Elizabeth Carper. Born Jan. 10, 1832; died Sept. 22, 1842.

Carrington, Gene Edward G. Born in Halifax Co., Va., Jan. 4, 1790; died Mar. 7, 1855.

Caldwell, Alice Gaunt. Born in 1807; died July 19, 1875 (Lies with Gaunt family).

Dame, Betsy. "Here lyeth the body of Betsy Dame". Born Mar. 11, 1797; died Apr. 1797.

Dakin, Jacob. Born Mar. 15, 1837; died June 30, 1877.

Ferguson, Joseph. "A native of the County Tyrane, Ireland, and emigrated to this Country in 1820; dept. this life Sept. 28, 1830, aged 36."

Ferguson, Jane (wife of above). Born Dec. 1812; died Feb. 16, 1838.

Ferguson, David Kyle; son of Joseph and Jane Ferguson. Died Sept. 9, 1846.

Ferguson, Robert H. "Young merchant of Fincastle". Died Sept. 11, 1853, aged 24 years, 5 months and three days.

Ferguson, Sarah; died Nov. 7, 1855.

Ferguson, Lydia; daughter of Joseph and Jane Ferguson. Died June 19, 1824. "She was a young Christian."

Ferguson, Margaret. Died Apr. 4, 1943

Fletcher, Jacob, Capt. Born Dec. 24, 1791; died Sept. 24, 1873.

Francis, Charles. Died Oct. 22, 1855, aged 29 yrs. 6 mo. 13 days.

Gaunt, Joseph. Born Sept. 14, 1815; died June 12, 1901.

Gaunt, Susan (wife of above). Died Mar 19, 1907, aged 81 yrs.

Giles, Martha Peyton, wife of Senator Wm. B. Giles. Born Oct. 1777; died July 1808.

Gordon, Margaret Mrs. Died Mar. 19, 1819, aged 19 yrs.

Harvey, Patsey. Died 1795.

Harvey, Matthew, Col. Died Sept. 19, 1823; aged 62 yrs.

Harvey, Magdalene, consort of Matthew Harvey; born July 24, 1775; died Apr. 20, 1845.

Harvey, Virginia B. "Youngest daughter of Matthew and Magdalene Harvey. The wife of Col. Thomas B. Mitchell: died in 37 year of her age".

Hickok, Morris. Born Amherst Co., Va., Feb. 5, 1795; died May 5, 1873.

Hickok, Sarah B. (wife of above). Born Feb. .... 1795; died Feb. 17, 1871.

Hancock, John. Died 2nd. Aug. 1798.

Kollock, Maria, Mrs. Wife of Dr. L. Kollock, (No dates.

Kyle, William. " A native of Ireland. Died June 25, 1832; aged 50 yrs." (Lies in plot with Fergusons).

Legan, Robert, "Who for nearly thirty years was a minister of the Presbyterian Church". Died Oct. 9, 1828, aged 50 years.

Logan, Margaret (wife of above) died May 10, 1830, aged 49.

McFerran, Martin. Born Nov. 28, 1858; died Nov. 23, 1886.

McFerran, Penelope W. (wife of above). Died Sept. 13, 1880.

Mays, Frances Jane. dau. Fletcher and Ellen Mays. Died June 8, 1853, aged 18 years.

Mays, Ellen; Consort of Fletcher Mays; died Mar. 23, 1840; aged 31, yrs. and 3 mo.

McPheeters, S. B. Rev. Born Sept. 18, 1819; died Mar. 9, 1870.

McPheeters, E. C. (wife of above). Born Sept. 6, 1827; died July 22, 1872.

Neville, John. Born Dec. 12, 1773; died Feb. 17, 1838.

Neville, George. Born Oct. 22, 1821; died July 22, 1855. "A Clerk of Bot. Co. Court".

Patton, Marcus G. Born Nov. 12, A. D. 1825; died Jan. 4, A. D. 1859.

Patton, Sarah A. (wife of above). Born May 5, 1830; died Oct. 16, 1852.

Patton, William. "Merchant of Fincastle". Was born in County Down, Ireland, A. D. 1790; died Sept. 21, 1851. "Survived by an affectionate wife, and three infant sons".

Patton, John A. Son of Wm. T. and Fanny R. Patton. Born Oct. 24, 1859. died 1860.

Patton, Mary W. (dau. as above). Born Feb. 23, 1840; died Jan. 22, 1841.

Patterson, Sam'l, son of Robert Patterson. Died Mar. 20, 1791; aged 20 yrs. 1 month.

Patterson, Timothy M. M. D. Died Sept. 5, 1828, aged 47 yrs., 28 days, 1 month.

Price, John H. Born Oct. 20, 1832; died Mar. 6, 1865.

Price, George S. Born June 1, 1841; killed in battle Feb. 1863.

Price, John D. Born Sept. 3, 1797; died Sept. 5, 1855.

Price, Eliza Hudisill (wife of above). Born Apr. 25, 1805; died Mar. 15, 1899.

Peck, William. Born Oct. 1796; died May 11, 1882.

Peck, Lumima(wife of above). Born Oct. 12, 1809; died Mar. 12, 1876.

Pitzer, Virginia E. L. Died Sept. 10, 1854, age 31 yrs. (see Weich).

Shanks, Thomas. Born July 15, 1796; died May 7, 1849.

Shanks, Mary T. (wife of above) Born Sept. 20, 1797. Died May 10, 1845.

Shanks, Grace M. Wife of Thomas Shanks. Died 26 July, 1833. Aged 88 years.

Shanks, Mary G. Died July 7, 1833, aged 26 yrs. Wife of Dr. Lewis Shanks and mother of six children.

Smith, Robert Parks (1849-1852) and Charles Wm. (1848-1848) Children of I. B. and R. A. Smith.

Steele, Sallie M., wife of J. M. Steele. Born Apr. 1, 1837; died Sept. 9, 1880.

Simpson, Levi. Born Mar. 5, 1809; died July 12, 1869.

Simpkins, John, M. D. Died July 15, 1838, aged 25 years.

Stoner, Louisa G., daughter of Sam'l and Catherine Stoner. Born Oct. 5, 1842, died June 3, 1852.

Thomas, Francis, Born 23 Mar. 1743; died June 27, 1835.

Thomas, Grace, consort of Francis Thomas. Born Mar. 14, O. S. 1741; died Sept. 6, 1829

Turner, Sarah Ann, R. Consort of D. P. Turner. Died May, 1842, aged 30 years.

Thrasher, William P. Born June 7, 1718 (?) Died Jan. 15, 1800 (Dates uncertain).

Thrasher, Mary. Wife of above. Dates obliterated.

Williams, Charles Dr. Born Dec. 27, 1806; died Nov. 10, 1870.

Williams, Jane Mrs. wife of above. Died at 83 yrs. (No other dates).

Williams, Maria Jane (dau. of two above) Died Jan. 1863, aged 10 yrs. 15 days.

Wax, Catherine Mrs. Daughter of Michael Bock, dec. and relic of Henry Wax. Born Dec. 15, 1784.

Word, Emily Messler, and Helen Early, twin daus. of Wm. M. and Helen D. Word; Born Nov. 1846, lived one month.

Word, Cyril Earnest. Son of above W. M. & Helen Word; born and died 1856.

Woodson, Nancy S. Dau. of H. W. and M. Bowyer. Died Apr. 2, 1845, aged 22 yrs.

Woodson, Mary Susa. Dau. of H. W. and M. Bowyer. Died Dec. 2, 1825.

Woodville, Mary Sophia, wife of James L. Woodville, and daughter of Col. John Lewis. Died Wed. the 8 June, 1836, aged 39 years.

Taken From Cemetery Near Daleville

Coffman, Jacob; died Sept. 29, 1838; aged 63 years and 9 months.

Denton, Anna, wife Robert A. Denton. Born Aug. 12, 1812; died Jan. 26, 1897.

Denton, Robert A. Born Sept. 30, 1815; died June 2, 1880.

Frantz, Jacog; Born July 7, 1801; died Aug. 19, 1861.

Gish, Abraham, born Apr. 25, 1769; died Mar. 15, 1859.

Gish, Abraham. Died Apr. 4, 1839, aged 44 yrs. 3 mo.

Gish, Anna. No dates—very old.

Cish, E. No dates—very old.

Gish, Jacob, born Feb. 5, 1761; died Aug. 2, 1836.

Gish, M. Born June 30, 1795; died Jan. 29, 1831.

Gish, Mary 2nd wife Abraham; born July 19, 1786; died July 19, 1823.

Gish, Rosannah, 1st. wife Abraham; born .... 1796; died July 9, 1810(?).

Gish, S. Born Aug. 12, 1818; died Aug. 27, 1831.

Gwaltney, Philadelphia. Born Sept. 18, 1830; died 1901.

Hanes, Moses, son of Nicholas and Pricilla Hanes; born Oct. 10, 1859; died July 1870.

Kenzie, Cassie; born Dec. 1, 1809; died Oct. 4, 1865.

Kenzie, Daniel, born Feb. 6, 1809; died March 8, 1885.

Kenzie, Isobel, wife Dan'l Kenzie; born Dec. 13, 1813; died July 23, 1883.

Kinsey, Catherine, consort, Abraham Kinsey. Died Nov. 12, 1839, aged 66 yrs. 25 days.

Kirby, Thomas; born Nov. 11, 1827; died Aug. 30, 1874.

Moomaw, Annie L., wife Simon J. Born Feb.

23, 1863, died June 10, 1888.

Moomaw, Catherine. Died May 5, 1864, aged 89 yrs., 1 mo. 21 days.

Moomaw, Christian. Died Oct. 8, 1847, aged 72 yrs. 9 mo., 22 days.

Moomaw, Joseph; died Apr. 21, 1894; aged 77 yrs. 10 mo. 28 days.

Moomaw, Mary, wife Joseph Moomaw; died Sept. 20, 1888, aged 68 yrs. 11 mo. 20 days.

Moomaw, Mary, dau. Christinah and Francis Moomaw; died Oct. 28, 1837, aged 3 years.

Moomaw, Matthew, son of Joseph and Mary. Died Apr. 14, 1855, aged 4 yrs. 29 days.

Moomaw, Samuel. Died Nov. 7, 1852, aged 52 yrs.

Nininger, Christian; died Feb. 1838, aged 70 yrs. 8 mo.

Nininger, Elizabeth; consort Christian; died Sept. 5, 1845, aged 75 yr. 3 mo. 2 days. R. E. Died 1826.

HILLSVILLE, CARROLL COUNTY.

Bedsaw, P. Born Mar. 3, 1778; died Aug. 1871.

Bobbett, John. No dates. Very old.

Coaltrane, Amanda, wife Col. Ira B. Coaltrane Born, Sept. 23; died Oct. 31, 1889.

Coaltrane, Col. Ira B. Born May 22, 1815; died May 13, 1894.

Cockran, Frances, wife of Robt. C. Born Mar. 10, 1825; died Mar. 26, 1856.

Cockran, Robert C. Born Mar. 1, 1823; died Jan. 22, 1907.

Covey, Catherine, wife Samuel S. Born Sept. 1809; died Nov. 20, 1891.

Covey, Samuel S. Born Pulaski Co., Va., Jan. 14, 1814; died July 9, 1904.

Dalton, John. Born Sept. 28, 1772; died Mar. 24, 1851.

Dalton, Keziah J. Born Feb. 18, 1843; died Jan. 28, 1892. (Wife Martin Dalton).

Dalton, Martin. Born July 4, 1810; died Aug. 6, 1893.

Durnel, Dianah. Died Mar. 4, 1822. Aged 55.

Durnel, John. Died June 11, 1843, aged 60.

D.... W..... Died 1807.

Early, Ann Eliza W., wife John Early. Born Nov. 12, 1828, died Feb. 1, 1880.

Early, John, born Feb. 8, 1820. died Oct. 16, 1881.

Early, Rhoda, wife James Early; born May 2, 1828; died Feb. 18, 1877.

Edwards, Annuel (?) Died 1846, aged 81.

Edwards, Elia (?). Died May 9, 1830; aged 77.

Edwards, Isaac. Born Feb. 25, 1772; died July 2, 1825.

Farmer, Elizabeth, dau. James Farmer. Born May 11, 1802; died Feb. 7, 1853.

Farmer, James. Born; died Aug. 12, 1838; aged 80.

Farmer, James (son of above). Born Apr. 13, 1805; died July 16, 1850.

Farmer, Nancy, dau. of J. R. Early, and wife of Isaac Farmer. Born Mar. 17, 1815; died Nov. 17, 1882.

Farmer, Susannah, wife of James Farmer. Died Sept. 30, 1840; aged 85.

Franklin, Henry Died. July 20, 1845, aged 34.

Hill, James. No dates-very old.

Hill, Keziah. Died Apr. 3, 1815, aged 64.

Huffman, Barnaem. Died Sept. 20, 1826.

Huffman, Reuben. Born May 6, 1815; died

aged 94 yrs. 2 mo. and 16 days.
Huffman, Roxana; died July 6, 1887, aged 69.
Johnson, Martha Lowry, wife of Robert Cave Johnson. Born Frederick Co., Va., 1803; died April 15, 1886. aged 83 yrs., 1 mo., 27 days.
McClure, J. 1821, aged 77.
McClure, J. 1813. aged 22.
McClure, Kora (?). 1821: aged 23.
McClure, Rea..(?). 1821. aged 25.
Motley, Nancy, wife Joel F. Motley, died July 27, 1858, aged 57.
Paul, Abraham, died Oct. 27, 1857, aged 52.
Starr, Jeremiah; died ...... 11, 1845, aged 57.
Starr, John W., died Mar. 4, 1847, at Old Point Comfort, aged 21.
Starr, Nancy, dau. Jeremiah and Tibbatha. Died 1833, aged 14.
Starr, Tabittha, wife, Jeremiah; died May 4, 1851, aged 66.
Straw, Rhoda L., dau. Lawrence and Joanna Stephens.. Born Apr. 20, 1794; died Mar. 1, 1884.
Thompson, Frances (wife Wm.) Born Mar. 2, 1800; died Nov. 28, 1887.
Thompson, Rev. William. Born Campbell Co., Va. Jan. 7, 1788; died Oct. 17, 1759.
Thornton, Martha Lowry; born Orange Co. Va. 11, June 1832; died Nov. 27, 1916.
Thornton, William Craig. Born Augusta Co., Va. Aug. 26, 1825. Died June 5, 1913.
Tipton, Joanna, wife John Tipton. Born Jan 1, 1812; died Apr. 7, 1889.
Tipton, John. Born Feb. 5, 1800; died Apr. 17, 1853.
Toncray, Alverda Robinson; born Orange Co. Va. Feb. 25, 1830; died Nov. 7, 1917.
Toncray, Dr. Robert L., born Wythe Co. Va., Aug. 7, 1814;died July 4, 1886.
Utley, Rev. C. M. Born April 9, 1810, at B.... ington, Vt,, died Apr. 21, 1875.
W. I. 1797.

MONTGOMERY COUNTY

Cemetery Near Christiansburg, Va.

Anderson, Dr. George. Born April 19, 1779; died Sept. 20, 1818.
Anderson, John. Born April 19, 1789; died March 16, 1821.
Anderson, Sarah Leek. Died March, 1833.
Bratton, Elizabeth M. July 25, 1806.
Bratton, Capt. James. Died Jan. 2, 1814.
Brown, James. Of Madison, Miss. Died July 3, 1866, aged 60 yrs.
Clark, James R. Born Dec. 16, 1827; died Apr. 1903.
Craig, Anne Montgomery, wife of Capt. James Craig; died Dec. 2, 1841, aged 74.
Craig, Emmaline, wife of John Craig; born Nov. 1, 1813; died Jan. 3, 1892.
Craig, Capt. James. Died Feb. 8, 1834, aged 72.
Craig, John. Born April. 25, 1794; died Aug. 27, 1852.
Craig, John Jr. Born Jan. 14, 1839; fell at the battle of Chancorsville, 1863.
Douglass, Charity, wife of Benjamin Douglass; died July, 1832. aged 90.yrs.
Haymaker, Marthey, wife of Phillip Haymaker, Sr. born Jan. 12, 1814; died June 26, 1888.
Holman, Mrs. Martha, wife of Geo. B. Holman. Born Feb. 22, 1819; died Nov. 3, 1868.

Millar, Dr. Joseph. Sept. 7, 1781; died ...... ,1812.
Miller, Lewis. Born May 3, 1796; died Sept. 15, 1882.
Norvill, Francis G. Born Dec. 25, 1813; died May 1, 1874.
Reid, Peter W. Born in Scotland, June 9, 1830; died Jan. 30, 1909.
Trigg, Col. Robert C. Died July 2, 1872.
Wade, Eliza F. Born May, 1799; died Oct. 30, 1839.
Wade, Hampton. Born May 28, 1789; died May 2, 1846.
Wade, James. Born Dec. 5, 1791; died Apr. 27, 1839.
Wade, Rebecca, widow of Davis L. Wade; Born June, 1764; died June 4, 1822.
Also two infant children of Hampton and Mary Wade (Geo. A. and Mary) dying 1835, 1833.

Private Cemetery In Christiansburg

B,ratton, Cary Allen. Born May 5, 1802; died Mar. 13, 1838.
Bratton, Mrs. Dorathea, wife Capt. James Bratton, and dau. of Col. Wm. Fleming, and Ann, his wife. Born Aug. 17, 1777. Died Aug. 6, 1852.
Hanks, Mrs. Malcolm. Born Feb. 10, 1809; died Feb. 15, 1891.
Kyle, Elizabeth McKelvey. Wife of Jeremiah Kyle, and daughter of David and Elizabeth Kyle of Buckingham Co., Va. Died July 13, 1856, aged 64.
Kyle, Jeremiah. Born in Tyrone Co., Ireland, Oct. 1791; died Dec. 5, 1807. Was son of Wm. and Margaret Kyle.

ROANOKE COUNTY

Private Cemetery Near Roanoke

Craig, Robert. Born 1792; died 1852.
Lewis, Mrs. Mary A. Born 1819; died June 8, 1848.
Neville, Willie H. Born 1840; died 1856.
Shanks, Robert Craig. Born 1841; died Jan. 16, 1835.
Shanks, William Henry. Born 1838; died Oct. 14, 1340.
Walton, Frances W. Born 1809; died Mar. 10, 1830.
Walton, John B. Born 1758; died Mar. 27, 1836.
Walton, Mary L. Born 1758; died Aug. 21, 1824.
Walton, Mrs. Nancy. Born 1796; died Sept. 20, 1856.
Walton, William. Born 1749; died Jan. 29 1845.

SALEM

Altizer, Marvin Harrison, son of J. H. and M. J. Altizer; Apr. 2, 1818; Mar. 3, 1914.
Armstrong, Jane B. Mrs. Born June, 1799, died Sept. 30, 1874.
Armstrong, Ellin Baxter. Born in Co., Devon, Ireland, and removed to this Co., 1818; died Oct. 6, 1880.
Barnett, Charles T. Born Aug. 8, 1825; died Jan. 19, 1897.
Barnett, Susan Deyerle. (wife above). Born Aug. 24, 1825; died May 23, 1887.

Barnett, Mary A. Wife of J. L. Barnett, and last child of Rev. Robt. Logan; born June 22, 1818; died July 14, 1891.

Board, Green B. Born Sept. 27, 1815; died Sept. 15, 1887.

Board, Martha G. Born Sept. 25, 1831; died Apr. 13, 1893.

Bryan, Margaret Watson; wife Wm. Bryan, Jr., 1724-1804.

Bryan, Wm. Jr., son of Wm. Bryan, Sr. 1716-1796.

Bryan, William, Sr. Emigrant from Ballejroney County Down, Ireland in 1718. 1685-1786.

Campbell, Joseph. Born Oct. 2, 1800; died May 20, 1863.

Campbell, Mildred S. Hurt (wife of above). Born Jan. 1, 1804; died Dec. 24, 1845.

Campbell, Robert H. Born Dec. 15, 1828; died Aug. 14, 1853.

Carnes, William. Born Dec. 18, 1811; died Apr. 27, 1882.

Chapman, Henry H. Born Oct. 16, 1793; died Oct. 4, 1862.

Chapman, Nancy, born Feb. 21, 1807; died Jan. 24, 1863.

Davis, Anna Caroline; born Jan. 27, 1827; died Feb. 27.

Davis, John B. Rev. Born May 26, 1808; died Dec. 26, 1895.

Deyerle, Annie Crawford. Born Aug. 22, 1800; died Nov. 30, 1871.

Deyerle, Joseph. Born Nov. 10, 1799; died Dec. 26, 1877.

Hupp, Abraham Col. 1818-1866.

Johnston, Ann Carter, wife of W. F. Johnston born June 7, 1810; died Nov. 1, 1861.

Johnston, George W. Born May 22, 1811; died in Confederate Army, May 22, 1862.

Johnston, James. Born Nov. 28, 1808; died Aug. 29, 1846.

Johnston, John Dr. Born Nov. 15, 1761; died April 8, 1815.

Johnston, Lucy A. McClanahan, wife Wm. Z. Johnston; born Nov. 1809; died Feb. 8, 1888.

Johnston, Margaret Galloway; wife of John W. Johnston. Born Frederick Co. Va., Nov. 8, 1813; died July 21, 1890.

Johnston, William Z. Born May 23, 1802; died June 8, 1853.

Kizer, Hannah (wife John P.) Born Nov. 3, 1813; died Jan. 4, 1884.

Kizer, John P. Born May 15, 1805; died Feb. 18, 1882.

Lewis, Andrew Gen. 1716-1781.

Logan, Eleanor Moore; eldest child of Robt. and Margaret Logan. Died Jan. 25, 1859 aged 57 years.

Logan, Eliza, wife of J. B. I. Logan. Born Dec. 28, 1822; died June 24, 1890.

Logan, J. B. I., born June 2, 1811; died Dec. 10, 1877.

Lyle, Annie Elizabeth Matilda Turnell; wife John N. Lyle. Born Sept. 29, 1835; died July 30, 1901.

Lyle, Catherine E., wife John N. Lyle. Born July 14, 1817; died July 7, 1857.

Lyle, John Newton, Born Rockbridge Co., Va., Sept. 20, 1806; died May 31, 1867.

McClanahan, Agatha L.; March 15, 1779-June 14, 1852.

McClanahan, Elijah Col. Apr. 20, 1770-Dec. 1, 1857.

McCutchen, John S. Rev. of Iredell Co., N. C. "Died suddenly in this place June 24, 1846, while on a journey to Rockbridge Co., his native Co. Aged 41 years."

Persinger, Jacob; died Nov. 4, 1879, aged 84 years.

Persinger, Mary F. (wife of above) Died Oct. 11, 1887, aged 75.

Pitzer, Bernard; born March 6, 1809; died July 11, 1895.

Pitzer, Frances L. Born Mar. 3, 1816; died May 21, 1898.

Pitzer, Mary Jane, consort J. K. Pitzer. Born Feb. 23, 1811; died Oct. 22, 1856.

Powers, Henretta (wife of Urias Powers) Born Camden Co., S. C. Nov. 17, 1801. died Salem Nov. 24, 1883.

Powers, Urias Rev. Born at Croyden N. H. May 12, 1791; died Feb. 12, 1870.

Shanks, David. Died Dec. 12, 1833, aged 41 years.

Shanks, David S. Born Feb. 16, 1825; died May 1, 1900.

Shanks, Sarah M. Born Apr. 27, 1829; died Jan. 19, 1914.

Smith, William M. Born Feb. 24, 1809; died Aug. 18, 1886.

Strouse, Peter. Born Oct. 16, 1796; died Nov. 17, 1872.

Sublett, Thomas G. Born Dec. 15, 1822; died Mar. 6, 1898.

Shirley, John. Born Apr. 21, 1779; died Aug. 2, 1855, aged 76.

Shirley, Mary A. Born Aug. 6, 1787; died June 25, 1863.

Tyree, Cornelius Rev. Sept. 22, 1813-Dec. 23, 1891.

Tyree, S. H. Mrs. (wife above) died Mar. 6, 1884, aged 65.

Wade, Mary Ann, wife D. David Wade, and dau. David and Susan W. Shanks. Born Apr. 25, 1827; died Apr. 22, 1850.

Wilson, Mary Lou. Dau. J. Mark and Phebe S. Died Mar. 21, 1839, aged 13 yr.

Williams. W. C. Born Sept. 11, 1785, died Aug. 18. 1852.

Williams, Margaret; born Oct. 23, 1795; died July 8, 1871.

www.ingramcontent.com/pod-product-compliance
Lightning Source LLC
Chambersburg PA
CBHW060809110426
42739CB00032BA/3152